D0061650

SECRETS OF THE KINGDOM

SECRETS

OF THE

KINGDOM

THE INSIDE STORY OF THE
SAUDI-U.S. CONNECTION

GERALD POSNER

RANDOM HOUSE TRADE PAPERBACKS

NEW YORK

2006 Random House Trade Paperback Edition

Copyright © 2005 by Gerald L. Posner

Published in the United States by Random House Trade Paperbacks,
an imprint of The Random House Publishing Group,
a division of Random House, Inc., New York.

RANDOM HOUSE TRADE PAPERBACKS and colophon are trademarks
of Random House, Inc.

Originally published in hardcover in the United States by Random
House, an imprint of The Random House Publishing Group,
a division of Random House, Inc., in 2005.

LIBRARY OF CONGRESS CATALOGING-IN-PUBLICATION DATA
Posner, Gerald.
Secrets of the kingdom: the inside story of the Saudi-U.S.
connection / Gerald Posner.
p.   cm.
Includes bibliographical references and index.
ISBN 0-8129-7310-0
1. Saudi Arabia—Foreign relations—United States.
2. United States—Foreign relations—Saudi Arabia.
3. Saudi Arabia—Politics and government.   4. âl Saᵒ'd,
House of—Political activity.   I. Title.
DS228.U6P67 2005
327.538073'09'0511—dc22   2005042926

Printed in the United States of America

www.atrandom.com

246897531

To Bob Loomis, my friend and editor,

who has the rare courage in publishing

to let me choose a subject without knowing what,

if anything, I will discover during my reporting.

His confidence that the simple pursuit of the truth

will produce a book worth reading is something

for which I will forever be grateful.

CONTENTS

The Saudi petrodollars that have flooded into the United States during the last thirty years have affected American business, politics, and society. That money has bought the House of Saud a coveted seat at the table with America's corporate and political elite, and the Saudis have assiduously courted the clout and access that result from such enormous influxes of cash. This book is not intended to be a complete history of Saudi Arabia, nor even a thorough primer to the Kingdom's intricate political intrigue. It instead focuses on Saudi power, as flexed with billions of dollars in oil revenues. It reveals some ways in which the Kingdom has manipulated American institutions and policies.

Saudi Arabia acts much like every other country trying to cultivate U.S. support, influence foreign policy on issues it considers important, and learn about what America might do that could affect its own national interests. But what makes the Kingdom different from many other countries with similar ambitions is the power of its money. It has succeeded on a scale unmatched by other countries. This is the inside story of its success.

SECRETS OF THE KINGDOM

CHAPTER 1

A FREE PASS
FOR THE SAUDIS

On August 31, 2003, *Time* published the first review of my book *Why America Slept,* and focused on the final chapter about the capture and interrogation of an al Qaeda terrorist, Abu Zubaydah. It revealed an American intelligence scheme to dupe Zubaydah into disclosing whatever he knew about imminent terrorist attacks. Using a room in a CIA-linked Afghan facility that was hastily converted to resemble a Saudi Arabian prison, U.S. officials concocted an elaborate ruse. Two Arab-American Special Forces soldiers pretended to be Saudi interrogators. The Saudis wanted Zubaydah—Osama bin Laden's number three man—for terrorist crimes, and they had a well-deserved reputation for using torture in interrogations. The thinking behind the *Mission Impossible*–type deception was that Zubaydah would be so frightened he would either divulge critical information to avoid torture or prefer to be handed over to, and cooperate with, American questioners to avoid the tougher fate with the Saudis.

It took almost three years before news leaked out confirming that the government had approved so-called "false flag" operations for terrorists. On January 29, 2005, *The New York Times,* in its coverage of Michael Chertoff's nomination to be the next homeland security chief, reported that in his former job at the Justice Department, Chertoff had advised the CIA on the legality of coercive interrogation methods for terror suspects under the federal antitorture statute. CIA officials evidently wanted legal protection so its officers minimized the risk of prosecution. "Other practices that would not present legal problems were those that did not involve the infliction of pain, like tricking a subject into believing he was being questioned by a member of a security service from another country," reported the *Times*.[1]

The subterfuge backfired. Zubaydah seemed relieved rather than frightened when confronted by the fake Saudi interrogators. From memory, he rattled off two telephone numbers and told the startled U.S. Special Forces agents, "He will tell you what to do." The numbers were private home and cell phone lines of Prince Ahmed bin Salman bin Abdul Aziz, the nephew of Saudi king Fahd. The Western-educated Ahmed was one of the wealthiest members of the royal family and chairman of the Research and Marketing Group, the Kingdom's largest publishing company. Although his media firm was responsible for virulent anti-American and anti-Israeli propaganda, he was considered by most observers simply a Westernized businessman with little apparent political interest. Ahmed was best known as a premier collector of Thoroughbred horses, including the 2002 Kentucky Derby winner, War Emblem. Since 1996, he had spent $126 million buying racehorses.[2]

The CIA officials running Zubaydah's interrogation directed the two American Special Forces agents to falsely tell the terrorist that the telephone numbers he had provided were wrong. By that time, Zubaydah had been deprived of sleep for days, maintained on minimum pain medication for gunshot wounds sustained in his capture, and had been secretly administered a "truth serum" by intravenous drip. Yet, when told his telephone numbers had not panned out, he did not panic. Instead, he gave the "Saudi" interrogators several more numbers, these belonging to two other Saudi princes as well as the chief of Pakistan's air force, the equivalent of being a member of America's Joint Chiefs of Staff. These were his key contacts inside Saudi Arabia and Pakistan, Zubaydah claimed. And in a rambling monologue that one investigator later dubbed "the Rosetta stone" of 9/11, Zubaydah told his American interrogators that two of those named, the king's nephew and the chief of Pakistan's air force, knew *before* 9/11 there would be an al Qaeda attack in America around that date. No one had warned the United States.

Zubaydah's astonishing information put American intelligence in a quandary. At the time, April 2002, the U.S. was working hard to convince the Saudi and Pakistani governments to cooperate with George Bush's declared war on terror. Pakistan had already allowed the U.S. to use its military bases to conduct the war in Afghanistan, and the Kingdom was slowly providing some minor intelligence on al Qaeda, as well as tacitly supporting the Americans in Afghanistan. There was no willingness in the Bush administration to confront either ally based only on the unproven word of an avowed terrorist, especially since Zubaydah recanted his entire confession once he learned he had been duped by the Americans.

Intelligence analysts speculated that Zubaydah's inclusion of Prince Ahmed raised the possibility that the supposedly apolitical prince might merely be a conduit of information for someone higher ranking. Ahmed's father, Prince Salman bin Abdul Aziz, is the governor of Riyadh, the Saudi capital, a post he has held since 1962. One of seven sons of the country's founder, he is one of the Kingdom's most influential ministers and a trusted advisor to King Fahd. Since Fahd's 1995 stroke, Salman rarely leaves his brother's side in Jeddah. According to diplomatic reports, Salman, along with his older brother Sultan, the defense minister, and his half brother Abdullah, the crown prince, are the de facto rulers of Saudi Arabia.

Besides his official position, Salman, whose Riyadh office overlooks Sahat al-Adl—"Justice Square"—where public beheadings take place on Fridays after noon prayers, is influential both with Saudi intelligence and in censoring the media. But there were several other roles that interested American investigators more. One was Salman's multiyear courtship of religious fundamentalists as his power base, especially after his born-again conversion to strict Islam in the 1990s. He has strong ties to the religious conservatives, particularly those in the regional strongholds of Buraydah and Darriya, places Salman frequently visits. The CIA was also intrigued that during the 1980s Afghan war against the Soviets, Salman was responsible for organizing transportation to Afghanistan for the militant armies (mujahideen) from various Arab countries. And finally, he controlled the Kingdom's charities that raised tens of millions for the mujahideen, and brought in billions for Muslim causes worldwide. And many of those charities were on the U.S. government's list of terror sponsors.[3]

But U.S. intelligence agencies were soon stymied in determining whether there was an al Qaeda link between the senior Salman and his son. So the Bush administration gambled. It authorized the CIA to pass along Zubaydah's charges to Saudi Arabia and Pakistan. By covertly monitoring the reactions inside those two countries, the administration thought it might determine the accuracy of Zubaydah's remarkable revelations.

Both countries quickly answered, however, with remarkably similar denials, feigning outrage at the very suggestion there could be any truth in the disclosures.

If that had been the end of it, Zubaydah's confession might just be a footnote to the 9/11 story. However, what happened next ensured that the questions raised by Zubaydah might forever remain unanswered. Only three months after the Saudis and Pakistanis learned of what he had told the Americans, the people he named started dying. Within a few days, all three Saudi princes were dead. Forty-three-year-old Prince Ahmed, the king's nephew, died after he voluntarily entered the best hospital in Riyadh for non-life-threatening surgery for a digestive problem, diverticulitis (one acquaintance says the prince actually went for liposuction, but that procedure is normally done on an outpatient basis). He was dead two days later, with Saudi officials and doctors flip-flopping over the cause of death from a heart attack to a blood clot. One of the doctors suggested that the portly Ahmed was himself responsible for a deadly clot because he was not active enough after his surgery. The doctors, he claimed, felt they could not advise Ahmed to move about since he was a prince, and as such could not be given orders, even by medical professionals.

The day after Ahmed's untimely death, the second prince named by Zubaydah—Sultan bin Faisal bin Turki al-Saud—a forty-one-year-old former military officer, was killed in a car accident. He was Ahmed's cousin, and was on his way to Ahmed's funeral. No other car was involved. He must have been driving too fast, concluded the Saudi police, when his car spun out of control and off the road. A week later, the third prince named by Zubaydah—Fahd bin Turki bin Saud al-Kabir—a twenty-five-year-old, was found dead near his car, only fifty-five miles outside Riyadh. According to the Saudi Royal Court, which took the unusual step of announcing the death, this prince had "died of thirst," a victim of dehydration in the brutal Saudi summer.

Zubaydah's Pakistani link, Air Marshal Mushaf Ali Mir, died on February 20, 2003, together with his wife and fifteen of his top aides, when his military aircraft crashed in Pakistan's rugged Northwest Frontier province. That plane had recently sailed through a thorough maintenance inspection. The weather was clear at the time. There are reports—which Pakistani authorities refuse to acknowledge—that another military officer replaced the air marshal's trusted private pilot at the last moment. Also, ear witnesses told investigators they had heard a loud explosion immediately before the crash.

If foul play was involved in the cluster of deaths, what could the victims have known that was so significant that someone wanted them dead? It might not be possible to answer that. Saudi Arabia, for instance, never even made a pretense of investigating the deaths of the princes. In Pakistan, a full investigation was announced into whether sabotage brought down the plane and killed the air marshal. Nearly two years later, no Pakistani official even acknowledges whether such an investigation took place.

Some U.S. officials felt the Saudis and Pakistanis were hiding something. But the overriding consensus was not to confront, at least publicly, two critical allies over such a strange confluence of deaths. There is no indication that Bush administration officials even privately raised either the deaths or Zubaydah's revelations.

When the news of Zubaydah's claims, and the strange fate of those he named, was made public, however, the reactions of the Saudis and Pakistanis were telling. Instead of acknowledging the seriousness of the charges, and conducting at least perfunctory probes to bolster their public proclamations that they were solid allies in the war on terror, both relied on various officials and surrogates to denigrate Zubaydah's information.

Pakistan's air force issued an official statement that did not mention the investigation into the likelihood of sabotage in the death of its former air marshal. Instead, it said, in part, "Pakistan Air Force is deeply pained by these baseless allegations" and that "while [the] PAF reserves its comments to identify the institutions who must be behind the plot to discredit the professional fighting force of Pakistan, we request the Pakistani nation not to pay any heed to these news which are being circulated to maintain the hysteria related to terrorists and terrorism. Individuals like Gerald Posner knit any number of scenarios to sell books and magazines by scaring American and Western public. Any sane person knows that non-state actors carried out the attacks on 9/11 and states or governments had nothing to do with the planning or execution of these attacks." That statement evidently was the sum and public substance of any Pakistani investigation into Zubaydah's charges.

As for the House of Saud, they summoned an assortment of friendly Arab journalists, together with relatives of Prince Ahmed, to attack Zubaydah's charges and the questions raised by the string of dead princes. Writing in the Saudi English-language daily *Arab News,* editor in chief Khaled al-Maeena dubbed the news of Zubaydah's accusations, and the untimely deaths, "Posner's Fairy Tales." While not disclosing that the *Arab News* was part of the late Prince Ahmed's media empire, al-Maeena charged that the news was merely "cheap shots used to advance careers, make a quick buck and to get invitations to advertise themselves on early morning TV talk shows across the US."

In defending Prince Ahmed, al-Maeena said he had personally known him for fifteen years, and that "to believe that he had any connection with Al-Qaeda would be as absurd as believing that my mother was the 'planner' of Sept. 11." Then he discussed the other princes. "Not only is Posner outrageously slanderous, but he goes off the deep end by naming two other individuals who are also dead. So none of these people are here to defend themselves. And even if they were, it should hardly be necessary to defend oneself against such absurd allegations."

The argument set forth in the *Arab News* was picked up widely in the Middle Eastern and Muslim press. Some went further. Typical was Bangladesh's *The New Nation,* in which Mamoun Fandy said the work had an extremist Israeli link. And typical of the family's response was that of Prince Ahmed's wife. In an official statement released by the Saudi government, she called the disclosures "deplorable," "preposterous," and "outlandish lies." It was, she charged, a "fabricated and outrageous conspiracy theory" that "shamelessly maligns the memory of a beloved member of our family without any substance or reason."

In June 2004, on the two-year anniversary of Prince Ahmed's Kentucky Derby victory, his younger brother, and director of Saudi education, Prince Faisal bin Salman, did what is commonly done by wealthy Saudis when confronted with difficult issues—he hired a public relations firm.* Keating Public Relations of New Jersey sent out thousands of press releases for its new client, again denigrating Zubaydah's charges as "ludicrous." The Keating firm offered Prince Faisal for media interviews, an unusual move for the normally private Saudi royal family. It also recruited American friends and employees of Prince Ahmed, most from his multimillion-dollar Thoroughbred operation, to speak in his defense.

---

*Ahmed's older brother Prince Fahd bin Salman had died in July 2001, at the age of forty-six, from heart failure. Although the Salman family claims that all the brothers were apolitical, in July 2001, Fahd had met with the revisionist British historian David Irving. The prince discussed financing the controversial writer after Irving had lost a libel action in a London court against an American Jewish professor, Deborah Lipstadt, who had labeled him a "Holocaust denier." The judge eventually branded Irving an anti-Semite, racist, and a pro-Nazi right-wing polemicist. Fahd evidently had no problem with the court's characterizations of Irving, and agreed to provide the money so Irving could continue his work. But Fahd died only a few days after they reached an agreement and before any money passed to Irving.[4]

While the Keating firm, and those defending the prince, did their best to minimize the charges from Zubaydah, journalist Craig Unger published his own investigation, *House of Bush, House of Saud,* in which he showed that members of the bin Laden family, and other high-ranking Saudi officials—*including* Prince Ahmed—were allowed to leave the United States in the week after the 9/11 attacks, most without even being interviewed by the FBI.[5]

The first flight, on September 13, was a private jet that ferried three young Saudis from Tampa, Florida, to Lexington, Kentucky. In Lexington, they joined Saudi royals attending the thrice-yearly Kneeland auction for racehorses. That is where Prince Ahmed was staying. He had been in Kentucky on September 11, and heard the news of the terror attacks while at breakfast in his hotel, the Griffin Gate Marriott Resort. Two acquaintances were with him. One, Richard Mulhall, the racing manager for Ahmed's Thoroughbred Corporation, told a friend that the prince was "terribly upset, more surprised than anyone." Ahmed seemed distraught and immediately dialed out on his cell phone, but did not say whom he called. According to Mulhall, Ahmed kept asking, "Who in the world would be crazy enough to do something like this?" Breakfast was cut short and Ahmed hurriedly returned to his suite. The next day he attended the Kneeland auction and spent $1.2 million on two more Thoroughbreds.

Lexington, Ahmed's base of operations on September 11, had now become the unofficial gathering spot for other ranking Saudis like the three who flew in from Tampa. According to some in Ahmed's entourage, the FBI visited the prince on September 13. They interviewed him for nearly an hour in his hotel suite. The FBI refuses still to acknowledge that interview. What is undeniable is that three days later, Ahmed flew out of the U.S. on an opulently fitted 727, returning to Saudi Arabia. Most private planes in U.S. airspace had been grounded, and his was the first personal jet to be allowed an international departure.*

The rationale later given by Bush administration officials for allowing

*At the post-9/11 Kentucky Derby and Preakness (which War Emblem also won), reporters asked Ahmed what he thought about the terrorist attacks on America. "I leave those questions to the politicians," he said. "I am a businessman, not a politician." John Jeremiah Sullivan, in his 2004 book, *Blood Horses: Notes of a Sportswriter's Son,* reported on those two races held after 9/11, noting that they "were patrolled by shadowy men in dark vests and sunglasses, carrying sniper rifles." Ahmed refused to go to New York for the Belmont in 2002, even though War Emblem was competing for racing's rare Triple Crown.

flights like Ahmed's to leave so quickly after 9/11 was fear of reprisals against bin Laden family members and Saudi royals, since fifteen of the nineteen suicide hijackers had been Saudi. But that does not explain why non-Arab British citizens Jack Rusbridge and Anthony John Stafford were also allowed to board the Lexington-to-London flight. They were two of Ahmed's employees, serving as everything from chauffeurs to personal security. Rusbridge later told an acquaintance that in light of the terror attacks only days earlier, he was surprised the FBI's only function prior to departure was to ensure that everyone who boarded the plane had a passport that matched a name on the passenger manifest. The FBI did not, incredibly, cross-check the manifests against all government terror watch lists. In addition, 142 Saudis left on six chartered flights within a week of the attacks, and another 150 ranking officials or royal family members left on commercial jets.[6]

The most comprehensive official investigation so far into what happened before 9/11 is the one by the National Commission on Terrorist Attacks upon the United States, known popularly as the 9/11 Commission. Its final report received bipartisan political praise, became a national bestseller with over a million copies in print, and was given the unusual accolade for a government report of being nominated for the prestigious National Book Award. And what did the 9/11 Commission conclude about Zubaydah's charges against three Saudi royals and the Pakistani air marshal? It failed to address—much less resolve—whether he was telling the truth. The final report, incredibly, did not even mention the dead Saudis or the air marshal. It cites Zubaydah only briefly, and then primarily to bolster the interrogations of an even higher-ranking al Qaeda prisoner, Khalid Shaikh Mohammed. While the 9/11 Commission does reference some of Zubaydah's interrogations, not one is from March, the month of his capture, when he made his accusations about high-ranking Saudis. Zubaydah, who was mentioned by name in the now infamous presidential daily briefing that was presented to President Bush while he was on vacation at his Crawford, Texas, ranch less than a month before the terror attacks, received little attention from the Commission.[7] The 9/11 panel was given restricted personal access to two of the highest-ranking al Qaeda suspects, Khalid Shaikh Mohammed and Ramzi Binalshibh, but either never asked, or was not allowed, to talk to Zubaydah.[8]

The 9/11 Commission acknowledged that the Kingdom was "a problematic ally in combating Islamic extremism," but concluded, "[W]e have found no evidence that the Saudi government as an institution or senior Saudi officials individually funded the organization [al Qaeda]."

While the Commission acknowledged that unnamed wealthy Saudi sympathizers and leading charities had for years funneled money to al Qaeda, it did not pursue widely available research establishing the extent to which many suspect charities were controlled directly by the Kingdom or its ministers.[9] The Commission ignored, for instance, an October 2002 study by the Council on Foreign Relations that drew directly opposite conclusions about Saudi government complicity: "Saudi officials have turned a blind eye to this problem."[10]

The Commission also missed an opportunity to examine fully an intelligence coup in 2002 in which American agents retrieved computer files in Bosnia of a so-called "Golden Chain," twenty of Osama bin Laden's early financial supporters. On that list were a former Saudi government minister, three billionaire banking tycoons, and several leading industrialists. The 9/11 Commission did not confirm or deny the list's accuracy, nor did it address what the Saudis did with the information.

These are errors of omission. The same is true with the way the Commission dealt with the matter of the early Saudi flights after 9/11. The final report concluded, "We found no evidence that any flights of Saudi nationals, domestic or international, took place before the reopening of national airspace on the morning of September 13, 2001. To the contrary, every flight we have identified occurred after national airspace reopened."[11]

Such a conclusion is disingenuous at best. For nearly three years, the White House, and aviation and law enforcement officials, had insisted that the private flight of three Saudis from Tampa to Lexington on September 13 never took place.[12] "It's not in our logs," a spokesman for the FAA said when first asked about that flight. "It didn't occur."[13] Officials were adamant that no private flights took place until, at the very earliest, the following day, September 14. "General aviation was still down," insisted a senior FAA representative, "and if it was a corporate jet, it would not have been allowed to fly."[14]

Journalist John Jeremiah Sullivan was working on a related story when Craig Unger's article about the flights was first published in *Vanity Fair*. "Every official I talked to was baffled and at pains to deny that the flight on the thirteenth ever took place," he recounts. "For months they tried hard to deny it happened at all."[15] A Lexington, Kentucky, FBI spokesman, David Beyer, assured Sullivan that his own notes confirmed the Tampa flight did not get to Lexington until the sixteenth, three days after it actually happened. When Sullivan spoke to Ed Cogswell, an FBI spokesman at headquarters in Washington, he was told, "This stuff is either case sensitive or the information is classified because I really can't provide it to you. Whatever the rules were on those particular days, those rules were followed. They've got the date or mode of transportation wrong. We don't have any indication of a flight at that point." When Sullivan said he had gathered some evidence that the flight had happened, Cogswell promised to check further. A few days later they again spoke. "I can tell you there was *not* a flight at that time, the thirteenth."[16]

It was not until June 2004—thirty-three months after the flight with the three Saudis happened—that officials at Tampa International Airport finally acknowledged it.[17]

The 9/11 Commission dismissed years of repeated denials by federal officials of an early flight as the result of merely a "misunderstanding" between federal and local officials. And it concluded that the matter was insignificant since, it said, national airspace had been technically reopened on the thirteenth. However, it failed to mention that the reopening was for commercial—not *private*—planes, and there is ample evidence that aviation officials actually considered the flight on the thirteenth extraordinary.

Sullivan had located an airport official at Lexington who was at first unwavering in his contention that airspace there was not open until the fourteenth. That person thought such a flight was impossible and dismissed it out of hand until he personally checked fuel records at Lexington and saw the plane had in fact landed and been refueled on the thirteenth.

A former FBI agent and a private investigator accompanied the three Saudis to Lexington on the thirteenth from Tampa. They had been asked by the Tampa police, who had been prodded by the Saudi embassy, to ensure that the three left safely. When the two men, Dan Grossi and Manuel Perez, were told about the pending flight, they didn't believe it would happen. "Forget about it," Perez told Grossi. "No one is flying today."[18]

When they arrived at Tampa's airport, an airport employee laughed at them for even thinking they would be flying that day. At 10:57 A.M. on September 13, the FAA had issued another notice reminding the nation's airports that while commercial traffic was slowly resuming that afternoon, private aviation was still banned. Three private planes that violated the ban on the thirteenth—in Texas, Maryland, and West Virginia—were forced down in each instance by jet fighters.[19] Thousands of business executives and wealthy travelers had been grounded since 9/11, their private jets and smaller planes forced to land at the nearest airport after the FAA had taken the extraordinary step of shutting down all the nation's air traffic. They were all anxious to get to their final destinations, and many were bombarding the FAA and local airports with requests to get airborne. Not even private flights transporting organs for medical transplants were cleared for takeoff on the thirteenth. But the 9/11 Commission finessed the issue of the flight of the three Saudis from Tampa by concluding that since the plane was chartered from defense contractor Raytheon—and had a pilot with a CIA security clearance—it really was more akin to a commercial flight and therefore was allowed in the air.

The Commission's simple conclusion that the flight on the thirteenth was not out of the ordinary since some planes were back in the air raises questions as to whether they knew about the surprise that people in Lexington had when a private jet landed there that day. Sullivan interviewed a woman who works at Lexington's Bluegrass Airport. She had called her mother to tell her how weird it was that a plane landed since nothing was flying in or out. Some people saw the plane arriving and called friends. "Can you believe there is a fucking plane landing at the airport?" one said. A few came to look at it. Nearby on the tarmac was the 727, with Arabic lettering on the tail, that would transport Prince Ahmed out of the country in three days.[20]

On September 13, at New York's three major area airports, Kennedy, La Guardia, and Newark, only incoming flights were allowed, and only after 11:00 A.M. Later in the afternoon, those airports were closed entirely after a security scare at JFK when a man was detained with phony pilot identification papers.[21]

Either the 9/11 Commission was aware that it fudged its conclusion that the private Saudi flight on September 13 was normal or it did not know how unusual that flight really was, and either scenario is not reassuring regarding the Commission's investigation into matters Saudi.

The flight that departed Tampa did so only hours after the Saudi ambassador to the United States, Prince Bandar bin Sultan bin Abdul Aziz, had gone to the White House for a private meeting—no aides permitted—with President Bush. Neither Bandar nor Bush has disclosed the details of what they discussed that morning. Bandar has, however, denied directly asking the president to authorize the rapid exit of his high-ranking colleagues, saying instead that he asked the FBI for permission. The Bureau, says spokesman John Iannarelli, had no "role in facilitating these flights one way or another."[22] The FBI actually gave personal escort to two prominent Saudi families who fled the U.S. from Los Angeles and Orlando. Several other Saudis were allowed to leave the country without even being interviewed by the FBI.

Did the 9/11 Commission ask the president about his meeting with Bandar? Did it pursue full disclosure from Raytheon, which provided the plane and pilot, about how the flight was arranged? If so, there is again no indication in the final report.

The 9/11 Commission wrote, "Our own independent review of the Saudi nationals involved confirms that no one with known links to terrorism departed on these flights."[23] Of course, Prince Ahmed is never mentioned. From conversations with investigators familiar with the 9/11 panel's probe, the portions of Zubaydah's interrogation in which he named the Saudi princes and the Pakistani air marshal were *not* provided to the Commission. The CIA has even withheld the March interrogations from the FBI, which is supposed to have access to all terror suspects' questioning.

Shortly after the 9/11 Commission's report was released, co-chairman Lee Hamilton, the former Democratic congressman from Indiana, testified before the House Committee on Financial Affairs. When Representative Maxine Waters (D-Calif.) expressed strong doubts about the accuracy of the Commission's conclusions regarding the Saudis, Hamilton went further in defending the Kingdom than the Commission's own report. He said that during the Commission's twenty-month investigation, it had not found *any* evidence that either the Saudi government or senior officials gave money to bin Laden or al Qaeda.[24]

"We sent investigators to Saudi Arabia," he said, "we researched all kinds of information and documents, we talked to many, many people, we followed every lead we could."[25]

Those in the Kingdom, who would prefer that no bright light of scrutiny be shined on Saudi ties to terrorism and al Qaeda, heralded the 9/11 report as the definitive account. The week following the report's release, Saudi foreign minister Prince Saud al Faisal issued a statement from Jeddah. In part, it said, "The 9-11 Commission has put to rest the false accusations that have cast fear and doubt over Saudi Arabia. For too long, Saudi Arabia stood morbidly accused of funding and supporting terrorism. . . . The 9-11 Commission has confirmed that there is no evidence that the government of Saudi Arabia supported or funded Al-Qaeda. . . .

[And] the falsehoods that were disseminated about the flights that carried some Saudis after 9-11 when American airports and airspace were closed were shown by the report for what they were: at best a figment of the imagination, and at worst an intent to incriminate. . . . We are pleased with the report and we feel vindicated."

In a *New York Times* opinion piece on July 27, 2004, "Scrutinizing the Saudi Connection," I wrote that while the 9/11 panel had done excellent work in establishing how the government failed to prevent the terror attacks on New York and the Pentagon, it had done a less than reassuring job when it came to important issues about Saudi Arabia. By not probing possible Saudi complicity in 9/11 and honestly addressing troubling questions about the September 13 flight, the panel risked damaging its otherwise fine work. The 9/11 Commission gave the Saudis a free pass. This book shows why.[26]

CHAPTER 2

A TRIBE CALLED SAUD

If it were not for an anomaly of geology, Saudi Arabia might be a country occasionally featured on a Discovery Channel documentary for its desert tribes, falcon hunting, and ancient architecture. But the barren terrain that makes up the eastern coast of the arid country covers the world's largest oil reserves, so there can be no discussion of Saudi Arabia without first acknowledging the economic power this creates in an industrial world dependent on petroleum.[1]

The Saudis have about a quarter of the world's oil reserves, producing about eight million barrels daily. They claim they could easily push production to fifteen million and maintain that for a remarkable fifty years.[2] At the near $50-a-barrel price that the market soared to by the autumn of 2004, the Kingdom was averaging $400 million daily in sales. Unlike many oil reserves in the United States, the known Saudi repository is close to the surface, so it can be pumped inexpensively (it is estimated that a trillion barrels may eventually be recoverable).[3] Through most of the 1990s, it cost the Saudis about fifty cents a barrel to get their oil out of the ground. Although extraction has become more expensive—recently near $2 a barrel—Saudi Arabia still earns over $300 million daily in profits. Those riches are concentrated among six thousand male princes in the enormous ruling family, the House of Saud, which just took control of the fragmented desert kingdom in 1932.

The story of the founding of modern-day Saudi Arabia has been told so many times that many Americans are becoming familiar with it. By understanding how the country was formed just over seventy years ago, it is possible to better appreciate many of its current policies and decisions that otherwise seem anachronistic to Westerners. Today's rift between the traditions of Saudi Arabia's strict Muslim adherents and a new generation that sees its future in coexistence and partnership with the West has its beginnings in the violent baptism that created the Kingdom.

Bounded on three sides by water, and separated in the north by rugged mountains from neighboring Iraq and Jordan, the Arabian peninsula was for hundreds of years a vast, mostly impenetrable desert of enormous, shifting sand dunes. Although some port cities, like Jeddah, prospered as trading stopovers during the Roman and Persian empires, the mystique of a land that could not be pierced by outsiders was not shattered for Westerners until 1917, when T. E. Lawrence (Lawrence of Arabia) crossed the giant desert to attack the Turkish-held city of Aqaba (now in Jordan).

At 900,000 square miles, Arabia is about a third the size of the United States, and has long been home to fiercely clannish tribes. Bloodlines, not geography, were key for centuries. Individuals were loyal only to their tribes and never identified through any national pride with the Arabian peninsula. Instead, they were proud only to be Bedouins, Otaybas, Harbs, Ajmans, Anazahs, or any of several dozen other clans. They fought each other for territory, trade routes, access to oases, and even tracts of date groves. Most considered neighboring tribes as rivals, not potential fellow countrymen united under a single flag. Couple that with the nomadic way of life that dominated the country, and the likelihood of forming a stable single government seems unrealistic.

For over a thousand years, the only common thread among the tribes was their religion, Islam. Muhammad, the faith's prophet, was born in about 570 to a reputable merchant family in Mecca. In his sixty years, Muhammad preached a monotheistic faith that slowly spread among the pagan tribes. Two years before his death in 632, Muhammad's Muslim followers were plentiful enough to attack and capture Mecca. After his death, two cities in Arabia became central to Islam. Mecca was its spiritual site, where the faith held its obligatory annual pilgrimage called the hajj. And Medina, which had been the seat of Muhammad's political and military power, transformed into an important hub for codifying Islamic law.

Over several hundred years, however, the heart of Islamic and "Arab" civilization moved farther away from Arabia, resulting in a deterioration of culture and order, particularly after the thirteenth-century Mongol invasions. As the overland trade routes between the Mediterranean and Asia changed to ocean shipping, the peninsula lost what little prosperity it had gained through its cities. Dozens of tribes devolved into bitterly opposed factions vying for power across large swaths of the desert, turning the country into a violent and chaotic hodgepodge of rival sheikhdoms. No one ruled the great arid plateau, the Najd. The Bedouin tribes that lived there did so in complete independence, and with little contact with the outside world. The Najd was the home of the Wahhabi Islamic sect, and of a tribal family called the Sauds.

The Saud family had settled in the center of Najd, near the modern capital of Riyadh, around 1500. The tribes of the Najd, isolated from the centers of Islamic life in Medina and Mecca, had largely resumed pagan practices. Some had even returned to ancient rites such as worshipping trees and rocks. It was in this environment, in the 1700s, that one local tribesman, Muhammad ibn Abd al-Wahhab, tried instilling a strict interpretation of Islam (*ibn* means "son of" in Arabic). Al-Wahhab had grown up in the Najd, where he was considered something of a child prodigy for his ability to memorize the entire Koran by the age of ten. By twelve he had married—not an uncommon age in Arabia for boys at that time—and settled down to studying Islam. As a teenager, he traveled to Iran and Iraq to learn more about Islamic law, and when he returned to the Najd he was preaching and writing against local paganism and advocating a pure Muslim faith. His core message was strict monotheism, that there is only one God, who does not share power with anyone. Nonbelievers were condemned as infidels. His students called themselves mujahideen ("holy warriors" is the literal Arabic translation). Their detractors referred to them as Wahhabis.

Al-Wahhab attached a militant political dimension to his religious preaching. Some local sheikhs were attracted to his cause, and with their help he destroyed some pagan sites before he was forced into exile in the tiny oasis principality of Ad Diriyah. There, the Saud family welcomed al-Wahhab. Muhammad Saud, head of the family, was also the local emir (chieftain). In 1744, Saud and Muhammad ibn Abd al-Wahhab swore a traditional Muslim *mithaq,* or covenant, promising to work together to establish a state based on the most austere Islamic principles. It was an oath that would change history.

By the time he died, twenty-one years later, Muhammad Saud's private militia had established his uncompromising puritanism and the authority of the Saud family over most of the Najd.[4] Tribal battles that had been a staple of the Arabian peninsula for many generations now had a religious imprimatur. Saud's son Abdul Aziz ibn Saud (called Ibn Saud, "son of Saud"), continued the aggressive Wahhabi onslaught. In 1801, the Saud-Wahhabi armies sacked the shrine of Hussein in Karbala, Iraq. Shiites, whom Wahhabis consider wayward Muslims, were massacred by the thousands.[5] When the city of Taif, at the edge of Mecca, resisted the Sauds, it was ransacked and all its inhabitants, including women and children, were slaughtered.[6] Medina and Mecca fell without a fight, the cities opening their gates in terror to the Sauds, who then embarked on what Wahhabi imams (clerics) called a "cleansing." They destroyed monuments and grave markers used for prayers to Muslim saints and for religious rituals. Thousands of books on Islamic law containing prayers the Wahhabis did not approve, and works of Islam's scientific tradition, were burned. The Sauds considered these acts to be a purification allowed by a central Wahhabi theme, *takfir*, the belief that even Muslims could degenerate into infidels by engaging in improper religious instruction. The destruction of venerated tombs and saint shrines, though, drew sharp criticism from many Muslim communities outside Arabia (similar to the rebuke by moderate Muslims that followed the Taliban's March 2001 destruction of centuries-old Buddhist figures carved into the Bamiyan Valley of Afghanistan).[7]

The Ottomans, the family who ran a sprawling empire from Turkey that covered half the Middle East, could not initially decide how to deal with the Sauds. But something had to be done, as many Muslims considered it an insult to the Ottoman sultan that Ibn Saud had deprived him of the honor of custodianship of the holy mosques in Arabia. And to compound the insult, the Wahhabis interpreted Islam in ways that affected pilgrims visiting the holy cities. For example, convinced of the impermissibility under correct Islamic principles of the traditional camel caravans that annually brought tens of thousands of Syrian and Egyptian pilgrims, the Wahhabis simply banned the caravans. They also condemned as idolaters those pilgrims from other countries who enjoyed playing musical instruments. It was one of many decisions that caused an uproar in more moderate Muslim communities.

Eventually, the Ottoman sultan decided he could no longer tolerate the Wahhabis. He sent an army, mostly Egyptian, to confront them. Conservative Wahhabis viewed the Muslim Ottomans as so liberal as to be nonbelievers. The strictest scholars pronounced the invading Muslim armies to be apostates, condemning the Ottomans and their surrogates as polytheists. The grandson of the founder of Wahhabism, Sulayman ibn Abd Allah, wrote an influential epistle maintaining that not only were the attackers no longer Muslims, but even those in Arabia who assisted them should be considered nonbelievers. Jews and Christians were sorcerers who believed in devil worship (al-shaitan). The letter advocated a rejectionist philosophy toward the outside world and nonbelievers, and became the harsh and uncompromising basis for many subsequent legal, theological, and political positions propounded by conservative Wahhabi scholars.

The Ottoman campaign to destroy the Wahhabis began in earnest in 1811, and was a prolonged and bloody conflict. The Ottoman invaders had orders to obliterate the Wahhabi capital, Diriyah, and they razed the city, murdered its residents, and even burned its lush palm groves (Diriyah never recovered, and its ruins can still be seen just north of Riyadh). The Saud Imam was taken to Istanbul, where he was publicly executed. The Sauds, badly battered, retreated to the then backwater town of Riyadh. The Sauds claimed Riyadh as their capital in 1824, and controlled the city and a very small surrounding territory.

Wahhabi scholars urged rebellion against those who had expelled them from the holy cities. A ranking sheikh, Abd al-Rahman ibn Hasan, set forth the doctrine sanctioning personal jihad as a religious duty to expel nonbelievers and foreign influences. The doctrine of jihad had finally obtained a religious sanction, and the Wahhabis elevated jihad to a central Islamic obligation which they based on interpretations of the Prophet Muhammad's sayings. To the Wahhabis, when Muhammad said "Jihad is the ultimate manifestation of Islam," it did not mean the inner struggle for the individual soul, as interpreted by moderate Muslim scholars, but instead meant nothing less than "armed struggle." But jihad would not help the Sauds repel the Ottomans and Egyptians.[8] Instead, over the next six decades, bitter and often violent interfamily rivalries further damaged the Sauds. In 1890, they were so weakened that the family fled to Kuwait as more moderate Muslim tribes swept into Riyadh.

But Abdul Aziz ibn Saud, the grandson of Muhammad Saud, was now the ruler of his battered tribe, and was determined to return to Arabia and restore his family's honor by recapturing Riyadh and spreading Wahhabism. By 1906, he had battled his way back to power in the Najd, where he became the Wahhabi imam. In the bloody battle for Riyadh, Ibn Saud terrorized local citizens by spiking the heads of his enemies and placing them in a ring surrounding the city's gates. Twelve hundred others were burned to death. And young women were either taken as slaves or given as gifts to powerful friends. But ruthlessness alone was not enough to win the loyalty of disparate tribes with no allegiance to each other. Ibn Saud consolidated his claim to fight for God and Wahhabism by marrying his first wife, the daughter of the leading Riyadh religious leader and a direct descendant of Muhammad ibn Abd al-Wahhab.* And he won over the elders who ran the city's Grand Mosque by giving full authority for all law and morality to the ulema, the religious leaders who claim to have direct knowledge of God's intent.

With the help of Wahhabi Bedouin tribesmen called the Ikhwan Brotherhood, desert survivalists who proudly called themselves "Soldiers of God" and espoused a holy war to spread their evangelism, the Sauds kept adding to the territory they controlled.[10] World War I presented them with a great opportunity, as the Ottoman Empire crumbled and, with its collapse, Ottoman control of eastern Arabia ended. Ibn Saud used the chaos to resume his advances, capturing a string of small cities before seizing Mecca in 1924 and Medina the following year. It was not long after that the Sauds had trouble with their allies the Ikhwan. They were even stricter in interpreting the Koran than the Sauds. Dressed in white robes, with long pointed beards and black antimony paste around their eyes, the Ikhwan attacked non-Muslims in the country. These Islamic purists also eschewed all twentieth-century machinery, ranging from diverse inventions like the telegraph and telephone to the railroad—the only modern device for which they found a Koranic exception was the rifle.

Ibn Saud set about to resolve the theological dispute. He hired an Egyptian religious sheikh, Muhammad Tammimi, to fabricate a family tree

---

*Muslims are allowed to take four wives at any one time, although that is not expressly stated in the Koran (the Prophet Muhammad had nine). Instead it was the solution of Islamic scholars to the large number of widows and orphaned daughters left from the many violent battles in the faith's history. As for female captives, Muslim men were told they could take, as slaves, "those that your right hand possesses." Ibn Saud liberally interpreted the number of wives he was permitted. While he only had four at any one time—in addition to four concubines and four slaves—he changed them regularly. Eventually he took more than one hundred wives, marrying women from each of the thirty major Arabian tribes, solidifying his support among those clans. He had 45 sons and an unknown number of daughters, although the best estimate is over 125.[9] Ibn Saud's sons married some 1,400 women.

to "prove" he was a direct descendant of the Prophet Muhammad. The sheikh's drafts were rejected several times until one finally showed Ibn Saud with a close enough connection to the Prophet that he could claim the upper hand in his religious squabble with the Ikhwan. The Ikhwan were not impressed. So Ibn Saud instead persuaded friendly clerics to issue a fatwa (religious order) condemning the Ikhwan,[11] and then attacked and defeated them in a series of bloody desert battles in 1929. (The combat at al-Sibila, where five thousand Ikhwan were slaughtered, was the last great Bedouin battle in history, shattering forever the military power of the independent tribes.) In those battles, Ibn Saud showed no mercy toward his enemy, personally taking part in public beheadings, floggings, and amputations.[12]

By 1932, the Sauds had consolidated their tribal control over the peninsula. Although his Wahhabi fanaticism had imbued him with the philosophy that he should establish a pure Islamic state as far west as Spain and to Indonesia in the east, Ibn Saud did not have the army to do so. Instead, he settled for establishing an absolute monarchy on the Arabian peninsula. It was a monarchy that had never existed before, and it was not recognized by a single government. Although he was still the fierce-looking desert warrior, with a dark beard, piercing jet-black eyes, and wrapped in the traditional robes and headdress of his clan, he now called himself king, and treated the state as his personal fiefdom.

"The state and its countries and lands are to God, and then they are mine."[13] In a single decree, he announced that all members of his extended family were of royal blood. And on September 22, 1932, Ibn Saud renamed the peninsula the United Kingdom of Saudi Arabia ("the Arabia of the Sauds" is the literal meaning). In the space of thirty years, Ibn Saud, who had started out in exile with a band of forty men, had created a country. For the first time in the peninsula's history, the Sauds supplanted all competing schools of Islamic study and thought with Wahhabism. The Koran was the new country's guidance. Tolerance was not part of their agenda. According to Ibn Saud, "The Arabs understand two things only: the Word of Allah and the sword."[14]

"Prior to the unification, in the great mosques of Mecca and in Medina, all the Islamic schools of thought were represented," says Mai Yamani, a research fellow at the Royal Institute for International Affairs in London. "They had all the Sunni schools of thought; they had the Shi'a; they had each one their own imam and somehow in different corners. . . .

It was after the unification of the Kingdom of Saudi Arabia in 1932 that a process of national homogeneity was attempted [with a move toward] the Wahhabi Islamic thought. . . . They regarded it as much purer because it's more fundamentalist, much more conservative than the people who are like in the south, the people in Mecca, who had more mystical religious trends."[15]

While most of the inhabitants of the Arabian peninsula could trace their families and tribes back for centuries, they had no reason to feel as though the newborn state was anything more than an annoyance. And there were numerous Arabists in Europe, especially in the United Kingdom, where British legations had long histories with Arabia, who thought the Saud family would be short-lived in their effort to create a unified country. The early predictors of disaster pointed out that the new country was teetering on the brink of bankruptcy only a year after it had been founded.

"Neither he [Ibn Saud] nor his government can be expected to last much longer without money," wrote an American diplomat in a 1933 cable to Washington. In an earlier cable, another diplomat stationed in the Kingdom said, "Undoubtedly the Wahhabi family, as it has done twice before, will abandon the Hijaz and retire to Najd, soon after Ibn Saud's death or possibly even earlier."[16]

King Ibn Saud had decided to finance his family's control of Arabia by taxing Muslim pilgrims who flocked annually to Mecca. But many resented the tax, and the number of visitors dramatically dropped during the Kingdom's first year (from 100,000 to fewer than 20,000).[17] Grinding poverty was quickly an overriding problem.

But no one, including the Sauds, could have foreseen the development that saved them. The Sauds' timing in taking control of Arabia could not have been better. A few years earlier, American oil giants had dispatched geological teams to several Middle Eastern countries in search of petroleum reserves. Oil had been discovered in neighboring Iraq in 1927. American geologists had pinpointed the Arabian peninsula as an area that might have its own reserves. In 1933, a year after the Sauds came to power, Ibn Saud, pressured by the country's dire finances, granted broad exploration rights to Standard Oil of California. Standard Oil received an oil concession that covered 360,000 square miles (over one third of the country) for a $35,000 annual fee and two loans totaling $350,000. There were some stiff religious objections from top scholars to allowing *agnabi* (foreigners) into the Kingdom, but Ibn Saud won the blessing of the ulema by convincing them it was permissible to use foreign experts to "extract for our benefit the metals, oil, and water placed by Allah beneath our land."[18]

The price paid by Standard Oil was soon realized to be a fraction of what the rights were worth when the company struck oil in 1936 in the country's eastern province. At first, the oil executives did not realize how stunning the reserves were that they had found. It would take three more years before the first commercially productive field was located. King Ibn Saud celebrated it by personally traveling to the oil field at Dhahran, and, in a simple ceremony on a blistering 110-degree day, opened the valves that then pumped oil into a docked tanker. American oil companies now knew the size of their strike in the Saudi desert was enormous, capable of producing at least twenty times a day more than the best American wells.[19] Geologists dubbed the porous limestone underneath the Arabian peninsula Arab-D. Unique to the eastern coast of Saudi Arabia, it is the richest oil-bearing rock on the planet. The Saudi oil discovery led to the formation of a giant consortium. Named Aramco (Arabian American Oil Company), it consisted of Standard Oil of California, Texas Company (now Texaco), Socony Vacuum (now Mobil), and Standard Oil of New Jersey (now Exxon). Because King Saud was so pleased with the first productive well, he agreed to give Aramco sixty-year leases on 400,000 miles of the peninsula, an area equal to Texas and California combined. For these rights, Aramco agreed to pay $700,000 in gold bullion, a lease fee of $100,000 a year, and another $500,000 when, and if, oil was discovered on the rest of the land.

But the companies and the Saudis were not able to immediately exploit the newfound reserves because World War II intervened. Production was suspended. The oil firms had been advancing Ibn Saud monies against future earnings. But during the war's long hiatus, they stopped the payments. The U.S. stepped in and kept Saudi Arabia solvent, with more than $33 million in government subsidies, until it could start pumping oil again.[20] After the war's end, a new wave of explorations uncovered more gigantic petroleum reserves across the Arabian deserts. By the end of the 1940s, Aramco had started its oil refinery business in earnest. Saudi oil not only turned Aramco into one of the world's largest and most profitable corporations (by the early 1980s, it employed over 50,000 people and had revenues of $50 billion, larger than the budgets of most third world countries), but it also turned out to be the glue that held Saudi Arabia together.[21] Although the Sauds would be the prime beneficiaries, they were smart enough to know that other tribes would have to share in the wealth in order to keep internal unity and peace.

The discovery of oil transformed the Kingdom.

CHAPTER 3

LEGACY OF EXTREMISM

The Arabian peninsula might have had a new name as a unified country with a self-proclaimed monarch and the world's most profitable natural resource in plentiful reserve, but it still held to social anachronisms that made it stand out as a place the twentieth century had seemingly passed by. The most glaring problem was the flourishing tradition of slavery.[1] Chattel slavery was not only protected but also encouraged by law, and children were routinely sold into slavery and prostitution.[2] The main source of slaves was the annual pilgrimage to Mecca, where poor Arabs, primarily Sudanese and Nigerian, sold their children in the holy city to pay for their journeys home. In all the Najd, as well as in the major Saudi cities and towns, every emir, sheikh, and prosperous merchant had at least one black slave family working in his household.

When Crown Prince Faisal ibn Abdul Aziz visited New York in 1944, the management at the Waldorf Astoria was startled to learn he had brought along one of his hundreds of personal slaves, Merzouk. Ibn Saud himself had a nasty reputation for abusing his slaves, wives, and concubines.[3] He maintained a harem of several hundred virgins, who he boasted of taking personally and then giving away as presents to friends.[4] Well into the 1940s, each of Ibn Saud's sons had an *akiwaya,* or "little brother," attached to him. In reality, they were young slave-entertainers whose sole purpose was to keep the king's sons amused and happy.

In such an atmosphere, where some people had been considered for generations as expendable chattel, it was not easy to quickly change the mind-set regarding slavery. Proponents of the trade argued convincingly for the vast majority of Saudis that it was a legitimate business that should not be abandoned merely because non-Islamic Western countries did not approve or understand. In 1962, after President Kennedy pointedly brought up the subject in a private meeting with Prince Faisal, and coordinated pressure from more moderate Arab countries like Egypt, the House of Saud finally abolished the open trade in slaves (it did not change the law allowing the purchase of wives). However, while technically illegal, the practice still flourished until the mid-1970s.[5] Although no longer with the government's stamp of approval, most of the four thousand slaves stayed where they had been before the decree freed them.[6]

Slavery was not the only social and cultural institution that marked Saudi Arabia as a country from a bygone era. The Kingdom's interpretation of Islam was the most radical in the Muslim world, one that longed for a simpler and isolated society that existed centuries earlier. Wahhabism viewed the progress of the modern world as a serious intrusion into the faith. At its core it was a doctrine of intolerance that allowed no dissent. It is not surprising that Wahhabism is the ideological underpinning of today's international terrorism, the succor to Osama bin Laden and his suicidal followers. When the Taliban led Afghanistan back to a feudal society reminiscent of the fourteenth century, Wahhabi ideology was their inspiration.

In Saudi Arabia, Islamic theology is unyielding. "The reason is that the religion is the law," says Prince Amr ibn Muhammad al-Faisal, the grandson of King Faisal. "It permeates the culture. It is rooted in the history. It is part of the DNA, if you like, of the Saudis."[7]

Islamic law based on the Koran is known as "sharia." Under the House of Saud, the civil courts that had existed since the eighth century were disbanded and replaced with ones administered by Islamic clerics. All public behavior is regulated, especially for women and foreigners.

Under the Wahhabi interpretation of Islam, non-Muslims are technically not permitted in the country. But the House of Saud realized early on it would have to welcome foreign diplomats (except in Mecca and Medina, the holy cities, where no non-Muslims are ever allowed). The royals circumvented the taboo by allowing non-Muslim workers and diplomats to enter as "guests" for extended stays. No foreigners, however, can ever become citizens. During the tenures of Ibn Saud and his successor, King

Saud, diplomats who arrived in Riyadh had to don traditional Arab robes before a royal audience. Women were not only barred from the visiting parties, but also not even permitted to wait in the outer chambers lest they contaminate the palace. Christians in the Kingdom, branded apostates, who worked at foreign embassies or with companies were banned from celebrating their religion or having any symbol of their faith, from cruci- fixes to rosaries. (When a supermarket once tried to import Christmas trees for its local foreign residents, the shipment was condemned as infi- del icons, seized, and burned.) When Aramco had a worker play Santa Claus over the holidays during its early days in the Kingdom, the religious police halted it.[8]

American military personnel were allowed to use the Saudi airbase at Dhahran since a deal had been struck between the two countries in 1945. Americans there organized their own religious services, attended by some local Aramco officials. Prince Faisal, feeling pressure from the ulema, fi- nally told the U.S. ambassador, J. Rives Childs, that it was a problem if Christianity was publicly observed anywhere in the Kingdom. Childs ca- bled the secretary of state with the complaint in 1950. Mass and the Chris- tian sacraments became word-of-mouth affairs held at private homes. In the mid-1950s, the Saudis tried, in vain, to penetrate the Dhahran contin- gent to determine whether infidel worship was still being practiced. These problems at Dhahran only concerned Christians. The Saudis would not, of course, allow the U.S. to post Jews there.

Since foreign faiths are considered not just false, but also dangerous to the purity of Wahhabism, mosques are the only religious buildings per- mitted. Into the late 1960s, Jews were prohibited from even entering the Kingdom. Also through the sixties, the Saudi capital, Riyadh, was virtually closed to Westerners. There were no more than three hundred foreigners, almost all diplomats, in Riyadh in 1970.

One of the House of Saud's duties that it considers sacred is *dawah,* the mandate to export Islam outside their own country. But they are con- cerned not only with exporting the extreme tenets of Wahhabism, but also with ensuring that the faithful inside the Kingdom do not stray far from its origins. In the Kingdom's early days, under Ibn Saud, the enforcers of the faith were called the Committee for the Advancement of Virtue and Elimi- nation of Sin, or more informally, the religious police. They ensured that the only version of the Koran enforced as the Kingdom's law was the one interpreted by Wahhabi scholars. Muslims caught with Shiite prayer books were sometimes arrested and jailed.[9]

The Wahhabi version of the Koran made Saudi society austere. Singing and musical instruments were banned. No plants or flowers were allowed in terraces or backyards. Laughing inside a home, if loud enough to be heard on the street, earned the offender a knock on the door and a warning from the religious police. People were punished for wearing gold, Western clothes, perfume, or silk.[10] Pet ownership was banned, and most pets, said religious authorities, were profane in any case.

By the mid-1930s, societies of the ultrareligious had formed citizen patrols in virtually every neighborhood in the country. Dubbing themselves, by then, Committees for the Propagation of Virtue and the Prevention of Vice, these bearded zealots dressed in pure white robes roamed the streets, wielding canes not only to distinguish themselves, but also to snap them at offenders of Wahhabi regulations. They enforced dress codes and sex segregation. Those who refused to obey their orders were often beaten and sometimes jailed. In Riyadh, as the sun set, the virtue patrols walked through the marketplace beating on the windows and yelling *"Salaat"* ("prayer") at any shopkeeper who was slow to close his doors. All Muslims must stop five times daily, at set intervals, kneel facing Mecca, and pray to Allah.

Excesses of Western civilizations, especially those viewed as corrupting influences by Wahhabi scholars, are forbidden. Alcohol is banned. When nonalcoholic drinks with tastes similar to beers and wines were invented, the Saudis promptly forbade those as well, lest citizens get a taste for liquor. Vanilla extract was forbidden since it contains a trace of alcohol.[11] Cigarettes were banned under King Saud and only allowed after he abdicated in 1964.

Technological advances have always been controversial, since modernity meant Westernization to the most conservative religious authorities. Radio was only let into the Kingdom after the religious authorities were convinced that they had to battle the godless radio then penetrating the Kingdom from Cairo stations. Therefore, they broadcast Koranic verses for hundreds of miles from their own stations. The only program was Radio Mecca, basically a nonstop recitation of Koranic verses. Telephones were given the Koranic blessing since they allowed imams in one city to talk to ulema in another, so they facilitated religious solidarity. But still the ulema warned against men and women talking directly to one another unless they were married or relatives.[12]

Cameras were originally banned from the Kingdom because the mullahs feared they might be able to take a picture of God, which would be heretical. Planes might provoke God's anger by flying too near the divinity in the sky. It took years of patient argument to win the necessary religious blessings for both technological innovations.*

When television arrived in 1965, King Faisal only got the blessing of the religious sheikhs for the innovation by calling it a "test," and programming a nonstop schedule of religious readings, prayers, and theological instruction. The equivalent of Saturday-morning cartoons for children was a show in which a jury of bearded, dark-spectacled sheikhs quizzed nine- and ten-year-old star pupils on how much of the Koran they had memorized. (Today, it is endless hours of European football, nature programs, and Islamic lessons.) Still, the introduction of television, though offering only strict Islamic fare, caused uproar among the ultrareligious. Even some members of the royal family dissented. Khalid ibn Musa'id, the king's nephew, and a group of fellow-minded Wahhabi zealots stormed the only television station. King Faisal was not a monarch accustomed to dissent, even from his family. He authorized the police to shoot his nephew dead at the demonstration. The protest against television fizzled after that.

Ibn Saud, after watching a U.S. propaganda documentary on board an American ship that took him to meet Franklin Roosevelt, said, "I doubt whether my people should have moving pictures like this. . . . It would give them an appetite for entertainment which might distract them from their religious duties." All of Ibn Saud's successors have agreed with him, and movies are not allowed in Saudi Arabia.[14]

Western books, magazines, and newspapers are permitted so long as any offending material is excised or covered. The Saudis employ hundreds of third-world laborers, armed with brushes and ink pots, to block out everything from ads for alcohol to articles containing pictures of scantily clad women. An article in *Time* about breast cancer was cut from copies distributed in the Kingdom since there was an anatomical drawing of a breast. An issue of *Newsweek* with a cover story on AIDS was banned. *Time* suffered the same fate when it ran a story that mentioned the laziness of the king.[15]

Women are singled out in Wahhabism for special restrictions. There

---

*Saudi Arabian Airlines, with a modern fleet of Airbuses and Boeing 777s, has a recording loudly repeating *"Allah akbar"*—"God is great"—as the plane taxis for takeoff or lands. TV screens in each cabin show a compass pointing to Mecca so passengers will know which way to face at prayer time. At the rear of each plane is a space where up to nine people can spread prayer rugs.[13]

is virtually no mobility outside their households, where they are supposed to focus solely on raising their children. No public contact is allowed between the men and women.* Even Valentine's Day is banned as a Christian holiday that might encourage unauthorized socializing between the sexes.

Women's activities are always segregated from men's. Women are banned from performing legal or financial transactions on their own. The Saudi American Bank, for instance, like other banks in the Kingdom, has women's branches, with separate entrances staffed by women.[16] Job opportunities are almost nonexistent, with women making up only 5 percent of the workforce, and most of those jobs are in retail sales and health care. A girl cannot accept a job in a rural area if it requires that she live apart from her family. Even at work, the sexes are segregated. Female employees can only deal with a male supervisor or client via telephone or fax (on Saudi Arabian Airlines, Saudi women cannot be flight attendants because it would require them to work with Saudi men, so all the airline's female flight attendants are from less strict Muslim countries, like Morocco or Jordan). At Herfy's, a Saudi-owned chain of fast-food restaurants, the booths in the "family section" are curtained so women can eat without being seen by male customers.

When parents in Riyadh take their children out for an evening, the men might head to the country's only ice-skating rink. No women are allowed. Even marriage ceremonies, usually held in rented wedding halls, are segregated. The groom enjoys dinner with his male friends and relatives in one room, while the bride and her female guests dine and dance in another. Bride and groom only get together to pose for wedding pictures with their families.

Saudi women can't travel abroad without a husband's permission. Daughters can inherit only half as much as sons, and a woman's testimony is given only half the weight of a man's in court.[17] Husbands who take additional spouses are not required to tell their wives about the new marriages.**

---

*The fact that contact between unrelated men and women is banned in Saudi Arabia has led to a boom in illicit phone sex, which the religious police have been unable to stamp out. Author Paul Theroux, who spent three years in the Kingdom, found that Saudi women often called him in the hope that, since he was a foreigner, he might be more willing to engage in the prohibited talk.
**Among educated urban dwellers in Saudi Arabia, polygamy has lost much favor. But senior royals still adhere to it. Crown Prince Abdullah, who effectively runs the country, always has his quota of four wives, but over time has had more than thirty.

Even after cars were allowed into the Kingdom, women were banned from driving and obtaining a driver's license. It is also against Wahhabism for women to ride motorcycles, or even bicycles, in public.[18] When, in November 1990, a group of forty-five Saudi women took their husbands' cars and drove them to downtown Riyadh to protest the ban on driving, they were detained and taken to hospitals where they were invasively tested for semen, alcohol, and drugs. Several lost their jobs, and some "ringleaders" were arrested, tried, and imprisoned.[19] Others had their passports confiscated. They were denounced in mosques around the Kingdom as "whores," their conduct was called "depraved," and many received harassing telephone calls.[20] The Saudi security service placed them under surveillance.[21]

The main role for women in Wahhabi Islam is to bear children. Contraception was banned by the government until 1980. Married life is spent mostly in the company of female relatives, raising the couple's children and tending to the husband's needs. A wife can seldom divorce her husband—only when a local imam, based on excessive physical abuse or the failure of a husband to support the family, grants a special dispensation. But a husband can divorce his wife simply by saying, "I divorce you, I divorce you, I divorce you." Children stay with the divorced mother until the age of seven, when they are turned over to the father.[22]

In 1980, when *Washington Post* editorial page editor Meg Greenfield took an extended trip through Saudi Arabia, she reported that what surprised her most was that "this is a public world without women. In Riyadh, you will see no woman in the restaurant, in the government office building, in the hotel lobby, in the lounge. You will see no women as hotel maids or as secretaries or as casual strollers-by. You will see no women in the heavy auto traffic, no women's pictures in the newspapers or in depiction on the walls. It's as if there are none."[23]

When Aramco established its extensive operations in the Kingdom in the late 1940s, foreign women who worked or accompanied their husbands to live in the Kingdom could only drive inside the company's walled compounds. Whenever they ventured outside the Aramco encampments, they had to cover their arms and legs so as not to offend the Committees of Public Morality, which were concerned with the insidious effects of Western culture, especially when it came to women. The uncovered legs of Western women were sometimes literally spray-painted with black paint by disapproving Saudis.[24]

In 1964, when King Faisal assumed the monarchy from his brother Saud, the fourth and last of Faisal's wives, Iffat al-Thunayan, tried fulfilling a long ambition of hers not only to open a school for girls, but also to introduce some Western subjects like science and foreign language into schools for boys. When the Kingdom was founded in 1932, there were no schools in the capital, Riyadh. Instead, local mosques served as schools, and under the Saudi system there was no Western-style effort to probe and inquire about different subjects. Instead, the goal of education in the Kingdom was to memorize long portions of the Koran. Higher education for men was not even available until 1957.[25] Under Ibn Saud, not a single girls' school had opened.[26]

It is not surprising that Ibn Saud did not put much emphasis on education. He himself was semiliterate, thought all Americans were Red Indians, that the world was flat, and never learned fundamental differences among other faiths, such as the distinction between Catholics and Protestants.[27] More than once Ibn Saud did not recognize the Saudi national anthem when it was played, and had to be instructed about what to do when it was. One of the few times he ventured out of Saudi Arabia was to Egypt, where he told the foreign minister, "This country is full of pretty women and I would like to buy some of them and take them back home. How about £100,000 worth of them?"* About women and education, he said, "Learning does not become women."[28] His son and successor, Saud, was little better. "People who dealt with him never considered him bright," recalls Mike Ameen, vice president of Aramco in the 1970s.[29] "I do not recall any substantive thing Saud ever said on any issue," says Hermann Eilts, U.S. ambassador to the Kingdom from 1965 to 1970.[30]

When the citizens of the town of Buraydah heard the rumors in 1964 that Faisal's wife wanted to open a school for girls and expand the curriculum for boys, they assaulted the building where they believed it might happen. Faisal had to send in the National Guard to quell the violent mobs. The headmistress of the first girls' school had to be installed by force.

*Evidently picking up their father's view of women, many of Ibn Saud's sons developed nasty reputations, especially outside the Kingdom. Typical was one son who thought any and all European women in bikinis were for sale and repeatedly tried to buy them to bring them back to Saudi Arabia. Some of the sons embarrassed other royals and the religious authorities by consorting frequently with the most expensive prostitutes in Paris and London and distributing like calling cards solid-gold watches with the picture of their father on the dial (Ibn Saud so liked the watches that he gave away 35,000 of them as gifts in a single year).

The only pupil during the first year was the headmistress's daughter.[31] But slowly, Iffat, with the approval of her husband, moved the Kingdom to accept the idea of girls attending school.

By 1975, a quarter million girls were enrolled in Saudi schools, although the chairman of the religious committee in charge of female schools had replaced the hours originally intended for scientific and mathematic study with simple Koranic repetition. Saudi schools for women were, for many years, merely religious study classes.* And even today, Saudi women are excluded from studying subjects such as journalism, architecture, and engineering. While men can study overseas, Saudi women can do so only if accompanied by a male relative.[32]

The harshness of rules applied to women may be illustrated best in a tragic incident in Mecca involving the *muttawa,* the religious police, on March 14, 2000. A fire broke out in a girls' school. While eight hundred students started fleeing the burning structure, the religious police arrived and stopped some schoolgirls from leaving because they were not wearing the head scarves and abayas (black robes) required by the Kingdom's strict interpretation. Fifteen girls died in the blaze and more than fifty others were injured. According to a Saudi newspaper, *al-Eqtisadiah,* firemen confronted police as they tried to keep the girls inside. One witness saw three policemen "beating young girls to prevent them from leaving the school because they were not wearing the abaya." The religious police also prevented men from helping the girls and warned, "It is sinful to approach them." The school had been locked at the time of the fire, a usual practice to ensure full segregation of the sexes.[33] Even some Saudis were outraged at the actions of the religious police, but no disciplinary action or prosecutions ever resulted.

———

While Faisal might have made small progress by allowing women into their own schools, on other fronts strict Wahhabis had a revival under Faisal, a power they maintain to this day. The Kingdom's leading Wahhabi

*While schools for girls were one of Faisal's reforms, it was one of the few moves toward liberalization he allowed. He dismissed every attempt at democratization, and filled the country's government and ministerial positions with his own family. Once, when asked after the opening of the first girls' school when he was going to grant women rights, Faisal said, "When we grant them to men."

cleric, the grand mufti, Sheikh Muhammad ibn Ibrahim, had urged Faisal in the beginning of his tenure to make "Saudi Arabia lead the Arab world," and maintained that "the ideology of Wahhabism should be exported."[34] Through organizations founded under Faisal's tenure, such as the Muslim World League and the World Assembly of Muslim Youth, the Saudis became aggressive in spreading Wahhabism beyond their borders. Since the early 1970s, billions of dollars have gone to support Wahhabi mosques, community centers, schools, and associations in dozens of countries.[35] The Saudi funds always come with a string: unless their version of Islam is the one taught or proselytized, the money will be cut off.

And Saudi universities have become major sources for instilling Wahhabism in a generation of students. Two of the most prominent, the Islamic University of Medina and King Abdul Aziz University, have student bodies that are up to 85 percent non-Saudi, making them effective tools for spreading Wahhabism among non-Saudi Muslims.[36]

Radicals in the Islamic world not only embrace the absolutist interpretation of Wahhabism, but also know that Saudi Arabia has traditionally been a safe haven when other Muslim countries have cracked down on hard-liners. When Egypt's Gamal Abdel Nasser promoted secular Arab nationalism and set about to crush the Muslim Brotherhood, Egypt's Islamic fundamentalists, Saudi Arabia gave the Brotherhood's leaders asylum. Most who sought safety in the Kingdom were given jobs at Saudi schools or Islamic organizations. That further commingled the Muslim Brotherhood's belief that the West's secularism was dangerous together with the Saudi view that Wahhabi Islam was the only true faith and all Muslims were duty bound to spread it. In this view, the West was not only the enemy of Islam, but there could be no coexistence with nonbelievers, only conflict until one side or the other prevailed. At Saudi universities, popular professors, like Dr. Ali Muhammad Jarishan and Muhammad Sharif al-Zubayq, taught that secularism itself was "aggression against Islamic legitimacy."[37]

One of those given refuge in Saudi Arabia was Muhammad Qutb, the brother of Sayyid, a prolific Muslim scholar who did a watershed six-volume commentary on the Koran, setting the guidelines for modern Wahhabi adherents. It was the anti-Western themes of Sayyid Qutb—executed by Nasser in Egypt in 1966—that became the trademark of the Kingdom's brand of faith. The term *salibi* (Crusader) was used to describe Christians, and Qutb concluded that "the Crusader spirit runs in the blood of all Occidentals."[38] To scholars like Qutb, the Crusades were still ongoing.[39] Typical of many virulently anti-Christian books was *The Facts That the Muslim Must Know About Christianity and Missionary Activity*. It declared, "The Crusader wars that were ignited by the enemies of Islam continue. We suffer from its influence in the Philippines, in Lebanon, Ethiopia, Nigeria, Sudan, Chad, Bulgaria, Thailand, Palestine, and others. These wars will continue until Allah will take possession of the earth, or until the reasons for these wars will be uprooted."[40]

In the years immediately before the attack on America, up until 9/11, when the House of Saud urged the Kingdom's religious leaders to tone down their harsh Wahhabi rhetoric, Saudi mosques were the breeding grounds for militant Islamic provocation. Leading imams condemned Christianity as a "distorted and twisted religion," and claimed that any interfaith dialogue was "sinful . . . and forbidden" since it would only distort Islam with "the satanic path of heresy." Since Christians and Jews were apostates, Saudi textbooks teach that it is acceptable in their interpretation of the faith to "demolish, burn or destroy [their] bastions."[41] (Wahhabi religious leaders have controlled Saudi education since the king ceded that right in 1963.)[42]

Saudi religious charities, long the cornerstone of fueling Wahhabi radicalism outside the Kingdom, sponsored firebrand religious leaders like Sheikh Mohammed al-Fazazi, who toured Europe before 9/11 giving thunderous sermons to standing-room-only crowds, condemning Christian and Jewish "infidels" and telling local Muslims about the necessity to fight a "jihad" against America.

"The Jews and Crusaders must have their throats slit," said Fazazi, as he implored those who listened to "fight the Americans as long as they are keeping Muslims in prison."

Many of Fazazi's preachings are recorded on videotapes. Some of those were seized by German police in a bookstore only two blocks from the Hamburg mosque frequented by Mohamed Atta, the lead hijacker in the 9/11 attacks. Other Fazazi hate-filled sermons were confiscated from the apartment of Atta's former roommate.[43]

Muslim extremists who found safe refuge in the Wahhabi Kingdom include the Palestinian firebrand Abdullah Azzam, dubbed "the Emir of Jihad," and Osama bin Laden's mentor. Hassan al-Turabi—who later welcomed Osama bin Laden to the Sudan for five years—sought refuge in the Kingdom when he was in exile during the 1970s. The blind Egyptian cleric

Sheikh Omar Abdel Rahman, who was convicted in 1995 for his role in an aborted day of terror in New York, spent safe years in Saudi Arabia teaching at a college. In the 1980s, the Saudis welcomed Ayman al-Zawahiri, bin Laden's number two man, who today has a $25 million bounty on his head for terrorism and his role in 9/11. The men who later led a terror war against America and the West found safety only in the Kingdom.

CHAPTER 4

THE EMBARGO

Wahhabism might be the unifying thread among the peninsula's historically rival tribes, but it provided little guidance when it came to modern issues confronting the monarchy about relations with the rest of the world,
especially the United States. What drove Saudi foreign policy from its earliest days was not so much religious fervor, but rather what the House of
Saud considered an incredibly effective American Jewish lobby. The assumption accepted as gospel in the Arab world is that the political muscle
of the small but powerful American Jewish community is the reason that
U.S. foreign policy is skewed pro-Israel and anti-Arab. The Saudis, sitting
on vast oil reserves that the West needs, decided early on to develop a
competitive Arab lobby.

They found a strong ally in Aramco. The oil companies and their Saudi
partners have tried—and sometimes succeeded—to be a factor in U.S.
politics since shortly after World War II. King Ibn Saud personally peti-
tioned Franklin Roosevelt before his death, as well as Winston Churchill,
beseeching them not to grant "the ambitions of the Zionists."[1] In 1948,
Aramco officials joined in opposing the creation of Israel, and lobbied the
Truman administration not to recognize the Jewish state. Truman listened
to both sides, and then told his aides, "I'm sorry, gentlemen, but I have
to answer to hundreds of thousands who are anxious for the success of
Zionism; I do not have hundreds of thousands of Arabs among my con-

stituents."[2] An angry Ibn Saud threatened to take away Aramco's oil concession and grant it to British firms, but he did not.[3]

Safe with its Saudi oil concession, Aramco turned to lobbying the Treasury Department to get special tax treatment of its revenues. In 1951 it succeeded. Treasury issued a unique ruling whereby the American oil firms in the Kingdom were given a special "oil tax credit." It was based on a creative interpretation of an overlooked 1918 tax law.[4] What it effectively did was allow the oil businesses to treat their royalty payments to the Saudis as taxes. Aramco's 1950 taxes were $50 million, but dropped to $6 million in the year following the Treasury Department ruling. The American taxpayer had unwittingly become the underwriter of Aramco's payments to Saudi Arabia.[5]*

In 1952, Saudi military forces occupied neighboring Oman's lush Buraimi Oasis over a long-simmering territorial dispute. Aramco provided free transportation for the Kingdom's soldiers.[6] And some government officials with whom the Saudis frequently dealt ended up at Aramco. Diplomat Terry Duce became Aramco's president. William Eddy, U.S. minister to Saudi Arabia, resigned to become a company advisor. His strong anti-Israel positions made him an instant favorite with the House of Saud.[7] The CIA's Joe Ellender and James Russell Barracks moved to Aramco's government relations department.

For Ibn Saud, those job switches reinforced his conviction that the U.S. government and the oil companies were closely allied. It was a partnership he approved. There was some temporary hand-wringing at Aramco, however, when Ibn Saud suddenly died in 1953. Under his rule, the state treasury had been the king's private purse, and Aramco had ensured that the king had plenty of money to spend. Ibn Saud had exhausted nearly $400 million of the country's oil revenues on himself and his family, with almost nothing going toward the country's infrastructure. Riyadh had no traffic lights. The electrical system was a patchwork that provided power only about half the day. The telephone system was often broken, with some customers waiting up to two years for service on lines that had stopped working. Urban towns that were desert market settlements before

---

*Aramco eventually treated more than $24 billion in payments to the Saudis as deductible foreign income tax rather than less tax-advantageous royalties. The American public only learned of the arrangement when muckraking syndicated columnist Jack Anderson disclosed in 1982 that Aramco's deal had allowed it to offset *all* its annual tax liability despite then having nearly $40 billion in annual revenues.

oil was discovered were still waiting for funds, planning, and technicians to bring them up-to-date.

The line of succession in Saudi Arabia is strictly based on seniority. Ibn Saud's eldest son and heir was also named Saud. By the age of fifty-two, he had taken more than one hundred wives.[8] As ignorant of statecraft as his father, and as morally and financially corrupt, Saud, to Aramco's relief, changed little after the transfer of power.[9] In his first year as king, Saud claimed the country's entire $234.8 million in oil revenues as personal income.

The Saudis were so close to Aramco officials that Saud asked them unofficially how to better deal with the U.S. government. At Aramco's suggestion, in 1957, even though he was still smarting over the U.S.'s support of Israel in its 1956 war with Arab countries, the new king agreed to a five-year extension for the American military's use of Dhahran as a staging post. President Eisenhower had also done his best to soothe Saud's feelings. When Saud visited the U.S. in 1957, the president drove to the airport to greet him, the first time Eisenhower had done so for a foreign leader. He also cleverly made Saud feel as though Saudi Arabia was an important part of America's anti-Communist camp.[10] After that summit, Saudi Arabia received a generous $180 million increase in economic and military aid. The CIA sent senior Washington-based agents like Kim Roosevelt and Harry Kern for frequent visits to the Kingdom to provide advice to the royal family on everything from foreign policy to military preparedness.[11] And as an added bonus for the Saudis, under the newly proclaimed "Eisenhower doctrine," the House of Saud was to be a moderating Middle Eastern influence, counterbalancing the radical rhetoric from Egypt's Gamal Abdel Nasser.[12] Aramco's advice to the royals to extend the U.S. military lease on Dhahran had been good.

And for its part, Aramco seemed eager to follow Saudi dictates even if they skirted the edge of legality in the U.S. For instance, until 1959, Aramco had successfully lobbied for an exemption from New York State's antidiscrimination laws and was allowed to ask prospective employees if they were Jews, on the grounds that Saudi Arabia refused to admit Jews. When this arrangement was finally challenged in a lawsuit, the State Department, incredibly, intervened on behalf of Aramco, fearing that to do otherwise might offend the Saudis. The New York State Supreme Court strongly condemned the practice, directing Aramco, "Go elsewhere to serve your Arab master—but not in New York State." The New York State

Commission Against Discrimination finally ordered Aramco to stop complying with the Saudi ban on Jews.[13] And although Aramco stopped directly asking the question about religious affiliation, the word in the oil industry was widespread for at least another decade that Jews need not apply for any of Aramco's Saudi projects.[14]

By the 1960s, Aramco and other Saudi watchers were fretting over Saud's tenure as king. He had become an utterly ineffective leader and his botched rule threatened the continuity of the monarchy.[15] He drank heavily, to the fury of the religious authorities who knew of his secret addiction.[16] Also, according to author Said Aburish, it was not a very well kept secret inside the royal family that Saud had a liking for young boys, and that the CIA willingly procured some for him, giving his critics the credible argument that it exposed the king to personal blackmail.[17] Finally, his extravagant lifestyle was literally threatening the Kingdom with bankruptcy. One episode particularly infuriating to many Saudis occurred when the construction of a water project and several bridges was delayed so government funds could instead be diverted to lavish simultaneous weddings for six of the king's sons.[18]

"They were making a lot of money," recalls Aramco vice president Mike Ameen, "but they were spending it foolishly. They were broke.'"[19]

The national treasury was almost empty after a decade of Saud's mismanagement. Saud had built a palace for $10 million, but didn't like the way it looked, so he tore it down and put up a new one for $30 million. He once drove a Cadillac, and when it ran out of gas the first time, he gave it away, and bought a new one with a full tank. He and his family set records in personal consumption from the beginning of his reign. In November 1964, Saud abdicated after the religious authorities and some seventy-two senior princes forced him out.[20]*

Saud's half brother Faisal ibn Abdul Aziz, who had served previously as foreign minister and prime minister, ascended to the throne. Faisal, in contrast to the country's first two kings, had traveled extensively, was well-read, and was worldly beyond the Kingdom. He was more effective at governing, but his taking of the throne initially did not change the cozy rela-

*Saud spent his last years exiled in Athens, Greece. As had his father, he flaunted his rights of marriage when he was king. He had at least fifty-two sons and fifty-five daughters. His eleven-year rule is now considered an embarrassment to most Saudi historians. In government buildings, while the walls are adorned with pictures of the country's different kings, Saud's is almost always missing. Until recently, no street or building had been named for him.

tionship between Aramco and the House of Saud. In June 1967, some of Aramco's compounds were damaged, and its workers threatened, by rampaging mobs furious over the six-day military debacle suffered by Egypt, Syria, and Jordan at the hands of Israel. Anything American, including local consulates, was the object of the crowd's anger as they blamed America's military support of Israel for the crushing Arab defeat.[21] But beyond that incident, there were no major problems in the relationship between the oil giants and the Sauds until the early 1970s.

Trouble did not originate inside the Kingdom. Instead, it began with a radical new Arab leader, a young Libyan colonel, Muammar al-Qaddafi. He demanded higher payments from the American oil firms pumping crude in his country. When they refused, relying on long-term contracts that spelled out cheap royalty rates, Qaddafi ordered the oil firm executives to slash their Libyan crude production in half. That sent shock waves through oil company boardrooms worldwide. Threatened with nationalization, the oil firms capitulated by the end of 1970 and agreed to pay Libya significantly more to run petroleum operations there.

Libya's breakthrough had a domino effect, encouraging other oil-rich countries to confront the American and European consortiums that had long benefited from inexpensive petroleum and cheap royalties. Although major oil producers, primarily Arab, had formed a cartel, OPEC (the Organization of Petroleum Exporting Countries), in 1960, it wasn't until Qaddafi stared down Occidental and other large multinationals that OPEC realized it too was in a strong bargaining position. Years earlier, having just emerged in many instances from colonial domination, these often backward countries were pleased to discover they were fortunate to have giant oil reserves, and they also considered their early deals with companies like Aramco to be good ones. The Western firms did all the work, extracted and exported the crude, and without any responsibilities the oil-rich countries raked in billions annually in royalties. Only when these countries realized that their natural resource was truly indispensable to an industrialized world that ran on petroleum did they begin to appreciate their own strength. So long as OPEC members could agree on a single price, they could magnify their negotiating power.

From 1970 to 1972, OPEC's members did not just want higher royalties, they also fought for partial control of the oil firms' assets. If the companies did not agree to give up partial equity, they knew nationalization of their assets was a possibility. In October 1972, the OPEC pressure succeeded, and all the parties signed a substantial new contract titled "The General Agreement." Each company transferred a quarter of its assets to its host country. Aramco and the Saudis, through the oil minister, Sheikh Ahmed Zaki Yamani, negotiated future ownership transfers on a sliding scale, culminating in 1983, when the House of Saud would own a controlling 51 percent of Aramco.

The Saudis understandably were emboldened. Before Faisal, the monarchy seemed incapable of coping with the growing complexities created by the rush of oil dollars and the lure of modernization. But Faisal was not at all intimidated by the challenge confronting him, and set about an ambitious program of economic and social development. The growing sense of power from controlling enormous oil reserves was something Faisal relished, and he encouraged his ministers to use it to Saudi Arabia's advantage. The Kingdom's smooth oil minister, Sheikh Yamani, soon ignored the General Agreement's terms and demanded that Aramco pay even more in royalties. It added to the tension between the House of Saud and the American conglomerate. Saudi oil ministry officials complained that Aramco placed too much stress on the physical infrastructure of large oil fields, since they excessively pumped enormous quantities of light crude. Had Aramco exceeded geologically prudent standards in order to produce as much oil as possible prior to a possible nationalization of its Saudi assets? Some Saudi nationalists demanded that all Aramco contracts be broken. The Oil Ministry launched a public affairs campaign, urging surrogates to give inflammatory press interviews attacking Aramco at international industry conferences.[22]

But Aramco executives saw a way out. It involved a completely separate political matter, but one the executives thought might endear them to the House of Saud and earn enough good capital inside the Kingdom that it could defuse the vexing oil dispute. The issue was Israel and the Jews. King Faisal had an undisguised hatred of both.

Even in a country based on an austere religion, Faisal was recognized as pious and stern. He was widely known in the Arab world for his asceticism. And he was also far more of an Islamic fundamentalist than his predecessor, Saud. Faisal was proud that his mother was a direct descendant of Muhammad al-Wahhab. His grandfather, who had raised him after his mother's death when he was only six, was himself a strict Wahhabi scholar. The religious authorities, the ulema, had been largely responsible for Saud's abdication and Faisal's rise to the throne. Faisal enthusiastically supported the recently formed Muslim World League, a Mecca-based outfit of religious dignitaries with a stated goal of spreading Wahhabism internationally, convincing non-Wahhabi Muslims to adopt the Saudi interpretation and to convert nonbelievers.[23] And he created new government ministries under the control of the religious leaders, the most important being education.*

New institutions, such as the Directorate of Religious Research, Islamic Legal Rulings, Islamic Propagation and Guidance, and the Ministry of Pilgrimage and Religious Endowment, among others, gave the Wahhabi scholars newfound power under Faisal. Top theological leaders, such as Sheikh Ibrahim bin Muhammad Al al-Sheik, the son of the grand mufti, and the future grand mufti, a blind Wahhabi cleric, Sheikh bin Baz, met weekly with Faisal (bin Baz was the epitome of a narrow-minded religious leader, long agreeing with Ibn Saud that the earth was flat, and refusing to believe that man had ever traveled to the moon).[24] It was as if Faisal had revitalized the oath made between Wahhab and the founder of the House of Saud in the 1700s.

The religious authorities encouraged Faisal's burning hatred of Jews and Israel, similar to the almost pathological feelings he shared with the first king, Ibn Saud. In 1937, Ibn Saud had told a reporter that "the word of God teaches us—and we implicitly believe this—that for a Muslim to kill a Jew, or for him to be killed by a Jew, ensures him an immediate entry in Heaven and into the august presence of God Almighty."[25] Ibn Saud had feared that Zionism would mean a Jewish empire stretching from Medina across the Persian Gulf, and bemoaned that the Nazi Holocaust had created such guilt in America and England that European Jews would now get a country at the expense of Arabs.

The Koran was used by Saudi clerics to legitimize the monarchy's anti-Jewish fever.[26] Portions of the Koran that condemned Jews—"The Jews are the enemies of Allah, of the prophet and of the angels" (2:97–98); "they lie against Allah" (4:50); "they have killed the prophets of Allah" (5:70); "they are enemies of the believers" (5:82); "they will receive the punishment of hell-fire (59:3)"—were given ever more prominence.

A mandatory Saudi textbook, *Introduction to the Science of History,* condemned Jews as intrinsically evil, and taught that they were a "corrupt

---

*About 125,000 students are enrolled in Saudi Arabia's six universities, three of which are strict religious institutions. Seventy percent major in Islamic studies, a curriculum set by the religious authorities.

and deceitful" race.[27] A 1968 conference of the Academy of Islamic Research had produced a body of virulent anti-Semitism from Muslim scholars, calling Jews a "pest and plague," "cursed by Satan," and "thirsty for drinking more blood of Muslims."

Faisal went beyond even what Ibn Saud thought of Jews. He contended that Zionism and communism were two sides of the same international conspiracy, a plot by Jews to take over the world.[28] When a reporter asked Faisal why the Soviet Union was not supporting Israel, but rather strenuously backing the Syrians, Egyptians, and Jordanians in Middle East politics, the king waved him off. "It's all part of a plot, a grand conspiracy. Communism, as I told you, is a Zionist creation designed to fulfill the aims of Zionism. They are only pretending to work against each other."

Faisal ordered that all hotels have the infamous anti-Semitic forgery, the *Protocols of Zion,* as bedside reading.[29] Foreign diplomats and titans of industry, whenever they had an audience with the king, were accustomed to hearing at least a thirty-minute monologue on the evils of Jews and how their Zionist plots were about to destroy the world.[30] Henry Kissinger was among those who received a copy of the *Protocols* from the king.[31]*

Faisal believed that Jews used the blood of Muslims and Christians in their religious holidays. In 1972, Faisal told an Arabic newspaper, "It happened that two years ago while I was in Paris on a visit, the police discovered five murdered children. Their blood had been drained, and it turned out that some Jews had murdered them in order to take their blood and mix it with the bread that you eat on this day [Passover]. This shows you what is the extent of their hatred and malice toward non-Jewish people." In 1973, Faisal attended a conference in Damascus and stressed the importance of understanding this alleged Jewish bloodlust in order to appreciate the magnitude of the "Zionist crime."[32]*

Protocols of the Learned Elders of Zion was published around 1900, and purported to set out a secret plot by Jewish leaders, gathering in 1897 at the first Zionist Congress in Basel, Switzerland, to dominate the world. Millions of copies of the *Protocols* have been translated into dozens of languages. American car magnate Henry Ford, himself a fervent anti-Semite, quoted from them freely and gave them as gifts to friends. It was not until 1921 that author Philip Graves convincingly demonstrated that the *Protocols* had been plagiarized, often word for word, from an obscure French satire of the 1800s. Later, Russian historian Vladimir Burtsev proved the *Protocols* had been forged by the czarist secret police to discredit Karl Marx and other Jewish opponents of the czar. The discovery that the *Protocols* were fakes hasn't stopped them from being widely distributed. Arabic translations are still widely available. The Palestinian terror group Hamas invokes the *Protocols* in its charter.

When Israel captured Jerusalem in the Six-Day War in 1967, an Australian Christian suffering from mental problems set fire to the al-Aqsa Mosque, Islam's holiest shrine there. Israeli firemen reacted quickly and saved the mosque. But for Faisal, it confirmed his worst suspicions. He viewed the incident as irrefutable evidence that Jews intended to destroy all Islamic sites, starting with those in Jerusalem. By 1972, Faisal was fed up with the continuing American support for Israel, and what he considered the political pandering for Jewish votes that had started in earnest in the 1968 Nixon-Humphrey presidential election.

The Aramco executives, who lived in a sprawling compound on a hilltop in Dhahran, had decided they needed to placate the king's anti-Jewish, anti-Israel anger. On May 3, 1973, Aramco's soft-spoken president, Frank Jungers, met with Faisal, Oil Minister Yamani, and Foreign Minister Ommar Saqqaf in Riyadh. On this occasion the discussion was not about increased royalty payments, reduced crude production, or possible nationalization of Aramco's assets. Instead, the king bluntly told Jungers that to keep Aramco's lucrative monopoly in the Kingdom, the consortium had to change American foreign policy on the Middle East.

"I'm going to have to tell you, you're simply not doing enough," Faisal told Jungers. "And I'm serious about this."[34]

The king insisted it was time for Aramco to unequivocally demonstrate its loyalty.[35]

Two weeks later, Faisal demanded that the Aramco board of directors fly to Switzerland to meet him in his lavish hotel suite during a break in an OPEC summit. They apprehensively complied. According to notes taken by W. J. McQuinn, Standard Oil of California's vice president in charge of foreign operations, the king reminded the oil executives that Aramco's concession was in jeopardy. "Time is running out," the king warned them, "you may lose everything." McQuinn noted, "Things we must do (1) inform U.S. public of their true interests in the area. They are now being misled by controlled news media; and (2) inform Government leaders—and promptly."[36]

---

*Even as late as 2002, an article in the prestigious Saudi daily *Al Riyadh* accused Jews of "consuming the blood of Christian and Muslim children during the holiday of Purim." The author, a professor of Islamic studies at King Faisal University, represented a widespread belief in the Saudi population, and called this medieval fiction a "well-established fact." The same professor, Dr. Umayma Jalahma, told an Arab League think tank in 2003 that "the U.S. war in Iraq was timed to coincide with the Jewish holiday Purim."[33]

It did not take much soul-searching for the oil officials to act to save their profitable arrangements in the Kingdom. Jungers promptly flew to the U.S., "during which I saw thirty-three CEOs of all the major companies in the United States at that time—General Motors; Ford, [where] I met with Henry Ford; IBM—the major oil companies, the major banks, one at a time and sometimes more than one, and tried to explain this issue."[37]

On May 30, 1973, a large contingent of executives flew to Washington. Among them were Texaco chairman A. C. DeCrane and Exxon, Standard Oil, and Aramco senior vice presidents Charles Hedlund, W. J. McQuinn, and J. J. Johnston.[38] The group spent the day shuttling among the White House, Pentagon, and State Department.[39] They met with the National Security Agency's General Brent Scowcroft, Henry Kissinger's top deputy; Joseph Sisco; and Deputy Secretary of Defense William Clements, Jr., among others.[40] They laid out Faisal's warning and asked for help.[41] The oil executives left the meetings with the feeling that everyone they spoke to thought Faisal was simply bluffing.[42]

"We tended to think that was just more hot air out of the King," recalls James Schlesinger, the secretary of defense at the time.[43]

Through the 1973 summer, the oil firms continued lobbying Washington for some token gesture to show the Saudis they were making progress. Aramco hired a group of powerful, well-connected lobbyists to further their cause. Chief among them was John McCloy, a named partner in the Wall Street law firm of Milbank, Tweed, Hadley & McCloy. He had previously been the high commissioner for Germany after World War II, and had brief stints as president of the World Bank, the Ford Foundation, and Chase Manhattan. McCloy, who later urged Nixon not to ship arms to Israel during the Yom Kippur War, now told oil executives they should concentrate on the energy crisis and demonstrate to Americans how bolstering relations with the Saudis and other Arab countries might ease it.[44] Israel was singled out as the source of instability and the reason for the U.S.'s deteriorating image in the Arab world.[45]

In June 1973, Mobil published a provocative "commentary" in *The New York Times,* arguing that the U.S. must improve relations with Arab countries. In New York, Exxon vice president Howard Page gave a speech appealing for better relations with Arabs. When Standard Oil chairman Otto Miller had a similar appeal published in the London-based *Middle East Economic Survey,* Saudi and other Arab newspapers carried his plea

for a change in U.S. foreign policy as front-page news.[46] Miller also sent a
letter to all Standard Oil stockholders informing them that "there now is
a growing feeling in much of the Arab world that the United States has
turned its back on the Arab people . . . It is highly important at this time
that the United States should work more closely with the Arab governments. . . ."[47]

American supporters of Israel reacted angrily, and when Miller gave a
speech in New York on August 9, demonstrators from the Jewish Defense
League protested at his hotel. Several were arrested in a melee. Aramco
executives, as reporter Steven Emerson reported in his 1985 book, *The
American House of Saud,* "were ecstatic."[48] Internal Aramco memos boasted
of the good fallout from provoking militant Jewish demonstrators, and how
pleased King Faisal was with the oil firms.[49]

The Saudis also did their part for the public relations campaign. Pre-
paid luxury junkets were launched, ostensibly to convince U.S. dignitaries
that Saudi Arabia was deserving of more equal treatment in America's
policy in the Middle East. Scores traveled to Saudi Arabia at the invitation
of the Kingdom, among them General Andrew Goodpaster, the Supreme
Allied Commander for Europe, and Rear Admiral Earl R. Crawford, deputy
chief of staff for the Allied Command. Corporate titans, from Bechtel to
General Dynamics, made the pilgrimage as well.

Faisal was satisfied that the Kingdom's joint lobbying efforts with
Aramco had shown good progress. The Saudis no longer threatened to na-
tionalize the oil refineries. Aramco thought it had mollified its Saudi hosts.
But on October 6, an event took place that would forever change the U.S.
relationship to Saudi Arabia and its oil. On that day, which was Yom Kippur, the holiest day of the Jewish calendar, Egypt and Syria launched a
massive military strike at Israel. The surprise attack caught the Jewish state
napping. Previously hapless Arab armies made unexpected gains during
the war's first week. Aramco officials had their lobbyist, John McCloy, hand-
deliver a letter to Nixon's chief of staff, General Alexander Haig, from the
chairmen of Exxon, Mobil, Texaco, and Standard Oil—the four oil firms
that controlled Aramco—imploring Nixon to avoid "any further demonstration of increased U.S. support for the Israeli position." "Increased military aid to Israel will have a critical and adverse effect on our relations
with moderate Arab oil producing countries," the letter continued.[50]

The oil companies hoped that their early intervention might prevent
Israel from getting any military help in fighting off the invading armies.

With the exception of the Netherlands, all Western Europe had frozen military equipment previously scheduled to be shipped to Israel. Moreover, the Europeans announced in unison that they refused to grant overflight access or air refueling rights in any effort to resupply Israel.

The Nixon administration initially hesitated, distracted in part by the Watergate scandal, then in full bloom.[51] But the first indication that the oil companies and their Arab allies might not get their way came when Haig sent a response to the plea from the oil chairmen, dodging any formal commitment and telling them instead that their note was being shuffled around the administration.

On October 13, a week after the war's start, the Nixon administration announced it would resupply Israel. The decision caused a firestorm in Saudi Arabia and other Arab capitals, as well as angst in the boardrooms of the oil conglomerates. King Faisal had Saudi financier and arms dealer Adnan Khashoggi deliver an appeal to Nixon to cease supplying jet aircraft to the Jewish state. Nixon and Khashoggi were friends, having met in 1967 at the Rasputin restaurant in Paris. Khashoggi had thrown grand receptions for Nixon in Saudi Arabia and Jordan, and Nixon had reciprocated by hosting a party for Khashoggi in Nixon's Fifth Avenue apartment in New York City, and introducing him to his close friend Charles "Bebe" Rebozo. Khashoggi was not only a guest at Nixon's inaugurations, but also met with Nixon, while president, in San Clemente, Paris, and even at Rebozo's Key Biscayne, Florida, house.[52] Watergate investigators questioned Khashoggi as to whether he had given Nixon secret campaign contributions totaling a million dollars (the story was reported in the French press), but nothing was proven, and all the parties denied it. On this occasion, however, Nixon politely told Khashoggi no, that the U.S. would not stop supplying arms to Israel.

By October 16, just three days later, Israel had turned the battle's tide, recaptured the Golan Heights, and was marching toward Damascus and Cairo when the Americans demanded they stop. Although the war was lost, the Saudis now decided that OPEC should teach the West, particularly America, a lesson for its support of Israel. On the day Israeli general Ariel Sharon broke through the 50,000-soldier Egyptian Third Army, OPEC raised the price of a barrel of oil by 70 percent, from $3.01 to $5.12. It did so unilaterally, without any consultation as had happened in the past with Aramco. In the previous twenty years, the price had increased a total of only one dollar.

When Saudi oil minister Sheikh Yamani left Geneva after the startling OPEC price increase, he told a colleague, "The moment has come. We are masters of our own commodity."[53] The importance of that decision was momentarily missed in the West. *The New York Times,* for instance, reported OPEC's historic move in a small Associated Press story on page 16.

As if the initial price shock was not enough, the following day OPEC adopted a Saudi proposal that it cut oil production by 5 percent monthly until Israel withdrew from all occupied territories. Then, on October 18, the Saudis went a step further. They unilaterally cut their production, then supplying about a quarter of the world's needs, by 10 percent. The Saudis and other Arab producers announced an embargo on all shipments of their oil to the United States. In the West, panic set in. Three days later, on October 21, King Faisal personally extended the embargo to the U.S. Sixth Fleet patrolling the Mediterranean, and to U.S. diplomatic outposts.[54] Then the Saudis cut off the U.S. Seventh Fleet in the Pacific and Indian oceans.[55]

Of course, Saudi Arabia could not enforce the embargo on its own. It needed the help of Aramco. The day after the United States had begun resupplying Israel, Aramco president Frank Jungers was summoned to see the king. Faisal told him about the embargo.

"I don't see how you are going to do it," Jungers said.

"You are going to do it," Faisal told him.[56]

Fearing nationalization, Aramco complied. It diverted all shipments of oil away from the United States. Aramco even supplied the Saudis with all its data for shipments of oil to American military and diplomatic bases worldwide. While company officials later claimed the Saudis forced them to provide the information, subsequent Senate investigations revealed that Aramco needed little prodding, and readily went along with the embargo, convinced that it would further ingratiate them to the Saudis.

In America, long gas lines formed for the first time since shortages had prompted them during World War II. The influx of cold weather early in the fall exacerbated concerns over supplies, and prices for winter heating oil soared. Cut off without warning from its supply of inexpensive oil, the U.S. economy went into a tailspin. Hundreds of thousands of jobs were lost. American workers demanded a retaliatory food embargo on Arab countries. Vice President Gerald Ford intimated that military action was not out of the question. "Throughout history, nations have gone to war over natural advantages such as water or food," he said shortly after the embargo began.[57] The embargo precipitated a deep recession in 1974 and 1975, the deepest slowdown since the Great Depression.

In November 1973, Henry Kissinger made one of several trips to Riyadh, this time to appeal personally to King Faisal to lift the embargo. As secretary of state, he was the obvious choice to head the diplomatic efforts, but some worried that the fact that he was Jewish could hinder what he might achieve. And indeed, prominent members of Faisal's government, including the king, thought that Kissinger's religion hampered his impartiality on Middle East issues.[58]

Two tall Saudi guards, in black robes and white headdresses, each carrying Saracen swords, escorted Kissinger to see Faisal, who was surrounded by dozens of royal princes, many wearing sunglasses and sipping tea. Kissinger, at Faisal's request, shook hands with each of the princes. Only then did the king agree to talk to him privately for two hours. At that meeting, Kissinger tried mollifying the king by suggesting that the U.S. would strongly support an international peace conference on the Israeli-Arab conflict, and that the embargo complicated American efforts to encourage Israel to withdraw from the occupied territories. But instead of being receptive to the American overture, Faisal gave Kissinger a tongue-lashing. The king complained, "Israel is advancing Communist objectives. . . . They want to establish a Communist base right in the Middle East. Now all over the world, the Jews are putting themselves into positions of authority." Faisal insisted he would only consider lifting the embargo after the U.S. forced Israel to first withdraw from its captured territory of 1967, and after the Palestinians had a homeland with Jerusalem as its capital. "The Jews have no right in Jerusalem," Faisal lectured Kissinger. Faisal had previously reprimanded U.S. ambassador George Ball, telling him that "Jews should visit their holy place in New York."[59]

Then Faisal launched into one of his outbursts of anti-Semitism. Staring at Kissinger, Faisal told him that the Jews were responsible for the 1917 Russian revolution, had an expansionist ideology they intended to fulfill through a greater Israel, and that "Jews all over the world are putting themselves into positions of authority . . . trying to run the world." Faisal told Kissinger that he, as king, would stop them with his "oil weapon."[60]

As they left the tense meeting, Kissinger walked stiffly through a room thick with incense and tried making small talk with Faisal. The secretary of state looked at a large painting and asked Faisal if it was a depiction of the Arabian desert. No, Faisal said, it was the Kingdom's "holy oasis."

Kissinger apologized. Later he told a colleague, "I guess I set back the lifting of the oil embargo by at least one month with that comment."[61]

That the American secretary of state not only could return home empty-handed from his meeting with the Saudi monarch, but would tolerate such a strong personal rebuke apparently so meekly, further emboldened Faisal and the Saudis.

In December, shortly after Kissinger left the Kingdom, Faisal and the Saudis orchestrated a doubling of OPEC's official barrel price, to a record $11.65.[62] Some Iranian crude, in the ensuing panic in the West, hit over $17.00 a barrel.[63]

Raymond Close, the CIA station chief in Saudi Arabia, worked diligently behind the scenes to find a way the U.S. could get the embargo lifted while giving Faisal something concrete to satisfy his demands. The Saudis demanded that Nixon link the lifting of the embargo to America's commitment to a Middle East peace deal based on United Nations Security Council resolution 242, that Israel withdraw from all occupied territories in return for Arab recognition of its right to exist. Nixon agreed, and in his January 1974 State of the Union address included almost precisely the language insisted upon by Faisal. Nixon also predicted, in that speech, that the embargo was about to end. It did in March.[64] But by that time the Saudis were awash in dollars, having raked in $60 billion in surplus profits from the price increases.[65]

CHAPTER 5

THE BOYCOTT

Not everyone was distressed by the economic shock waves from the 1973 oil embargo. In the short run, Aramco executives had cause to be delighted. Only five days after the embargo was announced, Aramco's president, Frank Jungers, learned that Faisal was quite pleased with the company's pro-Arab, anti-Israel position, and its reward was the unfettered right to sell crude oil originally destined for the United States to other countries, at much higher prices than first expected. As a result, the third and fourth quarters of 1973 were the most profitable in Aramco's history (Exxon's individual profits, $2.5 billion, were then a business record).

But the major benefit was to the Saudis and other large oil producers. It was as if overnight they received a crash course in appreciating the power they wielded through their natural resource. Oil had cost $3 a barrel in October 1973. By the early 1980s, oil was in the low-to-mid-$30 range. That price jump meant that a trillion and a half dollars flooded the economies of just a dozen countries. The Saudis' profits, slightly more than $2 billion annually pre-embargo, zoomed to over $100 billion a year. They exercised their muscle not only with fellow Arabs in OPEC, but also by buying more of Aramco. In 1973, the Saudi government acquired a 25 percent share in Aramco that increased to 60 percent a year later.[1]

The monarchy now recognized that while it could not exert any sway over foreign affairs with military might, it could combine the oil weapon, together with liberal amounts of the money flooding the Kingdom, to win influence. The grand mufti, Sheikh Muhammad ibn Ibrahim, urged Faisal to exert his power aggressively so "Saudi Arabia should lead the Arab world" and "Wahhabism should be exported." Faisal took the exhortation to heart. Although he had occasionally talked about reform in the early 1960s, he now become as conservative a ruler as the forty-year-old country had known. King Faisal and the religious leaders established the Muslim World League and funded it with $50 million to jump-start its mission of spreading Wahhabism and Saudi influence. The World Assembly of Muslim Youth, another proselytizing group, was also begun at this time.

In late 1973, at Faisal's direction, the Saudis began liberally spreading money around the United Nations, especially among several impoverished African delegations. This generosity came with a string. Faisal wanted support on important Islamic issues. And those matters soon became clear. In February 1974, he convened a pan-Islamic conference in Pakistan. A newcomer at the table given the status of a head of state was Yasir Arafat, representing his Palestinian Liberation Organization. Islamic solidarity was the message of the day. The oil embargo's success imbued the conference's participants with a confidence seldom manifest in the Arab world. Unified in confronting Israel, the conference emerged with a new goal of obtaining the imprimatur of the United Nations. Saudi money, often passed through low-cost loans or grants to other countries, was a factor in the 1974 UN General Assembly's decision to invite the PLO to participate in debates on Palestine, grant the then terrorist group observer status, and call for Palestinian self-determination. The Saudis led the successful Islamic effort to bar Israel from full UNESCO membership, and also got UNESCO to cut off all aid to the Jewish state. On March 19, 1974, when Faisal led OPEC in lifting its oil embargo, the Saudi king was convinced that he was steadily achieving his chief foreign policy objectives.

One month after the embargo was removed, the United States made a "surprise" announcement to sell the Kingdom naval vessels, armored vehicles, tanks, and fighter aircraft of a sophistication and power never before provided to an Arab country. Also, Kissinger promised a major initiative to transfer high-level technology to the Saudis. In November 1975, the United Nations approved a resolution—cosponsored by the Saudis—stating that Zionism equaled racism. The United States voted against it, but did not veto it.*

---

*Israel made revocation of the resolution a condition of its participation in the Madrid Peace Conference in 1991. On December 16, 1991, the UN General Assembly finally revoked the "Zionism equals racism" resolution by a vote of 111 to 25 (with 13 abstentions).

That same year, 1975, forty-five of America's corporate leaders, representing companies employing over one and a half million workers, and with revenues exceeding $100 billion annually, made a tour of the Middle East and Arab countries. The Saudis were a prime target for new business. The Kingdom was earning profits of almost $13 million an hour. By the end of 1975, Saudi foreign cash reserves had zoomed to number two in the world. For Western companies, the enormous revenues meant incredible opportunities for profit.

The Americans wanted to convince the Saudis that their desert kingdom needed a modern infrastructure, and that with its newfound money it could build state-of-the-art highways, hospitals, housing, power plants, shopping centers, airports, and schools. Businessmen packed the only habitable hotel in Riyadh, the Al Yamana, located on a narrow road between the town's center and the airport. Room reservations at the Al Yamana meant nothing. It was first come, first served, although the hotel quickly learned that businessmen were willing to pay bribes to guarantee a room. The managers at the Al Yamana, according to an American businessman then living in the Kingdom, were swimming in money from foreigners stumbling over one another trying to sell things to the newly rich Saudis.

Some of those who arrived were luxury-goods purveyors who envisioned a modern-day gold rush. They successfully convinced newly rich princes and their families that they needed private planes, yachts, second and third homes in places like the South of France and London, and jewelry that would soon compete with some of the world's largest private collections. A group of Scandinavian businessmen converted an enormous North Sea ferry into a floating showplace filled with luxurious furs, vintage cars, rare china, and hand-loomed carpets with Koranic verses on them. Its contents sold out within hours of docking in Saudi Arabia. And wealthy Saudis, even royals who had never seen so much money before, quickly delved into a frenzied competition of one-upsmanship. Consumer goods jammed the ports.[2] Luxury car imports tripled. Interior Minister Prince Nayef had his Stutz Bearcat reproduction car lined with mink, even in its trunk. Many new car buyers left the price stickers on the side windows to show others not only that the cars were new, but how much they cost. Rolls-Royces had the grills and flying-lady hood ornaments plated in gold. Mercedes made a special vehicle for falcon hunting by extending the wheelbase, cutting off the top, and putting in four black-and-white mink bucket seats.[3]

Although there was a Wahhabi rule against men wearing jewelry, shops sold out of gold watches encrusted with pavé diamonds, and matching gold ring, pencil and pen sets, and even prayer beads in gold and diamonds. In Riyadh and Jeddah's "gold souks," eighteen- and twenty-one-karat gold jewelry was sold by the weight from hundreds of shops, often with cars necessary to transport the largest purchases.[4] Tens of thousands of "petromigrants," manual workers from the Muslim third world—initially Yemenis, Palestinians, Lebanese, and Egyptians—were brought into the country to do the menial jobs that newly wealthy Saudis deemed beneath them.[5] One overly eager entrepreneurial Texan convinced Saudi sheikh Al-Aharif al-Hamdan that the Alamo was for sale, and the sheikh offered to buy it, sight unseen, for his son's amusement. When word of that leaked out, the outcry from Texans was so great that the sheikh claimed his offer was only in jest.

In 1974, property prices soared. The main beneficiary was the monarchy, which in the 1940s and 1950s bought more than 90 percent of the country, often at bargain prices from Bedouin chiefs who claimed heritage to the land. Only princes were allowed to own and register real estate in the desert provinces.[6] The royals had named those provinces after themselves, and actually owned so much land that they passed it around in business deals, as marriage gifts, and even as substitutes for cash.[7] Faisal himself often gave large tracts of arid land to family members so they could feel they shared in the Kingdom's resources without tapping into the government's treasury.[8] No one could have envisioned the explosion in land values after the embargo. A hectare (about 2.4 acres) that was worth about $3 when Faisal distributed it was commanding $6,000 within a few years.[9] Faisal's wife Iffat received prime properties in Jeddah, estimated to be worth $2 *billion* then. Several hundred million in land went to the oil minister, Sheikh Yamani.

One of the few people not thoroughly pleased with the flood of cash and the explosion in consumer spending was King Faisal himself. He worried that such material emphasis could damage the piety and spirituality that was supposed to be the Kingdom's trademark, and that the now easy-to-obtain affluence might be a harmful effect of the oil embargo. Just before the oil rush, Faisal had said, "My Kingdom will survive only insofar as it remains a country difficult of access, where the foreigner will have no other aim, with his task fulfilled, but to get out."

But personal luxuries were just the beginning of what American businesses wanted to sell to the House of Saud. American banks wanted Saudi cash deposits and aggressively sought petrodollars with enticements the Swiss and Europeans found difficult to match. The Saudis had long resisted international banking: Islam forbids the charging of interest, and the House of Saud considered it unseemly to have financial arrangements with foreign firms that made their living by loaning money. There was also a widely held bias that prominent Jewish families controlled international banking. During the first fifty years of the Kingdom's existence, there were no banking laws or regulations or foreign banks in the country.[10] Most business was still conducted by long-established families who controlled money changing in local bazaars. When petrodollars poured into the Kingdom after the embargo, the Saudi Arabian Monetary Agency (the equivalent of the American Federal Reserve) relocated from the converted rustic apartment house it occupied near Jeddah's airport and switched from its manual bookkeeping to rudimentary computers in order to keep track of the billions pouring in. The House of Saud arranged with the religious authorities to adapt the ancient rules barring interest so that it was permissible to collect "service charges" on loans or provide "commissions" on deposits. That opened the floodgate to Western banks.

Bank of America created a new bank in 1975, Misr America International, with the First Arabian Corporation. It quickly became an outlet for money from the House of Saud and leading Saudi businessmen.[11] Citibank opened branches in Jeddah and Riyadh, and established a special international division to offer investment advice to wealthy Saudis. J. P. Morgan bought 20 percent of Saudi International Bank, a London-based merchant bank, with the Kingdom's central bank as the majority owner. Chase Manhattan bought 20 percent of the Saudi Investment Banking Corporation, headquartered in Riyadh. Chase, with personal lobbying from its chairman, David Rockefeller, got the nod from the Saudi central bank to become the American financial institution where all money invested into other U.S. banks or businesses would first be deposited. Although Chase only held the funds, totaling billions of dollars, for a day or two while they were settled into dollars and then transferred out to other banks, it still meant millions of dollars in interest, called "the float."[12]

Meanwhile, American industry titans told the Saudis and other oil-producing nations they visited that they could help them create modern nations within a decade, societies that would rival any Western country, even America, in terms of progress and technology.

While King Faisal was interested, he first wanted the American business chiefs to understand what was important to Saudi Arabia. The king
often delivered his now standard monologue on the "evils" of Zionism, the
international Jewish conspiracy, and how the U.S. must be more evenhanded in dealing with Arabs and Middle East politics.[13]

Some of the executives understood the quid pro quo and adopted it.
For instance, when Robert Malott, the chairman of the diversified industrial production company FMC, returned to the States, he gave speeches
to business groups condemning America's pro-Israel bias, urged a more
evenhanded U.S. policy toward the Arabs, and regaled his audiences with
stories of how friendly King Faisal was, and how stubborn and inflexible
he had found the Israelis. During the decade following Malott's conversion to a critic of Israel and a friend of the Saudis, FMC won more than
$600 million in contracts with Arab countries, most of it in Saudi Arabia.
These included everything from armored personnel carriers to food-
processing equipment.

In 1974, the Saudis approved a $142 billion five-year plan (cost overruns
eventually pushed it to $180 billion) to transform the backward Arabian
peninsula. The country desperately needed modernization, and only Western companies could help—the Soviet Union had too many of its own infrastructure and industrialization problems to lend a hand. By the end of
the 1950s, the only public works completed in the Kingdom were a railway
from Dhahran to Riyadh, a jetty in Jeddah, and a network of water wells.
Many towns still did not have morgues, only fences around the cemeter-
ies to keep out wild desert dogs.[14] In the 1960s, schools, some airports, and
housing had been constructed. But the new plans called for a complete
redo of the nation. American companies almost stepped over one another
trying to win the work.* More than 500,000 foreign laborers, managers,
and technicians were to be imported to help implement the massive transformation (the Saudi Finance Ministry in 1950 had ruled that visas could
be issued to foreign workers so long as "those for whom the visas are required are not undesirable persons," it being understood that undesirable
persons include Jews).[15]

And FMC was just one of dozens of companies that cashed in,

*The plan is technically known as the Second Five-Year Plan. The First Five-Year Plan came
before the embargo brought oil riches to the Kingdom. It had only a $9.2 billion budget, a frac-
tion of that of the new proposal. The plan itself was thousands of pages long, weighed over two
hundred pounds, and was scheduled to cost 3.5 times more than the Apollo space program.

many championing public positions approved by the Saudis. The San Francisco–based Bechtel not only built King Khalid Airport in Riyadh, but also landed the $40 billion petrochemical complex in Jubail. On that project alone, Bechtel had 1,500 architects, technicians, and construction managers overseeing a workforce of 40,000 laborers. And to protect its relations with the Saudis, Bechtel employed the former U.S. ambassador to the Kingdom Parker Hart, as well as two former CIA directors, Richard Helms and John McCone, both of whom had friendly relationships with the House of Saud. The Justice Department would eventually charge Bechtel with having excluded companies and persons the Saudis did not want in any of its deals, primarily Jews, and the company signed a consent decree not to comply further with the discriminatory practices.[16]

George Shultz, when secretary of the treasury in 1973, encouraged the formation of a Treasury Joint Economic Commission, JECOR, a government commission with no congressional oversight, as a joint venture between the Treasury Department and Saudi Arabia. The committee, established the following year, focused on keeping petrodollars in the U.S. The Saudis bought U.S. treasury securities as investments and the interest on them was often paid to U.S. companies to develop the Kingdom. It was another windfall for American businesses. The first JECOR contract went to Waste Management for technical assistance and 280 garbage trucks to replace goats that otherwise roamed Riyadh picking up garbage. Bechtel Corporation, of which George Shultz later became a director, was again a huge beneficiary.[17]

The Saudis did not just wait at home for American businessmen to visit and pitch new ideas. By the time JECOR was formed, among other prominent Saudi investments, Saudi middleman Adnan Khashoggi had acquired a controlling interest in a huge conglomerate, Arizona-Colorado Land and Cattle; Prince Khalid Abdullah invested in First Chicago Corp. and Bank, as well as former Nixon cabinet secretary James Baker III's family bank, Texas Commerce Bancshares. The House of Saud, in 1975, also sent seven officials to crisscross the United States and pitch reasons why American companies should invest in Saudi Arabia, and why they should support Saudi policies in the Middle East. The Saudi delegation ran at the pace of a U.S. presidential campaign, covering ninety cities in six weeks.[18] American business executives, over twenty thousand by the tour's end, clamored to hear a promise that if they established Saudi subsidiaries, the House of Saud would give them a five-year tax moratorium,

fifteen-year interest-free loans, and free land on which to build their businesses. And coupled with the commercial inducements, the delegation
was under orders from the king to ensure that Americans got a basic lesson in the Saudi view of Middle East history. Islamic Associations were
started in both Chicago and Tucson, with the idea of educating Americans
about the "real" issues facing Arabs from "Israeli aggression."[19]

The delegation's chairman, Dr. Abdelraham al-Zamel, an educator who
later became a senior cabinet official, regularly explained to the standing-
room-only business crowds about the Damascus-headquartered Arab
League's official boycott of Israel, in place since the 1948 war that broke
out when the Jewish state was created. "It is no different than the American embargo on Cuba" was one of Zamel's favorite lines, warning the
Americans that the boycott was simply a "fact of political life."[20]

Zamel made it clear to his audiences that while the Saudis wanted to
do business with America, and were dangling out incredibly tempting
incentives, such deals depended on "political realities."[21] The delegation
pulled no punches when it came to flexing its newfound oil muscles. Oil
is a legitimate instrument of foreign policy, they told the American business leaders, and they sent a chill through the crowds when they warned
that another oil embargo was possible, depending on how the U.S. dealt
with Israel.[22]

At New York's St. Regis Sheraton hotel, Zamel told 250 Manhattan
business leaders, "Any new embargo would be a reaction to United States
behavior. We know that Israel cannot go to war without the approval of the
United States." And if business leaders had any doubt about the Saudis'
commitment to their political cause, in the middle of the American junket,
the European Union signed an agreement to provide Israel with technology and trade assistance. Zamel told *The New York Times* that the
Saudis would soon "retaliate" against the EU, using oil as their weapon.[23]

The Saudi rules were different from anything that had previously confronted U.S. companies. The trip was a not very subtle form of blackmail,
urging companies to pursue profits so long as they played by the House of
Saud's anti-Israel, anti-Jewish line. In other global hot spots where individual countries maintained economic boycotts of bitter enemies, they did
not ask American companies to join the boycott as a condition of doing
business. For instance, Taiwan boycotted both China and the Soviet Union,
but did not ask American companies doing business in Taiwan to stop
doing business with China or the Soviets. The same was true of India,

which boycotted Pakistan, and the many black African nations that shunned South Africa but for many years gladly did business with American companies without ever asking them to boycott Pretoria.

Not only were the Saudis asking U.S. companies to abandon business with Israel, but they also had strict policies to ensure that Israel did not get a portion of any business indirectly. They demanded certification that exports to Arab countries contained no Israeli components.

Before the 1974 oil embargo, the Arab boycott had no teeth, and most companies ignored it.[24] But emboldened by their oil weapon, the Damascus Central Office for the Boycott of Israel issued a fifty-seven-page book of instructions called *General Principles for Boycott of Israel.* The Central Office began blacklisting not only U.S. companies that traded directly with, or invested in, Israel, but also even some who did business with other U.S. companies that dealt with Israel.[25]

At the time the Saudis made their pitch inside the U.S., the master list of boycotted companies already included Coca-Cola, Sears Roebuck, Bantam Books, and Zenith. By the time of the oil embargo, several thousand firms had been "blacked."[26]

Ford, whose founder, Henry Ford, was a notorious anti-Semite and author of *The Eternal Jew,* a conspiracy theory propounding that Jews intended to take control of the world, ironically not only was blacklisted, but made a point of taking a strong stance against the Arab boycott, even at the risk of losing Arab business. Hilton Hotels, Hertz, General Motors, AT&T, and RCA are other blacklisted companies that made firm declarations against the boycott—such corporate courage, unfortunately, was the exception.

Companies that did business with Israel were not, however, the only ones to suffer the wrath of the boycott. The Saudis were unequivocal they would refuse to do business not only with any firm that dealt with Israel but also with companies that had prominent Jews or "Zionists" in ranking positions. It was the first time a business boycott was directed not just at a country but at a religion as well. A common declaration on the forms sent to Western companies wanting to do business in Saudi Arabia and other Arab countries was "We hereby solemnly declare that the company is not a Jewish company nor controlled by Jews or Zionists and it has no relations with Israel which may contradict the boycott principles." At times, firms with officers with apparently Jewish surnames had to provide evidence that they were in fact not Jewish. (Later in the decade, the

Saudis agreed to remove the words "Jews" and "Zionists" after the U.S. negotiated a new economic cooperation agreement with the Kingdom.)

One leading American firm of architects tried making itself acceptable to Arab business by eliminating twelve Jewish names on its letterhead, while others deleted work they had done for Jewish-owned buildings or businesses.[27] American films deemed to be "biased in favor of Israel," or "too Jewish," were also banned.[28] Jewish performers like Kirk Douglas, Paul Newman, Isaac Stern, and Jerry Lewis were blacklisted under the prohibition of "pro-Zionist foreign actors," as were Elizabeth Taylor (she converted to Judaism for one of her marriages), Helen Hayes, and even such unlikely choices as Harry Belafonte. Sophia Loren was banned for making a film in Israel.[29] Otto Preminger was verboten because he directed *Exodus*. A scene in *Funny Girl* in which the Jewish Barbra Streisand kissed the Arab Omar Sharif caused great offense. Joan Baez was "blacked" for "Zionist lyrics," including one song in which she referred to waiting at a train station "with a ticket to the Promised Land" and another where she sang about "the children Moses led through the desert." The Disney film *Snow White and the Seven Dwarfs* was banned because the prince's horse was named Samson, after the Jewish biblical hero. The Central Boycott Office suggested that the film could correct this "Zionistic allusion" if it renamed the horse "Simpson."[30]

Verdi's opera *Nabuco* was blacklisted because one scene included biblical Israelites asking King Nebuchadnezzar to be released from Babylonian captivity. Such a scene, it was feared, could be used to justify current Jewish claims to Israel. A Yale Glee Club recording was banned when someone brought to the attention of the Boycott's Central Office that reprinted on the album was Hebrew writing on the university's official seal. The works of Émile Zola were blacklisted because Zola's efforts helped free Captain Dreyfus, a Jew, from Devil's Island in the nineteenth century. Foreign printed matter was boycotted if it "contain[ed] propaganda for Occupied Palestine." That covered any atlas, almanac, or map that included Israel.[31]

The Saudis added some additional provisions to the boycott that were unique to the Kingdom. Any oil destined for Israel should be confiscated, undefined Israeli "money bags" were banned, and any media deemed to have "smeared" any Arab state should be boycotted or destroyed.[32] The Saudis led an effort to officially bar both CBS and NBC from covering news inside the Arab world in February 1975, but the boycott office decided to put them only "under supervision" to ensure that their coverage was "beneficial to the Arab cause."[33]

The U.S. government had a mild antiboycott provision included since 1969 in the Export Administration Act, but there were no substantive fines or penalties for violating it, and hence few U.S. corporate officials objected in running over one another to get a piece of the Saudi billions. In 1973, right before the embargo, there were only 785 business deals done between American companies and the Saudis in which the U.S. firm was asked to comply with the boycott. By the end of 1974, in just a six-month period, there were more than 25,000 such contracts, and in 90 percent of the cases, the U.S. firms acquiesced to some part of the boycott.[34] Commerce Department documents reveal that more than 1,400 major U.S. companies complied at some time with the boycott.[35] Among them were Westinghouse, General Electric, Texas Instruments, Du Pont, John Deere, 3M, and the defense manufacturer Rockwell International. Some firms, like Avon, General Mills, Scott Paper, Bendix, and American Can, questioned about their compliance in a random survey, lied about participating, though their required "exporter's reports" filed with the Commerce Department proved otherwise. Others, like American Express, closed their Israeli operations and avoided being placed on the boycott list.[36] And still other firms anticipated boycott pressures and voluntarily conducted business in a way they thought made them more acceptable for Arab trade. Banks and shipping companies favored such an approach and became adherents to a "voluntary boycott," cleaning themselves of Israeli and Jewish connections without ever being asked by any Arab country.[37]

The allure of Saudi wealth even affected American educational institutions, where the response to the boycott was mixed. When the Association of Colleges and Universities invited Saudi Arabia in 1975 to finance a $5.5 million teacher-training program, the Kingdom made it clear that all Jewish professors and staff members were banned from entering the country. The deal went through, even though some schools, like Harvard, protested and dropped out. The Massachusetts Institute of Technology, also in 1975, lost a $2 million contract to train Saudi technicians and graduate students because the Kingdom would not agree to MIT's stipulation that Jewish teachers should be part of the visiting faculty. And that same year, the Midwest Universities Consortium for International Activities (composed of the universities of Illinois, Indiana, Wisconsin, Michigan State, and Minnesota) won a contract to advise the University of Riyadh on an expanded curriculum, but later withdrew after four Jewish professors were denied entrance to the Kingdom.[38] When Prince Talal bin Abdul Aziz, one of the king's sons, paid the University of Houston to provide a college education for his daughter Princess Rima within the confines of his Riyadh palace, the American university selected two female professors who were neither Jews nor married to Jewish spouses.[39]

This stampede to do business in Saudi Arabia led to the start of what was to become an endemic problem: bribes disguised as business commissions—between U.S. companies desiring to profit from the explosion in petrodollars and extended relatives and friends of the House of Saud who wanted to greedily amass personal fortunes. In a government founded on patronage, the Saudis saw nothing wrong with this arrangement. If a desalting plant contract worth several hundred million dollars was about to be assigned from Riyadh and there were several equally competent firms from America and Europe all bidding for the deal, why shouldn't the one that wanted it most pay something for the right? All the "commission" did was reduce the amount of the profit that the Western company earned, so as far as the Saudis were concerned, it did not hurt anyone.

There was also a unique element to the Saudi component of the corruption. Although the various tribes that made up the Kingdom had been unified under a single national flag for a few decades, most government workers still counted their allegiance to their family lineage. As a result, personal relationships were critical in navigating the Saudi bureaucracy.[40] Not only did many bureaucrats earn miserable salaries, but promotion was often determined by family connection alone, not merit. As a result, low-level civil servants resorted to petty corruption, such as selling visas, whereas senior officials made sizable fortunes from peddling their influence and personal contacts to eager foreign contractors.

The House of Saud was itself not immune to the corruption that quickly permeated the government. In fact, the royals were the chief proponents and beneficiaries. There are approximately six thousand princes (every son or daughter descended from the Kingdom's founder, Ibn Saud, automatically has a royal title). The most prominent ones consider it their birthright to share in the country's wealth. Their accumulation of huge personal fortunes is critical to an intricate system of patronage that has created widespread support for the monarchy. The closer a prince is related to the king of the moment, the greater his profits from the endemic corruption. For instance, Prince Muhammad ibn Abdul Aziz, the older brother of kings Khalid and Fahd, renounced his claim to the throne. In return for doing so, his agents then became the official middlemen to arrange contracts with foreign companies for the Saudi firm that was slated to eventually take control of Aramco. Just a single deal, rejected by an American company as too pricey, would have netted the prince $1.2 million daily in secret payments.[41] In other instances, Aramco was told to sell oil to Japanese refiners at more than two million dollars over the going price, with the extra profit representing a "commission" pocketed by the prince.[42]

The briberies—or commissions, as the Saudis prefer to call them—came into practice after Faisal took the throne in 1964. Before that, the princes lived off huge government stipends. Ibn Saud, when king, just raked off a portion of the country's oil profits for his own income and that of his close family. It averaged about $250 million annually, even in the 1950s (billions a year in today's value). Tens of millions were regularly withdrawn from the country's coffers to build lavish palaces in Riyadh and Jeddah. When Ibn Saud's twelve-year-old son, Prince Mubarak, married in 1959 (marrying before teenage years was not then uncommon in the House of Saud), he received a $1 million palace as a wedding gift.[43] Fleets of Rolls-Royces were bought with government stipends, and Ibn Saud set the tone for the conspicuous consumption and dependence on large government doles to which other princes became addicted.

Faisal, however, wanted to wean the extended royal family off direct government generosity, so he gradually made them "work" for their millions. Work, as defined by the royal family, meant allowing them to collect commissions—sometimes hundreds of millions of dollars—on deals they negotiated.[44] These payments were legal, and there were no controls over them in Saudi Arabia until 1978. After that, the House of Saud declared that any foreign company doing business with the Kingdom could only do so with a Saudi, whose fee would be no more than 5 percent of a contract's value.

The wealthiest middlemen and royals ensured that the bureaucrats they dealt with regularly were inundated with lavish gifts, including even homes; became wealthy as partners in other business ventures; and had easy access to fleets of private planes, yachts, luxury cars, and, for those who wanted them, prostitutes and other Western indulgences on trips outside of the Kingdom.[45]

As American companies learned it was not possible to do business in the Kingdom without paying money to obtain access to decision makers, they built the multimillion-dollar payoffs into the contract bids themselves. "These kickbacks as we have labeled them," Daniel J. Haughton, Lockheed's chairman, told a Senate investigating committee in 1975, "they are paid by the customer in the main. This is not coming out of Lockheed's P and L [profit and loss] or cash. . . . The price is increased by the amount of the payment."[46] This practice, of making the end customer pay for the bribe, resulted in bloated contracts.

And every major company that did business in the Kingdom also understood that it needed to have members of the monarchy as "partners." Saudi princes owned the companies that had the exclusive concessions for everything from hospitals and road works to telecommunications. No work could be done unless these companies received payments as local partners. Many of these activities barely skirted the antibribery laws in the U.S., specifically the Foreign Corrupt Practices Act.*

What Faisal had essentially done was to keep the thousands of princes and their hangers-on drawing money from the government, but instead of doing so directly each year with a check written from the Saudi treasury, the king now hid the stipends by making them a portion of every major business contract in the country. The Saudi government was still paying the princes by overpaying on the inflated contracts, but it was less obvious to those in Saudi society who were not fortunate enough to be part of the monarchy or its wide circle of business acquaintances. The government-sanctioned bribery meant that a rich merchant class, nonroy-

---

*The problem over payments to do business in Saudi Arabia continues to this day. The methods of concealment have improved, but the process—money paid by American corporations to Saudi princes and middlemen for obtaining business—remains largely unchanged. On the front page of *The Wall Street Journal* in September 2004 was a headline, "Royal Treatment: Lucent Faces Bribery Allegations in Giant Saudi Telecom Project."[47] The article detailed how from the late 1990s to 2003, Lucent and its partners paid Dr. Ali Al-Johani, then the Kingdom's telecommunications director, between $15 million and $21 million to maintain a $4 billion contract to upgrade the Saudi phone system, one of the largest telecom deals ever. Lucent, according to documents filed in a private lawsuit, not only paid Dr. Johani cash, but also gave him additional perks he demanded, such as unlimited use of the company's Gulfstream jet for his family's shopping sprees in Europe and the U.S. In 1997, Dr. Johani showed his "philanthropic" nature, in a great fanfare of publicity, by giving $2 million to Seattle's prestigious Fred Hutchinson Cancer Research Center. The lawsuit alleges, however, that the money did not come from Dr. Johani, but rather was secretly paid by Lucent. And the methods used by Lucent to hide the money trail, complex arrangements involving a Lucent partner company and its affiliates, show the extent to which payment of "commissions" to Saudi officials is much more sophisticated than during the days of the boycott, when suitcases of cash often passed over a coffee table in a Riyadh hotel suite.

als, but connected through the right tribal affiliations and friendships, also fell into incredible wealth. Eventually, families like the Olayans, Mahfouzes, bin Ladens, Zamils, and Jamils, among others, would become billionaires by importing everything from luxury cars to gourmet food and helping to become partners, or commissioned agents, with Western companies.

Prince Bandar bin Sultan, the well-liked Saudi ambassador in Washington, has freely acknowledged that widespread corruption afflicts the Kingdom. When talking about his country's $400 billion development program that stretched over several decades, he said, "You could not have done all of that for less than, let's say, $350 billion. If you tell me that building this whole country, and spending $350 billion out of $400 billion, that we misused or got corrupted with $50 billion, I'll tell you, yes," he said. "So what? We did not invent corruption."[48]

The money earned could be seen in unlikely places. The harems of the leading princes became small villages unto themselves, with the women inside wearing the traditional black robes mandated by Wahhabism but having them designed by French fashion designer Christian Dior, for instance. Under the sleeves of their robes were hundreds of thousands of dollars in fine jewelry, hidden from public view.[49] Petrodollars paid for beach houses in the South of Spain, gambling in London casinos, villas in the South of France, and chasing starlets in Hollywood. (A Budget rental car location in Beverly Hills that carried Ferraris, Lamborghinis, Rolls-Royces, and other exotic cars was nicknamed "the Sand Lot" for its Saudi business, with customers often dropping more than $40,000 for multiple rentals on a several-week visit.)[50]

The American government, not wanting to be left out of the petrodollar hordes, set up the Joint Economic Commission, whose sole purpose was to help the Saudis establish government bureaucracies, ranging from transportation, customs, and census to taxation. The Saudis paid the salaries of the 1,500 American officials working on the project. Inside the Treasury Department, to accommodate Saudi needs, the Office of Saudi Arabian Affairs was established, the only such office for any foreign country.[51] At taxpayer expense, the Department of Commerce held seminars and mailed out thousands of invitations to U.S. business leaders encouraging them to take advantage of the "unprecedented . . . business in the Arab world."[52] The Commerce Department, entrusted by Congress with enforcing the rules against American companies participating in the Arab boycott, instead made available information on "Arab trade opportunities" that were dependent on complying with that very boycott.[53]

In 1976, the Commerce Department played a key role in a business conference that provided American firms with ways to evade the reporting requirements set forth in the Export Administration Act. The State Department also sent representatives who gave pointers on how to avoid the government's reporting rules.[54] Moreover, although the government's ban on American companies participating in the boycott covered every type of firm, Commerce only asked for statements from exporters, leaving banks, insurance companies, and even freight forwarders free to do as they pleased.

And while Commerce might have been ineffectual in enforcing the ban on American participation in the boycott, other U.S. government divisions actually took part in it. Since the mid-1950s, the Saudis had refused to allow the U.S. to station any Jewish servicemen at the Dhahran airbase. Although successive presidential administrations since Eisenhower had asked for the policy to be changed, Kings Saud and then Faisal rebuffed the U.S. efforts.

Until public pressure forced its elimination, the U.S. Navy's Military Sea Transportation Service had a Haifa Clause, which ensured that it never contracted with a tanker that had been to Israel whenever it carried fuel or equipment to the Kingdom.

By the 1970s, however, the issues of U.S. government compliance with the Arab boycott and Saudi exclusionary rules about Jews had spread far beyond a single airbase inside the Kingdom or the question of whether ships had previously docked at Israeli ports. The U.S. Army Corps of Engineers, it was revealed in Senate hearings, included explicit boycott stipulations in its dealings with Saudi Arabia.[55] In 1975, the year the Saudi business delegation toured America drumming up more commerce for the Kingdom, the Army Corps of Engineers already had $4 billion in military and civilian construction projects under way there. Governed by a 1964 agreement that was intended to maintain the purity of the boycott and the Kingdom's anti-Jewish stance, the Saudis had veto power over any American contractor chosen by the Corps of Engineers. No other country had such clout over the selection process for a U.S. government agency.[56] But the Saudis did not have to utilize their veto since the Engineers willingly excluded Jewish soldiers and civilian employees of American companies from working on any of its Saudi projects. Colonel William L. Durham, deputy director of military construction in the Office of the Chief of Engineers, told a Senate investigating committee that requests for visas to Saudi Arabia had to be accompanied by the applicant's baptism certificate, a birth certificate showing religion, a marriage license demonstrating a church wedding, or a letter from a church confirming membership.[57] "We don't make policy here," he said. "We only execute orders we get from the Defense Department and the State Department. The Arabs make the rules and it would be unwise to send a Jew out there."[58] The fallout from the public hearings prompted demands from several U.S. senators that the government stop doing Saudi Arabia's dirty work when it came to discrimination.

In addition to blocking Jews, at this time the Saudis also forbade women from entering the country on their own and from working on U.S. projects inside the Kingdom. American blacks, although not officially banned, were discouraged, and entrance into the Kingdom was often denied by the refusal to grant a visa. (American black Muslims were considered less than pure followers of the faith, and even they were not welcome.)[59] Secretary of Defense James Schlesinger reacted to the public criticism by ruling that U.S. government agencies should no longer anticipate Saudi objections by weeding out Jews, but should instead let the Saudis do their own screening.

That rule certainly did not apply, however, to American firms that supplied military technology and weapons systems, often with the blessing of the U.S. government. They focused solely on convincing the House of Saud that it should become a more potent military power. It took little persuasion, as Faisal thought from the start of his tenure as king that the country needed to have its own military might or it would forever be dependent on Western benevolence for its defense. The Kingdom's 1973 military budget was $2 billion, but in five years was nearly $11 billion. The Saudis were rich at a fortuitous time. The Nixon administration had decided to make Iran, run by the American-installed leader Mohammad Reza Shah Pahlavi, and Saudi Arabia the two towers of stability in the Arab world. An almost childlike fascination by Saudi military officers with the latest and flashiest gadgets fueled the Kingdom's massive military buying binge. Coupled with multimillion-dollar bribes disguised as commissions, American companies from Boeing to General Dynamics lined up at the royal palace in Riyadh to pitch their weapons and the reasons they were best for the region's new "superpower."

Saudi Arabia let them know from the start that they would have to adhere not only to the boycott but also to the Kingdom's policies regarding Jews. Most American firms were willing to comply in order to get the business. Typical was Lockheed, which in 1975 refused to allow a Jewish U.S.

Air Force sergeant to even apply for a job in the Kingdom.[60] Vinnell Corporation, which had a lucrative contract to train Saudi national guardsmen, adhered to clauses that banned it from employing anyone from a country not recognized by the House of Saud. That excluded Israel. Then the contract also banned hiring anyone "with a history of personal contact or interest in unrecognized countries." That excluded Jews and their supporters.[61] The Pentagon, in response to public criticism of this type of arrangement, inserted a federally mandated antidiscrimination clause into its contract with Vinnell, but only after an official complaint was lodged by the American Jewish Committee with the defense secretary. But besides specific cases like Vinnell, the Defense Department's overall view was that it was powerless to stop the Saudi discrimination since "a sovereign state has the right to determine to whom it will issue visas."[62] The Defense Department passed the buck to the State Department, which took no action on the Saudi policies.

Although the State Department might have been too timid when it came to confronting the Saudi discriminatory policies, individual U.S. states were not so craven. In November 1975, California's governor, Jerry Brown, ordered the state's Department of Transportation to cut off contract negotiations with Saudi Arabia on possibly hiring five hundred highway engineers about to be laid off by the state. The Saudis wanted those engineers to help build roads inside the Kingdom, but refused to accept Jewish, black, or female workers. The Saudi government lost the contract, but denounced the reports as false, saying it would not block blacks and women, but only "Zionists."

As with their commercial counterparts, defense firms were soon enmeshed in corruption. The same year that it refused to allow a Jew to apply for a contracted job inside Saudi Arabia, Lockheed paid more than $106 million in "commissions" to the forty-year-old Saudi financier Adnan Khashoggi to procure rewarding contracts throughout the Kingdom.[63] Northrop promised Khashoggi, who was in business with senior members of the royal family, a $45 million commission on an $850 million arms sale to the Kingdom.[64] Raytheon paid him almost $23 million, in 1974 and 1985, for the sale of Hawk missiles.[65]*

---

*Khashoggi, and one of his many companies, Lebanon-based Triad Financial, also offered occasionally to "fix it" for a blacklisted company to be removed from the boycott list. General Tire and Rubber, for example, successfully paid $150,000 to Triad to be removed from the boycott list in 1970.

A failed lawsuit by a fired employee of Litton Industries alleged the company paid members of the royal family between $47 million and $183 million to obtain $2.3 billion in contracts, including $1.5 billion to provide control systems for the Saudi Air Defense Command Center. As part of that deal, Litton had to provide housing for its personnel in Saudi Arabia for eight years. That deal alone, according to the lawsuit, allowed for pass-throughs of $115 million to Saudi royals.[66]

Another lawsuit, by a Sikorsky Aircraft employee, charged that his own firm, and its parent company, United Technologies, paid Saudi officials, including two senior princes, millions in commissions on the sale of Black Hawk helicopters.

But in these matters, and many other similar examples, Justice Department lawyers invariably found no conclusive violation of the Foreign Corrupt Practices Act. Proving bribery is difficult. Especially when the host country, Saudi Arabia, has given it official sanction.

Although the terms were never spelled out to American businessmen or government officials in a way that would create legal problems in the U.S., the Saudi delegation visiting the States in 1975, during the peak of the Arab boycott, made it clear that in order to play for profits in Saudi Arabia, companies had to pay, and the U.S. government had to ignore any unsettling details. And to emphasize the power of their oil weapon, in September 1975, at a Vienna conference, OPEC boosted the price of oil by another 10 percent, again jolting Western companies and governments.

By the time the Saudi delegation visiting the United States returned to Riyadh and reported to King Faisal on the enthusiastic reception they had received in the U.S., the House of Saud thought it had successfully flexed its oil muscles and changed the course of U.S. policy in the Middle East. Around the corner, however, they were about to get a lesson in American politics from an even more organized and effective group, the American Jewish lobby.

CHAPTER 6

FIGHTING THE
"JEWISH LOBBY"

On March 24, 1975, America woke to the disquieting news from Riyadh that King Faisal had been assassinated. The assassin was the king's twenty-seven-year-old nephew, Faisal ibn Musa'id Abdel Aziz. He was the younger brother of the prince who had been shot by the police a decade earlier in the aborted religious takeover of the Kingdom's first television station.

The assassin had spent much of the previous decade in the United States, attending school first at San Francisco State and then at the University of Colorado. A poor student, he was known for twin addictions—gambling and Scotch—and was eventually arrested in Colorado, with his Western girlfriend, for selling fifty-two LSD tabs and half an ounce of hashish to an undercover policeman. After pleading no contest, in 1973 he went to Berkeley, where he majored in political science before flunking out the following year. Friends there remember him with long hair, smoking marijuana, and talking often about his embarrassment at being a member of the House of Saud and his bitterness over the death of his brother.[1]

The royal family was so embarrassed that they ordered the young Faisal to return to Saudi Arabia and imposed a travel ban so he could not leave. He underwent treatment to kick his addiction, but evidently failed to do so. According to Saudi authorities, the night before he killed Faisal he met a group of "wanton" friends and drank whiskey, played cards, and watched television. At the palace the next day, while the king welcomed a Kuwaiti oil delegation, his nephew pulled out a small pistol and pumped three bullets into Faisal.[2]

Although some press reports speculated the CIA might have been behind the assassin in payback for Kissinger's recent personal rebuke from Faisal, most Saudis thought the killer was unbalanced.[3] The general consensus was that given his fragile mental state, his sinful life in the non-Islamic West, particularly America, had led to the metamorphosis from loyal family member to murderer.[4] Bolstering this conclusion was that the assassin confessed that he killed the king to end the rule of Islam in Saudi Arabia because it "was standing in the way of development in the country."[5] After a determination that there was no conspiracy among a rival faction of the enormous Saud family, or among external foes like Shiite Iranians, there was an immediate and strong backlash against what the official Saudi media called the "debilitating" and "corruptive" influence of the West. Only three months after Faisal's murder, the assassin was publicly beheaded in Riyadh's main square in front of twenty thousand Saudis. Significantly, standing beside the prince at the moment of his execution was a senior member of the ulema. The absolutists among the Wahhabis had reinforced their control in the religious councils.

This was the first time the Saudi system of succession had been tested in a crisis. The new king, Faisal's half brother, Khalid ibn Abdul al-Aziz, was a pious Muslim, introspective and quiet, and did not even want the job. His passion was falconry rather than governing. Khalid had an older brother, Muhammad, who was technically ahead of him for succession, but the Saud family had forced that brother, with a well-earned reputation for violence and drinking, to pass his right to Khalid.[6] Khalid had no choice but to accept; to refuse ran a risk of reviving ancient blood rifts inside the family. He kept a low profile, though, and let his half brother Fahd ibn Abdul Aziz, who became crown prince, control many of the day-to-day operations of the government. Most of the ministers, policies, and programs remained unchanged from Faisal's tenure. Two of the most important of the former were Princes Sultan and Nayef as ministers of defense and the interior.*

---

*Although Khalid was a remarkably uninvolved king, he did have one pet public project, a grand plan to move all Saudi tribesmen out of tents and into permanent housing. Despite advisors who told him the rural classes would never move to high-rise apartments because

Crown Prince Fahd was one of the most pro-American of the senior royals. He was also a prince who had, to the disapproval of the religious authorities, indulged often and publicly in what they considered decadent Western behavior. His passion for roulette, for instance, had been chronicled in the 1974 *Point International* magazine, in which it described how Fahd, with a large entourage of beautiful women, had taken over the casino at the Hotel Majestic in Cannes and spent millions on gambling, bowls of caviar, and magnums of vintage Champagne (the story was not reported inside Saudi Arabia).[7] In one evening at Monte Carlo, he lost nearly $5 million, and was recalled home temporarily by his brother King Faisal.[8] Fahd had built seven enormous palaces in Saudi Arabia, each grander than the one it replaced. One that he never moved into in Riyadh was a near replica of the White House (his advisors thought it too risky politically to imitate the American president, and it sat empty).[9] His "official" palace was a throwback to when the Kingdom's first kings lived behind small walled cities. It was essentially a tiny Vatican City, with opulent furnishings and walls that ran several miles around the perimeter. Architects who worked on the palaces estimated they were worth several *billion* dollars in the 1980s.

When Fahd traveled outside the Kingdom, he stayed in his own one-hundred-room palace in Marbella, Spain; a spectacular estate outside Paris, originally built for the eighteenth-century French kings; a mansion near London on which he had spent nearly $60 million in refurbishments; and a sprawling palacio in Geneva, in which, he was fond of boasting, he had 1,500 telephone lines. He flew between cities in a private 747-SP fitted with an enormous pink master bedroom, gold bathroom fixtures, a mahogany elevator, a sauna, and Baccarat crystal chandeliers. Fahd's lavish yacht—the size of a luxury liner—cost $50 million, and he kept over two dozen Rolls-Royces, fitted with gold hood ornaments and grills, in his different homes (the British firm of Wood and Barrett custom-fitted a Rolls-Royce Carmargue into a one-of-a-kind dune buggy). Fahd's personal wealth was estimated to be near $30 billion.[10]

Washington was generally pleased with the change in power, although the view was that while competent, Fahd was lazy and still a heavy gambler. Some intelligence reports about him claimed that in private, in viola-

---

there was no space for their livestock and too little room for their sprawling families, Khalid pressed ahead. He spent nearly $600 million on three enormous housing projects, each including mosques, playgrounds, retail stores, and schools. They remained empty years after their completion, tributes to the independence of the desert tribes.

tion of one of the strictest Koranic prohibitions, he was a secret drinker.[11] The same was true of some of his brothers as well as his father, King Ibn Saud.[12] The drinking rumors worried the White House because Fahd suffered from diabetes, a condition that was a potential killer when combined with too much alcohol.

At a White House state dinner in May 1975, President Ford welcomed Crown Prince Fahd, oil minister Yamani, and a coterie of senior princes. There was, of course, no hint of the intelligence the administration had gathered on the crown prince, although he lived up to his reputation by arriving at the White House nearly forty-five minutes late.

Ford ignored the tardiness and instead acknowledged how the Kingdom's international stature had changed since the embargo.

"Saudi Arabia is a nation which has grown in many ways in the last few years in world importance," he said. "Their supplies of energy are crucial to the well-being of people in many nations." With no mention of the embargo itself, he thanked the Saudi dignitaries for keeping oil flowing, and for having "saved the entire economic structure of the world from disruption."[13] No American president before or since had been so blunt in assessing the special nature of the U.S. energy dependence on the House of Saud.

Compliments to the Saudis like the one from Ford worried Israeli politicians and American Jewish groups, who saw a spike in Arab influence on the United States. The enhanced success of the boycott was also strong evidence of a new Arab standing in Western capitals. Jewish groups had talked about organizing a counterboycott to the Arab one, but consensus ran against that.[14] In July, only three months after Faisal's assassination, leaders of prominent Jewish advocacy groups gathered in Oxford, England, to devise the best way of breaking the Arab boycott and thereby reversing the rise in Arab prestige.

In late 1975, a number of Jewish organizations, led by the American Jewish Congress, the Anti-Defamation League of B'nai B'rith, and the American Jewish Committee, launched an official antiboycott effort. Their concerted campaign paid some quick dividends. Congressional hearings, prompted by the lobbying, led to embarrassing disclosures about American companies and government departments that had willingly participated in the boycott. The revelations prompted President Ford to issue several executive branch directives aimed at eliminating any further U.S. collaboration in the discrimination. The Commerce and State departments agreed to no longer circulate foreign trade opportunities if they contained boycott provisions, nor would they certify papers that supported the boycott. The Federal Reserve Board warned banks that even "passive participation" could violate U.S. antitrust laws.

But the Ford administration had no intention of striking a mortal blow to the boycott by passing any tough new laws, which is what the Jewish advocacy groups wanted. The Saudi monarchy was under attack from some Arab nationalists who thought the royals were too pro-Western. The Ford administration did not want to take any strong action that made the Saudis appear weak. Part of the reason for the sensitivity in Washington was that on December 21, 1975, the terrorist Carlos the Jackal and a gang of German Marxists shot their way into OPEC's headquarters in Vienna and seized eleven oil ministers and twenty-nine other industry officials. In a manifesto read to the press, the terrorists condemned Saudi Arabia and Iran for not aggressively using their oil profits to help the "Arab nation." The Saudis, Iran, the United Arab Emirates, and Qatar were castigated as "the criminal group" for their pro-U.S. policies. After arranging for a DC9 to fly his armed commandos and captives to Algeria, the Jackal released fifteen hostages in return for a multimillion-dollar ransom. Although the Saudis paid the ransom through back channels, rumors later persisted that Aramco had really put up the money.[15] After the Algerian stopover, the remaining hostages, including the prize catch of Saudi oil minister Sheikh Yamani, were flown on an odyssey to Tripoli, Tunis, and finally back to Algeria. There, after coming close to killing Yamani, the Jackal received a Saudi ransom offer so large that he freed the remaining captives. Aramco, which had a Learjet trailing the hostage plane, immediately flew the freed Yamani back to Riyadh, where the king welcomed him with the gift of a new Rolls-Royce.

But the terror kidnapping, and the fact that Saudis were being accused publicly of being too soft on Israel and too accepting of American policies, strengthened the Kingdom's hard-liners. Although they did not persuade King Khalid to modify his tacit promise that America would receive the oil it needed to maintain its economy, decision makers in Washington were increasingly worried about House of Saud concerned that they appeared too pro-American.

American Jewish lobbying organizations, however, viewed the time as opportune to launch a far more aggressive campaign to counter the influence of petrodollars and the possibility that business and government dependence on such money would force realignment in American policies toward Israel.

In 1975, when Saudi middleman and financier Ghaith Pharaon tried buying the Michigan-based Bank of the Commonwealth, FDIC chairman Frank Willie said Pharaon would be "treated as if he were another American" during the applications and approval process.[16] But public news of Pharaon's interest caused some Jewish activists to picket the bank, while others threatened withdrawals.[17] Max Fisher, a prominent Jewish financier in Detroit, publicly opposed the sale. "If they get into one bank, they can get into more," he said. "They could put a stranglehold on us. I don't think it's a Jewish matter, I think it's a national matter."[18] Pharaon countered the criticism by hiring Chase Manhattan to steer the deal to completion, and also employing the powerhouse Houston law firm of Vinson, Elkins, Searls, Connally & Smith (where John Connally, former Texas governor and secretary of the treasury under Nixon, was a senior partner).[19] Pharaon prevailed in his takeover, but the monarchy was infuriated by the extra battle he had to wage because he was a Saudi.

Saudis were further incensed by the Senate Subcommittee on Multinational Corporations hearings (1975–76) on the staggering amount of petrodollars that had been pumped by the Saudis and other OPEC producers into American banks and corporations. They threatened to withdraw their substantial American investments—over $20 billion at that time—should their money not be welcome.[20]

Arms dealer Adnan Khashoggi had to abandon his effort to buy the First National Bank in California after a storm of protest. "Zionists were trying to use the deal to create a new wave of hatred for the Arabs among the American public," he told an English-language magazine in Beirut. "I decided not to give them that satisfaction."[21] Khashoggi decried the increasing hostility to Arab investments, and said that it was the first time in history that money had been given an "ethnic tag." He also threatened to yank his money from the States.

Despite these threats, by 1977 the movement to confront the Arab boycott had grown. The American Jewish Congress, an independent group of prominent American Jewish businessmen and social leaders, had filed a successful lawsuit against the Commerce Department that year. They won the right to release the names of the U.S. companies that had complied with the Arab boycott, including some who had done so after the Ford administration rules had barred such conduct. The Commerce Department had estimated, before the suit, that only about $10 million was involved in boycott-related deals in 1974 and 1975. When the department released its files, the real figure was a disquieting $45 billion. There was outrage in Congress that American companies had so cavalierly ignored rules against the boycott—but probably not enough to pass stronger laws, if it had not been for an even more concerted effort by the American Jewish community.

Earlier efforts had failed because they were seen as putting American businesses at a disadvantage against foreign competitors. Stronger restrictions might damage U.S. interests in the Middle East. But now, armed with a list of major American corporations that had aided the boycott, leading Jewish groups concentrated on getting a tough new law enacted.[22] And with the change of administrations from Gerald Ford's to Jimmy Carter's, they had a better chance. Irving Shapiro, chairman of E. I. du Pont & Company as well as the head of the prestigious panel the Business Roundtable, and Burton Joseph, the chairman of the Anti-Defamation League, met to see if the two sides could reach a compromise. Small preliminary talks expanded to larger meetings in hotels and offices from New York to Palm Beach, as more Jewish advocacy groups and representatives of top corporations painstakingly bargained. Twice the talks broke up in arguments. But the two sides finally agreed to formal bargaining with professional negotiators.

The White House had noticed, and Carter took the unprecedented step of announcing that he would support whatever compromise was reached between the business representatives and the Jewish groups. They bickered for several months before resolving the impasse in April. Congress, acting on their recommendations, passed a tough new anti-boycott bill, and Jimmy Carter signed it into law on June 10, 1977.

As *U.S. News & World Report* later commented on the uniqueness of the new law, "What's unusual is that key portions of the legislation were hammered out not by the nation's elected lawmakers, but by private citizens from the American business and Jewish communities. Special-interest groups often have an active voice in the lawmaking process. But observers could recall no previous instance of Congress and the White House openly inviting such outsiders, in effect, to write their own statute."

The success of the Jewish lobbying in passing a robust statute that gutted the Arab boycott was not the only aspect of an invigorated American Jewish effort to go on the offensive against Arab policies. The Anti-

Defamation League (ADL) and the American Jewish Congress successfully lobbied members of Congress to appeal to the Defense and Commerce Departments to issue new regulations banning cooperation with companies that followed any discriminatory racial and religious practices demanded by foreign countries. And the ADL created national headlines when it charged that twenty-five U.S. banks were "waging war against Israel in collaboration with the Arabs."[23] The central thesis was that the banks named had acceded to more than eighteen thousand boycott requests by not paying more than a billion dollars in exporters' letters of credit without first obtaining proof of boycott compliance. These disclosures forced the Federal Reserve Bank chairman, Arthur Burns, to send a stern letter to the banks requesting that they not participate further in the boycott, and the Commerce Department took up the task of drafting strict new regulations for the banks.

Crown Prince Fahd was personally incensed by these events.[24] He told the London *Sunday Times* that the Kingdom was "fully committed to the principles of the boycott," and that the Saudis would not have "meek acceptance of American anti-boycott legislation."[25] But it did not take long before cooler heads prevailed, and the idea of boycotting American goods and companies, which Fahd suggested, was not realistic. "Certainly it would be disruptive to our five-year development plan to switch to other suppliers," said Saudi Arabia's minister of industry and electricity, Dr. Ghazi al-Gosaibi. "It would hurt us. No country is indispensable, not even the greatest. But American technology is superior, Saudi Arabia has had a long experience with Americans through Aramco, and we like Americans."[26]

By mid-1977, the Saudis not only had about $27 billion in contracts with U.S. companies for products and services, but they also had about $30 billion invested in America in real estate, government securities, and company stocks. Meanwhile, the U.S. economy was increasingly reliant on Saudi efforts to moderate oil prices. The economic intertwining had made it almost impossible for either country to sever its relations with the other in a pique.

Awash in billions of dollars in annual surpluses, the House of Saud decided to counter the Jewish efforts with a lobby of its own.[27] It had already hired public relations polling whiz kid Patrick Caddell to provide details about how Americans felt about Saudi Arabia, and what might be done to improve the Kingdom's image (Caddell was Jimmy Carter's pollster).[28] The embargo had left Americans with poor opinions of Saudi Arabia as an ally.

The royals turned for help to Sheikh Kamal Adham, who had run al Istakhbarat al Amiyyah (the General Intelligence Network), the Saudi equivalent of the CIA, since its inception. Adham's sister Queen Iffat was married to the late King Faisal. Adham had been a close advisor to Faisal, and the king had given him a then unprecedented 2 percent of the oil concession with Japan (he was dubbed "Mr. 2 Percent" in Middle Eastern business circles).[29] Adham, whose CIA intelligence moniker was Tumbleweed, advised the royals that they had to hire men who had the savvy to provide the information and analysis necessary to explain the political and economic rules of the game. In that way they would gain an advantage in dealing with the Washington labyrinth and prevail on issues important to the Kingdom. It was also necessary to create and fund a Wahhabi lobby. The orders from the royal family were unequivocal: the Jewish lobby must be fought with every tool available. Adham, with his understanding of both overt efforts needed in public relations and politics as well as covert methods from the intelligence world, seemed the ideal choice to initiate the program.

For over a decade Adham had built a remarkably close covert relationship with the CIA. Many at Langley thought of him as their most solid link to the Saudi monarchy.[30] In his private home he maintained communications equipment that allowed him to talk securely to the Pentagon.[31] *The Washington Post,* in February 1977, called him one of the two most important Arab policy makers with CIA ties (the other being the late King Hussein of Jordan).[32] Not only did Adham serve as the Kingdom's intelligence chief, but he had also, since 1973, been an integral partner in major Saudi commercial undertakings with the West. There were no conflict of interest laws in Saudi Arabia that barred someone of his position from using his government post to foster business. Instead, the House of Saud encouraged it. As a result, Adham was partners with Khashoggi in a British-Arab merchant bank, and turned up as one of the middlemen on arms deals with Northrop, Lockheed, and Boeing.[33] He was also a major shareholder (17.9 percent), with middleman Ghaith Pharaon, in the giant holding company First Arabian, which was the conduit for billions in Western investments, such as gobbling up U.S. banks, shopping centers, and office towers. Half a dozen royal princes had smaller shares of First Arabian, and Salem bin Laden, one of Osama bin Laden's brothers, had 5.4 percent, which he managed for the bin Laden clan. The bin Laden family, operating as the Mohamed bin Laden Organization, had become the de facto public works department in the Kingdom, holding almost all the contracts for building the nation's roads, airports, streets, and commercial complexes.*

But the Saudi royals did not now need Adham for his business acumen. Instead, his unequivocal brief from the king was to ensure that the Saudis did not lose the public relations war with American Jewish political lobbyists. He was also to try to prevent the Kingdom from getting blindsided by negative publicity from Western media, something to which the Saudis had previously paid little attention.[34] So that Adham could concentrate solely on his new assignment, he resigned his position as chief of intelligence and handed the post over to his thirty-two-year-old protégé and nephew, Prince Turki bin Faisal bin Abdul Aziz.

By 1978, a year after the successful American Jewish lobbying effort, the Saudis had made considerable progress of their own. They had won over, or hired, a great number of influential new friends.

Bert Lance, for instance, once Jimmy Carter's budget director, sold his National Bank of Georgia stock for $20 per share, $9 above the market, to thirty-eight-year-old Ghaith Pharaon, the Saudi investor who had started a giant investment holding company—the Saudi Research and Development Corporation—in 1966 with two of King Faisal's sons as partners. Senior Saudi officials were personally ecstatic with the Lance deal. It helped Lance, whose bank was seriously floundering, pocket a needed infusion of cash, $2.4 million.[35] Pharaon denied he made the investment to buy influence with the White House. "We have influence where we come from," he said, "so I don't think we have to buy it here."[36] But few believed it was from bad judgment or a coincidence that he paid nearly double the market price for stock from the former budget director.

Pharaon employed former Texas governor John Connally's law firm on the deal. Pharaon also went into business deals with Connally in 1978.[37] Houston, where Connally was based, became the American beachhead of the U.S. pro-Arab forces. Saudi Arabia replaced Japan as Houston's number one trading partner, with approximately $2 billion in goods (much of it imported crude oil) flowing back and forth through the Port of Houston.[38]

---

*Adham's eventual downfall came from his later investment in the Bank of Credit and Commerce International (BCCI), the largest bank fraud in history. Adham was indicted in 1992 for violating the New York Bank Holding Company Act and agreed to cooperate with prosecutors by providing testimony as well as paying $105 million in fines and restitution.

The Saudi Education Mission, which processes all Saudi students studying in the U.S., moved to Houston from New York. Shortly after that came
the Saudi consulate. A leading Saudi publishing company also relocated
there, and firms specializing in advertising and translation services for
American and Saudi companies doing business with one another made
Houston their base. Also, the Saudi government–owned petroleum and
minerals company Petromin opened up its U.S. office near the town's Gal-
leria Mall. The likable Connally, well connected in politics and business,
became the chief "introducer" for the new Saudi lobby, and *Newsweek*
dubbed him the "top Arab money lawyer."[39]*

Bert Lance had established a new venture, a Georgia-based consulting firm that for years would earn a substantial portion of its revenue from
advising Arab investors. Joining Lance and Connally in giving legal, financial, and political advice to Saudi investors was former vice president
Spiro Agnew. Agnew had, in 1975, taken over the presidency of Education
for Democracy, a group blasted by the Anti-Defamation League as a movement dedicated solely to anti-Israel, pro-Arab views. Over time, Agnew's
pronouncements sounded more like those of an Arab diplomat than a
former American vice president: "I see no reason why nearly half of the
foreign aid this nation has to give has to go to Israel, except for the influence of the Zionist lobby."[40] On NBC's *Today* show, on May 11, 1976,
Agnew warned that "Zionist influences in the United States are dragging
the U.S. into a rather disorganized approach in the Middle East."[41] In his
1976 publicity tour for a novel, *The Canfield Decision,* he often launched
into diatribes about what he considered a Jewish cabal in the U.S. His
comments complemented one of the major themes of his novel, that Jews
wielded tremendous manipulative power. He claimed that Jews owned or
managed 50 percent of the national media, including the wire services,
Time, Newsweek, The Washington Post, The New York Times, and *The International Herald Tribune.* Agnew often cited CBS's William Paley and
NBC's Julian Goodman as examples of the media's "tremendous Jewish
voice." And beyond the media, he complained publicly about Jewish influ-

*When Connally ran for the 1980 Republican presidential nomination, his nine-point Mid-
dle East peace plan showed the influence of his Arab clients and friends. He not only called
for complete Israeli withdrawal from the occupied territories and the dismantling of all set-
tlements, but also linked Israel's willingness to compromise to the willingness of Arab nations to "return to stable oil prices." Felix Rohatyn, a widely respected New York investment
banker, himself a critic of many Israeli government policies, told *The New York Times,* "To
think you can trade Israel for oil is totally impractical, in addition to being immoral."

ence in academia, the financial community, and public and charitable foundations.[42]

Agnew earned hundreds of thousands of dollars in commissions for arranging business deals between the Saudis and Western business interests. Many former government officials wanted a part of the new Arab business that Agnew found so lucrative. Richard Helms, former CIA director and ex-ambassador to Iran, started his own company, Safeer, which means "ambassador" in Farsi.[43] Others included former Nixon secretary of state William P. Rogers, ex–Kennedy speechwriter Theodore Sorenson, and Agnew. William Simon, Nixon's secretary of the treasury, became a middleman for some key Arab investors, including Saudi financier Suliman Olayan and his multibillion-dollar Crescent Diversified portfolio.[44]

The Saudis gave Frederick G. Dutton, assistant secretary of state for legislative affairs under JFK and LBJ, a six-figure retainer that obligated him to meet several times a week with the Saudi ambassador to the U.S. and pass along "basic intelligence" on what was happening in Washington that might affect Saudi interests.[45] Also, Dutton used his connections— he had been an advisor to Robert Kennedy and George McGovern—to arrange private meetings between his Saudi clients and American lawmakers like Illinois senator Adlai Stevenson III and South Dakota's James Abourezk.[46] In addition to his legal advice, for which he earned about $200,000 annually in the late 1970s, Dutton also performed personal jobs for his Saudi clients, from locating doctors to treat members of the royal family, to helping Saudi students in America who got in legal scrapes, to buying chairs for King Khalid's personal residences. He even tried helping Prince Saud al-Faisal, the Saudi foreign minister, buy a New York co-op apartment.[47]

Gerald Parsky, today a prominent California investment banker, had been assistant secretary of the treasury for monetary affairs in both the Nixon and Ford administrations. In that role, he traveled extensively to Saudi Arabia during a three-year span and became a promoter of Arab investments in the U.S., even emerging as a leading opponent of any anti-boycott legislation. After he left government service, Parsky became the Washington, D.C., head of a noted Los Angeles–based law firm, Gibson, Dunn & Crutcher, and the firm and Parsky were hired as registered foreign agents for Saudi Arabia and the United Arab Emirates. The year after Ronald Reagan's election, Parsky's law firm opened a Riyadh office to handle all the new business.[48]

Raymond Close, former CIA station chief in Jeddah, left to become a paid advisor to Kamal Adham, and later to the Faisal Foundation, the Saudi royal family's repository for medical research and philanthropic endeavors.[49] Ron Ziegler, Richard Nixon's pugnacious press spokesman, used his new role as managing director of New York's Syska & Hennessy Engineers to make frequent visits to Saudi Arabia and land the contracts to design new palaces.[50] Willis Armstrong, former assistant secretary of state for economic affairs, became a Washington-watcher for Saudi arms middleman Adnan Khashoggi. Former South Carolina governor John C. West, soon after leaving the governor's mansion, founded the Arab-American Development Services Company, a one-stop consulting service for U.S. firms trying to drum up business in Arab countries. But West had to temporarily leave his new venture when in June 1977, a year after founding it, he was appointed ambassador to Saudi Arabia (West was embroiled in controversy during his four-year tenure, sometimes for getting former South Carolina acquaintances lavish business deals in the Kingdom—when he retired from public service in 1981, he started the West Advisory Services firm, designed to help U.S. companies get Saudi business).[51]

Talcott Seelye, former ambassador to Syria, left thirty-two years of government service and became a consultant to Rezayat America Inc., a Saudi-owned company that coordinated multibillion-dollar service contracts between American firms and the Kingdom.[52] Clark Clifford, the Democratic party elder statesman, who had served both Truman and Kennedy before becoming LBJ's secretary of defense, had begun advising Arab governments and investors on how best to flourish in the U.S. Clifford was retained, among just one of many deals, by Adnan Khashoggi to fend off an SEC investigation into questionable payments by American defense contractors.[53] And Clifford served as chairman of Financial General Bankshares, Inc., a multibillion-dollar bank holding company with 150 branches in five states. Financial General had been taken over by Arab investors, including Saudi intelligence chief Kamal Adham.[54]

John J. McCloy II, son of the former U.S. high commissioner to Germany, represented the Wall Street private banking firm Brown Brothers Harriman & Co. in a joint fifty-fifty venture with Prince Mohamed, one of King Faisal's sons, in Middle East Financial Consulting Associates, a consulting firm whose aim was to put together large international commercial ventures.[55] Michael Moynihan, Senator Daniel Patrick Moynihan's brother, became a paid public relations advisor to the Saudis.[56] And Senator J. William Fulbright, whose law firm, Hogan & Harston, was registered as a foreign agent for the United Arab Emirates, aided many of the ex-officials who were on the Saudi payroll. Fulbright, former chairman of the Foreign Relations Committee, was one of the most prominent voices on behalf of Saudi issues, and one of Israel's strongest critics.[57] (When Fulbright lost his Senate seat in a 1974 election, he commented, "Any member of Congress who does not follow the wishes of the Israel lobby is bitterly denounced and can be assured of finding his opponent richly funded in the next election.")[58]

As the later Saudi ambassador to the United States, Prince Bandar bin Sultan, noted about the Saudi effort to cultivate and hire former American government officials, "If the reputation builds that the Saudis take care of friends when they leave office, you'd be surprised how much better friends you have who are just coming into office."[59]

The Saudis, completely outmaneuvered so handily by the American Jewish lobby on the antiboycott law, had vowed not to let it happen again. And they soon had a test of their new power, as eight separate government probes into the special Saudi-Aramco relationship had sprung up in Washington. American politicians wanted to know if Aramco had placed its loyalty to profits and the Kingdom above its allegiance to the United States.

Senator Frank Church (D-Idaho) summarized the essence of the investigations: "We Americans must uncover the trail that led the United States into dependency on Arab sheikhdoms for so much of its oil. Why did our Government support and encourage the movement of the huge American-owned oil companies into the Middle East in the first place? We must reexamine the premise that what's good for the oil companies is good for the United States . . . We must demystify the inner sanctum of this most secret of industries, especially Aramco. . . ."[60]

Aramco had raised concerns with some congressional investigators by its funding of pro-Arab think tanks that passed themselves off as unbiased institutes but instead advanced only the Saudi political line. While those grants supporting the House of Saud might have been controversial, they did not, however, violate any law.[61] A bigger problem arose when the Justice Department's antitrust division filed charges contending that Aramco had violated anticartel laws when it reaped record profits during the embargo.[62] Besides the legal broadside, probes had commenced in the

Senate Committee on Energy and Natural Resources; the House Sub-committee on Commerce, Consumer, and Monetary Affairs; the Senate Subcommittee on Antitrust, Monopoly and Business Rights; the Senate Judiciary Committee; and the State Department's Bureau of Intelligence and Research.[63]

The Saudis considered themselves to have been unfairly targeted. The royals complained bitterly about Jewish staff workers they considered anti-Saudi on Capitol Hill. They included Scott Cohen, Illinois senator Charles Percy's aide; Michael Kraft from New Jersey senator Clifford Case's office; Stephen Bryen of the Middle East Subcommittee of the Senate Foreign Relations Committee; Richard Perle, then working with Washington senator Henry "Scoop" Jackson, who was chairman of the all-important Senate Committee on Energy and Natural Resources; Richard D. Siegel from Pennsylvania senator Richard Schweicker's office; Mel Grossman, who had served as an aide to the recently resigned Florida senator Edward J. Gurney; Daniel L. Spiegel, an aide to Senator Hubert Humphrey (and later to his wife, Muriel, who finished his term in the Senate); Jay Berman from Indiana senator Birch Bayh's office; and Mel Levine, a top aide to California senator John V. Tunney.

Saudi officials were particularly incensed when congressional investigators asked for their internal figures on oil reserves and production capacity, matters the House of Saud considered their own national security.

"In some countries," said oil minister Sheikh Yamani, "information about oil reserves and reservoir behavior are not only classified but to reveal that is a crime covered by capital punishment. In this case we were singled out from all the other oil producers in the world by a group of Americans working for the Zionist lobby. Their aim was to show that Saudi Arabia is not really a country which can solve America's energy problems."[64]

War had been declared on the Saudis. It is little wonder that when the Carter administration soon lobbied them to support the historic Camp David peace agreement between Egypt and Israel, declaring a formal peace between the two countries, the Saudis opposed it. The House of Saud did the same when Egyptian president Anwar Sadat made his unprecedented trip to Jerusalem in December 1977 and gave an optimistic speech about a possible peace to the Israeli Knesset. And the Saudis repeatedly rebuffed the Carter administration's Middle East peace efforts. U.S. ambassador to Saudi Arabia John C. West had tried but failed to convince the House of Saud that its endorsement was necessary to encourage other moderate Arab nations to support the Egyptian-Israeli accord. Then Carter's national security advisor, Zbigniew Brzezinski, visited the Kingdom but also returned home empty-handed. The State Department's third-ranking official, David D. Newsom, held a secret meeting in Spain with Crown Prince Fahd but was unable to make headway. And finally, Carter himself sent a private letter to King Khalid, but it also failed to move the Saudis.[65] The monarchy had no reason, it concluded, to help the Americans in the Middle East if the U.S. was not willing to openly welcome Saudi investments in the States.*

When a proposed sale in 1978 of sixty F-15s to the Kingdom was opposed by many in Congress as a potential threat to Israel, Oil Minister Yamani warned that a refusal by Washington to sell the planes to his country would have an adverse effect on Saudi Arabia's oil production and support for the dollar. "We place great importance and significance on this transaction. We feel we badly need it. It's for our security. It is to defend Saudi Arabia. If we don't get it, then we will have a feeling you are not concerned with our security and you don't appreciate our friendship."[66]

The House of Saud was no longer hiding the fact that it linked its oil weapon to U.S. decisions concerning its national security. The royals leaned on former intelligence chief Adham. What was being done to counter the efforts of the American Jews? he was asked. Adham knew the king would not long tolerate continuing public embarrassments.

While publicly the Saudis were losing the public relations battle, there were some significant behind-the-scenes victories. Back in 1974 and 1975, the Senate Subcommittee on Multinationals of the Senate Foreign Relations Committee had launched an extensive probe into Saudi oil production and the Kingdom's relations with Aramco. The investigation slogged on for four years, with congressional subpoenas in 1978 to the oil companies causing the Saudis to claim all relevant documents belonged to the Kingdom, not Aramco. When the subcommittee finally completed a 130-page draft report that was highly critical of the Aramco-Saudi partnership, the Wahhabi lobby began to work to ensure that it was not released

---

*It also did not help that a year earlier, the Carter administration had ignored Saudi warnings that troops and supplies were pouring into Ethiopia. By the time of the Camp David peace accords, the Saudis faced a Marxist government installed directly across the Red Sea, and were having second thoughts about the reliability of America's defense commitment.

in its entirety. The oil industry chiefs, and Sheikh Yamani, made it clear that the future of Saudi investments in the U.S. were at risk if they were publicly embarrassed by the congressional report. The Saudis also let congressional staffers know they would view the report's release as interfering with their sovereign rights, and that given its pending release, they had zero incentive to reconsider helping the U.S. on the Egyptian-Israeli peace talks.

The full report was killed—an unprecedented victory for the Saudis— when it came to Congress. On April 14, 1979, a sanitized thirty-seven-page document, cleared by the Saudis beforehand, was publicly released. The king sent a personal congratulation note to Adham.

The Saudi success on the Senate subcommittee report would be repeated on a massive Justice Department antitrust investigation of Aramco and the international oil market. Saudi Arabia again aggressively warned officials in both the Carter and Reagan administrations that there would be serious repercussions if the antitrust probe, which had begun in 1977, produced embarrassing revelations. By that time, for instance, over ninety American colleges and universities had asked the Saudis for financial assistance and grants. The not very subtle word from Riyadh was that the Saudis would not be inclined to help higher-education facilities in a country that thought of them as being involved in criminal activity.[67] Some of the schools, like the University of Southern California, rushed to gain favor with the Saudis. USC actually created a King Faisal Chair of Islamic and Arab Studies, and after giving the Kingdom the veto power over the chair's occupant, the school got a $1 million grant from Saudi Arabia. And the Saudis showered schools with sympathetic study programs, as at Georgetown, and significant grants, as at Duke.

Sheik Yamani unequivocally told Treasury Secretary William Miller, during a December 1979 visit to Riyadh, that he expected Treasury's assistance in halting the Justice probe.[68] The National Security Council and State Department, both fearing negative fallout from the investigation, tried to stop Justice from pursuing its subpoenas. In March 1980, Deputy Attorney General John Shenefield, in charge of the probe, traveled to Saudi Arabia to ask for the Kingdom's permission to release certain documents relating to Aramco. The Saudis refused, and Shenefield left empty-handed. When the Reagan administration took office, it did not take long before the Justice Department voluntarily terminated the case.

Petrodollars also let the Saudis get their way when it came to cultural events. In the 1980s, the Smithsonian canceled a long-awaited exhibition titled "Archaeology of Israel." Although the Smithsonian had invested eighteen months in preparing for the exhibit, it changed its mind at the last moment since eleven of the items to be displayed came from the Rockefeller Museum, in a district of Jerusalem occupied by Israel. The turnaround came coincidentally after Saudi Arabia announced its donation of $5 million to build a Center for Islamic Study at the Smithsonian.

And even on social issues the Saudis made progress with their new lobbying efforts. A $430,000 film, *Death of a Princess,* was an American public television and British co-production about the 1977 execution of a Saudi princess who had eloped with a commoner instead of marrying the man selected by her family. The execution of the princess and her lover for violations of Islamic law had been ordered by Prince Muhammad ibn Abdul Aziz, who happened to be the oldest surviving son of the Kingdom's founder, Ibn Saud. The pending broadcast kicked off a firestorm in Saudi Arabia, where the film was viewed as a Zionist-backed attack on Islamic heritage. When it aired in Britain, Saudi Arabia expelled the British ambassador, and the British Foreign Office tried to mend diplomatic fences by later apologizing. When the American Public Broadcasting Corporation prepared to air it, the Saudis commenced a concerted effort to have it canceled. The Saudis lobbied friendly members of Congress—such as Charles Percy, the Illinois Republican on the Senate Foreign Relations Committee—urging that the show not be aired. Percy told President Carter that "there would be support in Congress should the President make a determination that the showing of the program would not be in the national interest."[69]

Others on Capitol Hill lashed out at the film. The Saudis, and their American friends and representatives, urged the State Department to get involved. The former chairman of the Joint Chiefs, Admiral Thomas Moorer, a director of Texaco, one of the four Aramco companies, urged that the film be banned unless the U.S. wanted "gas lines" and enough controversy to "blow up the free world."[70] The result was that although PBS aired *Death of a Princess,* Mobil withdrew its normal underwriting money, and not all of the 142 PBS affiliates ran the show. PBS followed the program with a one-hour panel discussion, described by a senior PBS official as "sixty minutes of Arab apologia."[71] Also, PBS committed to, and ran a year later, a documentary made with the wife of the Saudi ambassador to the

U.S. It presented a remarkably different perspective of the role of women in Saudi Arabia from the one presented in *Princess*. Moreover, the State Department launched negotiations with Saudi officials to produce a major documentary on Saudi society and foreign policy. That hagiographic film was finished two years after *Death of a Princess* aired, and it ran repeatedly on PBS.

As the 1970s closed, there was little doubt that, from congressional investigations to the airing of controversial films, the Saudis had begun to understand not only how to counter the pro-Israeli lobby, but also how to advance their own issues and interests.

By mid-1979, the Carter administration had reluctantly given up on persuading Saudi Arabia to support the Egyptian-Israeli peace treaty and instead turned its attention to, as *The Washington Post* reported, "repairing the substantial damage done over the past six months to the special relationship Washington and Riyadh have sought to build."[72] As part of the reconciliation, the United States stopped asking the Saudis to pay for fifty U.S.-manufactured F-5E jet fighters for Cairo, a reward to Egypt for signing a peace deal with Israel. The Saudis had been reluctant to pick up the $525 million price tag for the planes, and the issue had become a sore point between the countries.

And the Saudis were exhibiting new boldness in the Washington-Riyadh relationship as they expelled the CIA's station chief from the country. *The Washington Post* had run an article citing U.S. intelligence reports that concluded that Crown Prince Fahd's authority was waning. Banishing the American CIA station chief was as visible a sign of their displeasure over such anonymous attributions as the Saudis could show their American allies.[73]

Coupled with its other signs of strength, Riyadh had rebuffed repeated requests from the Carter administration to increase oil production in an effort to lower oil prices. Instead, the Saudis, in 1979, did the opposite. The Kingdom sharply reduced the amount of oil it sold—from 7 million to 6.1 million barrels daily—to American oil companies. The Saudi Council of Ministers publicly announced an examination of a policy put in place in the early 1970s to buy U.S. Treasury securities. The nearly $7 billion Saudi Arabia had invested in American government securities by 1979 was one of the most visible symbols of the unique relationship between the two countries.[74]

The Wahhabi lobby had begun working in the U.S. And it had imparted confidence to the House of Saud in its dealings with the American government. The Saudis were adamant that no longer would they allow themselves to be easily beaten in the U.S. by their Jewish rivals.

CHAPTER 7

INSURRECTION AND IRAN

The Saudi efforts to win influence in America seemed suddenly less important to the House of Saud in 1979 when several events shook the ruling clan's sense of security. On February 11, in the Kingdom's neighbor, Iran, Ayatollah Ruholla Khomeini swept to power on the back of a Shiite religious revolution that forced the shah of Iran, Mohammad Reza Pahlavi, to flee for his life. The shah had ruled since 1941. In order to counter Soviet influence when the British left the Gulf after World War II, the United States armed Iran as it had no other country, not even Israel. The rabidly anti-Communist House of Saud prized the shah as a buffer against the Soviets. And since the shah was a secular rather than religious ruler, he had not threatened the Wahhabis with Iran's traditionally competitive Shiite branch of Islam.

But the shah's swift fall from power, and his replacement by the Shiite equivalent of Wahhabi fundamentalists, sent shock waves through Riyadh. The House of Saud had, before the shah's fall, repeatedly criticized Khomeini, then in exile in France, and his followers as un-Islamic.[1] The Saudis could not fathom how the U.S. allowed the shah's government to topple so easily, and they thought it incomprehensible that the Carter administration refused the shah immediate asylum.[2] They wondered whether, if they found themselves in a similar crisis, America might as cavalierly accept their demise.[3]

Just seven months earlier, in July 1978, President Carter had issued Presidential Directive 18, which designated a 100,000-soldier strike force to respond quickly to regional conflicts that might endanger Saudi oil. The Pentagon had assigned two army divisions, one heavy and one light, and a marine amphibious force to fulfill Carter's directive. Two aircraft carriers and three air force tactical wings, totaling about two hundred fighters and bombers, supported the strike force. At the time, the Saudis thought it cemented their safety under the American military umbrella. Although the House of Saud still had considerable differences with American policies toward Israel and much of the rest of the Muslim world—not to mention their displeasure with Carter's persistent theme of "human rights"—it was satisfied with the president's explicit promise of military protection. It was especially pleased that it had come from a Democratic president. Until 9/11, the Saudis usually preferred Republican administrations. They considered the Republicans less controlled by American Jewish interests, less likely to promote issues like human rights, and friendlier to Arab issues because of their traditionally stronger oil industry connections. Even Eisenhower's pressuring of Israel to withdraw from the Sinai peninsula in 1956 is cited to this day in Saudi Arabia as an example of Republican receptiveness.

Now, however, with the collapse of the shah catching the CIA and Pentagon completely off guard, the Saudis were worried that instability in Iran might spread over their border and infect a growing population inside the Kingdom who were not members of the royal family nor had shared in the enormous wealth enriching a top few percent. The Iranian mobs, urged on by Khomeini's mullahs, had seized the U.S. embassy and taken hostages. Fifty-two of them would be held for 444 days. If that was the best America could do for its own citizens, what could it manage for the House of Saud if it was threatened? The grand ayatollah added to the region's anxiety in a series of inflammatory sermons in which he threatened to revolutionize Saudi Arabia, take control of Mecca, make war against Israel, and return Jerusalem and Riyadh to the Shiite fold.

The Saudis, thinking regional instability was enough of a justification, asked to buy missiles from the United States. Congress again refused. To the chagrin of the Carter administration, the Saudis bought similar missiles—"East Wind Heavy Rockets"—from China.[4] The U.S., paralyzed over the hostage crisis—and despite its promise to protect the oil fields with military force if needed—seemed unwilling to warn the ayatollah that it would be a serious mistake to meddle in Saudi affairs. The Saudis were furious, and not pacified by messages meant to be reassuring that were sent from the State Department to the crown prince.

Tensions increased when in the summer of 1979, only months after sweeping to power, Khomeini began a campaign to revolutionize the Shiite minority in Hasa, a tiny Saudi province just across the Persian Gulf from Iran. Hasa's population was only 200,000, but its people made up almost 40 percent of Aramco's workforce in a nearby Shiite township, Qatif. They were among the most underprivileged in Saudi society, and local Shiite leaders, even before Khomeini's ascension, had been restless. Now, a new fundamentalist radio station—the Voice of Free Iran—regularly denounced King Khalid, the House of Saud, and Aramco, and pushed the Saudi Shi'a to action. A typical program broadcast these words: "The Saudi authorities are carrying out the same treacherous role that the deposed Shah carried out in Iran . . . The ruling regime in Saudi Arabia wears Muslim clothing, but inwardly represents the U.S. body, mind, and terrorism. . . . Funds are robbed from the people and squandered . . . for the luxurious, frivolous and shameless way of life of the Saudi royal family and its entourage."[5]

On November 20, 1979, New Year's Day in the Muslim calendar, the annual pilgrimage to Mecca was under way, including the largest Iranian delegation ever. Some spoke openly of "exporting the revolution" to the Kingdom. Saudi security forces intermingled with the crowds, but the sheer size—more than two million pilgrims—made them impossible to completely control. At 5:20 A.M., Sheikh Muhammad bin Subayal, the imam of Mecca's Grand Mosque, approached the microphone to begin a special day of prayers. He had barely finished his intonations when a man standing near the imam whipped out a pistol and fired three times, missing Subayal but killing his acolyte. Another man, with wild eyes and a heavy, matted beard, then shoved Subayal to the ground, grabbed the microphone, and screamed that he was the "expected Mahdi."[6] The return of the Mahdi, a divinely guided messenger who will restore Muslim doctrines on earth and usher in a brief golden age before the end of the world, is an essential Shiite doctrine.[7]

This was murder and heresy at Saudi Arabia's most revered site, at the start of the calendar's holiest period. But the worst was to come. The assassin grabbed the microphone and shouted for the Mahdi's followers to seize the Grand Mosque. Suddenly from the crowd a heavily armed group, including women and children, stormed the mosque. They occupied it, locked its heavy front wooden doors with chains, and blocked other entrances with makeshift barricades.

For King Khalid, who was responsible for maintaining and protecting Islam's holy sites, the attempted assassination of the chief imam, and the occupation of the mosque by armed radicals, ignited fears that the seizure was the beginning of planned insurrections throughout the Kingdom by the ayatollah's agents. The next two weeks were as nerve-wracking for the royal family as Saudi observers ever recalled. All communication with the outside world was cut in the Kingdom. Civilian aircraft were grounded. A day after the mosque's seizure, a rampaging mob in Islamabad, Pakistan, burned the American embassy, blaming the U.S. for the crisis in Mecca.

It turned out that the assassin and his nearly two hundred followers were not Iranians, as first feared.[8] But almost as bad, most of them were Saudis—born-again Muslim zealots who condemned the Saudi royals as corrupt and greedy rulers who consorted with infidels. Among the armed militants who stormed the Grand Mosque, beyond the core of Saudis, were Egyptians, Kuwaitis, Yemenis, and Pakistanis.[9] All were fundamentalists who had come to believe that armed struggle against the monarchy was the only way to restore a pure Islamic theocracy in the Kingdom. This strident view of Wahhabism is remarkably similar to that of Osama bin Laden and al Qaeda, reflecting an identical goal of using violence to topple the House of Saud.

King Khalid asked the ulema, the religious sages, for permission to send troops into the Grand Mosque. Once given the green light, security chief Prince Nayef and the intelligence director, Prince Turki, ordered nearly one thousand specially trained assault troops to take the holy site without inflicting too much damage to the structure itself. But the mosque was a great fortress, and the insurgents held them off. At times, Saudi troops seemed hesitant to fight fellow Wahhabis inside the holy grounds, so Prince Nayef arranged for two battalions of Pakistani Muslim commandos, under contract to the Saudi government, to show no mercy to the rebels. After nearly two weeks of gunfire, tear gas, burning tires to smoke them out, and even efforts at electrocuting them, the assassin and several score of surviving resisters surrendered before Saudi TV cameras.[10]

While the international press focused on the uprising at the Grand Mosque, the House of Saud was paying almost as much attention to disturbing events a thousand miles away in Hasa. There, the Shiites of Qatif

had taken to the streets by the thousands to mark the holy day commemo-
rating the death of the Prophet's grandson Hussein. The ayatollah's short-
wave radio service bitterly attacked King Khalid and the Saudi royals, and
continued to announce to Shiite crowds that a general uprising had begun
throughout the Kingdom and those in the streets should consider themselves Allah's advance armies. Doped on a potent mixture of fermented
dates and spices, the crowd was already in a frenzy of self-mutilation and
-flagellation. In al-Khobar and Qatif they rioted, burned buses and cars,
and trashed shops, homes, and businesses. Aramco shut its doors in Qatif.
Interior secretary Prince Nayef, with the king's blessing, sent in a sea-
soned special army corps to harshly subdue the uprising. By January 9,
after six weeks of resistance, the Shiite insurgents were either dead or had
melted quietly back into their local towns. There was no longer any sign of
insurgency in the Kingdom. And to make the point that none would be tol-
erated in the future, sixty-three of the key agitators in Mecca and Hasa
were rounded up, split into smaller groups, and sent to Riyadh's "Chop-
Chop" Square, as well as to Medina, Mecca, Hail, Dammam, Buraida,
Abha, and Tabuk. All were then publicly beheaded before nearly 500,000
Saudis—a clear warning to potential political dissidents that the House of
Saud would not abide such rebellion.[11]

The uprisings in Mecca and Hasa, although never a serious threat to
the royal family, nevertheless added to their sense of vulnerability, especially in light of the agitation of the Iranian Shiites. As a result, the Saudis
adopted measures on two separate fronts to appease their own fundamentalists.

The House of Saud became more conservative on matters of Wahhabism, essentially implementing many of the positions of the extremists
they had just defeated at the Grand Mosque.

"A few months after we killed them, we adopted their ideology," says
Dr. Sulaiman al-Hattlan, a columnist for the Saudi daily *Al Watan*. "We
gave them what they wanted when they were alive. In every level in our
society—I'm talking about the educational system, I'm talking about the
needed discourse, I'm talking about the relationship between the government and the people, I'm talking about even the relationship between
people and the people—we started competing on how to appear more
conservative just to protect our reputation and to protect sometimes our
safety. Terms like 'liberals,' 'seculars,' 'Americanized' were and still [are], in
fact, terms of alienation, terms of exclusion. We had to act. We had to pre-

tend we were something that we actually were not. And this culture of hypocrisy was a result of our reaction to 1979, I think."[12]

Strict interpretations were reimposed in areas in which rules had gradually relaxed over the years. For instance, music was again forbidden in Saudi media. Women were prohibited from appearing on television. All stores and malls had to close completely during the five daily prayers.[13] And on the matter of their sacred duty to export Wahhabism, a royal directive stated that there were to be "no limits . . . put on expenditures for the propagation of Islam."[14] Oil revenue was set aside in a grand plan to build Islamic centers, mosques, and schools, literally by the thousands, around the world.

In the midst of these Saudi upheavals, more instability struck the region on December 24, 1979. The Soviet army invaded Afghanistan to prop up Babrak Karmal's puppet government. Moscow's leaders predicted its soldiers would leave Afghanistan by the following spring. To Muslims, not only in Afghanistan but also around the Arab world, the Soviet invasion constituted the first time an infidel army had occupied an Islamic country since the Crusades. Within weeks of the assault, thousands of fundamentalist volunteers were making a holy pilgrimage to Afghanistan to fight the foreign invader. Among them was Osama bin Laden, the twenty-two-year-old son of a privileged Saudi Arabian business family.

The invasion of Afghanistan was not the six-month picnic Soviet planners had boldly forecast. The White House did its best to ensure that the Soviets got caught in a quagmire similar to the one that entrapped America for more than a decade in Vietnam. The United States organized an international boycott of the 1980 Summer Olympics in Moscow and ordered the CIA to fund, arm, and support the Afghan resistance through Pakistan and northern Afghanistan. The CIA channeled aid and weapons to the mujahideen fighters, all the while denying that America had any role. American money was critical to sustaining the resistance, and U.S. arms in the rebels' hands—notably Stinger antiaircraft missiles, introduced in the mid-1980s by the Reagan administration—changed the course of battle. The Saudis, meanwhile, provided enormous sums of money and used their influence with Pakistan's version of the CIA, InterServices Intelligence (ISI), which was compromised with Wahhabi-style fundamentalists. For the Saudis, a Wahhabi-based government in Afghanistan would be a strong buffer against their new enemy, Iran's Khomeini.

But the results the House of Saud hoped for would not happen, even after ten years of brutal conflict. By the time it was over, a million Afghans were dead, six million more having fled as refugees to Pakistan and Iran. The Soviets suffered nearly 15,000 dead and 53,000 wounded.[15] When they withdrew in defeat in 1989, the power vacuum they left was quickly filled by civil war, eventually leading to the establishment of a purist Islamic government headed by the Taliban, rivaling the rigidness of the most conservative Wahhabis. Osama bin Laden had been key in raising money for the Taliban and fighting by their side. The decade-long war in Afghanistan had given bin Laden and thousands of his fellow Muslim warriors from several continents confidence that they could defeat great powers like the Soviets. They also felt Allah had personally anointed them to return the faith to its early, pure roots by waging a jihad against nonbelievers, as well as those Muslims who had lost their devotion over generations. Afghanistan was the training ground for the terrorists the West is fighting today.

But the raging battles and bloodshed north of Saudi Arabia were not the only incidents of unsettling military conflict that seized the Gulf region. On September 22, 1980, less than a year after the Soviets had rolled into Afghanistan, the Iraqi army invaded Iran. The pretext for the invasion was Iran's claim to a disputed region of land, the Shatt al Arab. But the war was one Iraq's dictator, Saddam Hussein, had wanted. He longed for an imperial Iraq stretching along the borders of the old Ottoman Empire. But behind the scenes, it was also very much a proxy war for the Saudis and Kuwaitis, who backed Iraq. Those two countries had agreed, prodded by America, to bankroll a war that became far more extensive than the three-to six-month battle plan royal advisors had told King Khalid was likely.* The king's aides were as wrong as the Soviet ones in the Kremlin had been. Instead, the Iran-Iraq war would last an agonizing eight years, with both countries eventually resorting to chemical weapons and dozens of bloody suicide attacks. More than a million died on each side. The conflict cost the Saudis over $38 billion, badly draining their own treasury, and it was all spent only to maintain a bloody stalemate. The House of Saud

---

*Saudi Arabia's relationship with Iraq, as with many of its neighbors, was complicated. On one hand, the religious authorities despised the ruling Baath party, which was a secular movement with no sympathy for religion. On the other hand, Saddam Hussein, a Sunni Muslim, detested Shiites, and as a result the House of Saud could reconcile supporting Iraq with its Wahhabi philosophy, since it meant stopping the suddenly greater threat of the new Iranian regime and its spreading Shiite doctrine.

justified its great cost in sentiments expressed by interior minister Prince Nayef: "Iraq is protecting the Arab nation."[16]

No sooner had the war started than both sides incessantly attacked the other's oil production facilities, hoping to cut off energy supplies and the ability to raise money and buy weapons. Tankers in the Persian Gulf were targets. The U.S., against its wishes, committed warships to escort the tankers after Khomeini threatened to sink one to close the strategic Strait of Hormuz, the only sea route from Dhahran in the west into the Indian Ocean.

As a result of the precipitous drop in Iraqi and Iranian oil production, prices spiked to record highs, reaching $42 a barrel (the equivalent of $95 a barrel in 2005). Panic again spread in the West. The U.S. Federal Reserve Board raised interest rates fast and sharp, not stopping until the prime rate reached its highest in history, 21.5 percent. Tight money from the government, coupled with dwindling corporate spending because of the sky-high oil prices, plummeted the country into a deep recession by the end of 1980 and early 1981. Finally, the Saudis doubled their oil production and the price of crude stabilized. It was in 1980 that America finally earned the title of the world's largest importer of Saudi oil (it had been only tenth a decade earlier).* The U.S. began pulling out of recession later that year, only to bottom out once again in 1982, with the second recession being even more severe.[17]

=====

The massive instability that began in late 1979—the seizure of the Grand Mosque and the violent riots in Hasa; the Iran-Iraq war; and the Soviet invasion of Afghanistan resulting in the war waged by the mujahideen— prompted the Saudis to strengthen their own control in the Kingdom and to protect their most valuable asset, oil. And adding to their anxiety over the confluence of troubling events, there was tension building inside the House of Saud. King Khalid, never the most forceful ruler, had been hobbled by poor health since the early 1970s. In 1972, in Cleveland, he had

---

*In 1974, six years earlier, Richard Nixon had launched with great fanfare a national program—Project Independence—to make the U.S. energy self-sufficient by 1980. Each year after that program had been launched, America actually relied on Saudi Arabia for increasing percentages of its imports, and OPEC's share of world crude exports zoomed to nearly 90 percent.

open-heart surgery; in 1977, a hip replacement in London; and in 1979, a few months after the ayatollah seized control in Iran, heart surgery again in Cleveland. Crown Prince Fahd, who had been running many of the day-to-day government operations, personally oversaw most of the crises, together with the tough Prince Nayef, responsible for security as the interior minister.

Although Khalid was only sixty-eight, his poor health had prompted early jockeying behind the throne for control, and speculation about whether a transition would be violence-free. The royal family was deeply divided over a renewed effort by the Reagan administration to get the Kingdom's approval for the Camp David peace process, something Carter had failed to do despite his own strenuous efforts. Reagan tempted the Saudis with the sale of highly sophisticated radar planes, AWACS— Boeing's airborne warning and control system, advanced spy planes and early radar warning systems rolled into one—that the House of Saud had long wanted. But not even that carrot brought a consensus in the royal family over Camp David. It was asking too much of the Saudis, the monarchy concluded, and Khalid was too weak to force a compromise. In the absence of strong leadership from the king, Crown Prince Fahd proposed his own eight-point program calling for the return of all Israeli-occupied Arab land and creation of an independent Palestine with East Jerusalem as its capital. Hard-liners inside the Kingdom and other Arab capitals were privately furious with Fahd's plan since it hinted at eventually acknowledging Israel's right to exist. But still, the very fact that he offered it unilaterally was a sign of the power the crown prince had consolidated.[18]

Although there were then over four thousand fathers, sons, brothers, uncles, nephews, and cousins, each with the title of prince, they understood that for all their bickering, without a consensus on who would lead after Khalid there could be serious obstacles to their retention of power. Fahd had the right bloodline—that of the Sudairi tribe, the clan from which Ibn Saud's favorite wife came. (Fahd is one of the so-called "Sudairi Seven," the seven sons of King Ibn Saud by one of his fourteen wives.) Fahd had also given up his extravagant playboy lifestyle that had so offended the religious authorities when he was first appointed crown prince. But some were still skeptical of his devotion to Wahhabism (they certainly could not be skeptical of his adherence to the Koranic exception to taking multiple wives, as Fahd has taken scores of wives—but never more than four at a time—a fact kept secret from the Saudi people for nearly twenty years, as the number was deemed extravagant by religious authorities).[19] His potential rivals for the crown were two relatives, also his brothers. Prince Abdullah, fifty-seven, head of the powerful National Guard and Fahd's half brother, was the favorite of many fundamentalists as he advocated a slower, more conservative approach to modernization. Prince Sultan, although behind Abdullah in the unofficial line of succession, commanded the armed forces, and while aloof and reserved, was decidedly more U.S.-oriented than the other two.

Organized opposition from the National Guard or the regular armed forces was considered unlikely. Abdullah's National Guard units were drawn exclusively from the nomadic tribes that are tied closely to the royal family through blood and tradition. The monarchy goes to considerable lengths to keep Sultan's armed forces well equipped, well paid, and well watched.

But all the speculation about who might take the reins of power ended abruptly with the unexpected death of King Khalid on June 13, 1982. He died of a heart attack at his summer palace. Fahd told the rest of the royal family that the uncertainty caused by the Iranian revolution, and the dissension inside Saudi Arabia, meant this was no time to hesitate in picking a successor. As crown prince, he should be king. There was no opposition. And once installed as king, Fahd lost no time consolidating power. Sultan, his brother and defense minister, became second deputy prime minister, next in line for the throne. And Fahd's half brother Abdullah was elevated to crown prince. Securing the loyalty of his two potential rivals, Fahd instantly revoked all of the small reforms that King Faisal had instituted. Overnight, full and unquestionable powers of state were returned to the king alone. Fahd assumed the roles of head of the royal family, prime minister, chief government executive, supreme religious imam, chief justice, and commander in chief of the armed forces. He adopted the title "Guardian of Islam's Holy Shrines," originally coined for the sixteenth-century Grand Sultan Selim I of the Ottoman Empire. There was no executive, legislative, or judicial authority to question Fahd's directives. He controlled completely the country's oil income, essentially reverting Saudi Arabia once again into the world's largest family-run business, just one that happened to have a flag at the United Nations. At the time Fahd took the crown, the untapped oil wealth of Saudi Arabia was estimated to be between six and seventeen *trillion* dollars.[20]

Primarily to appease Western Allies, Fahd created the Consultative

Council, an Islamic parliament, as a sign that he intended to slowly de-mocratize the Kingdom. It would take ten years before it became official state policy, and fifteen until the first one was actually formed.[21]

The only authorities Fahd had to appease, because of their own tre-mendous influence in the population, were the religious leaders. Whereas Khalid had been a true believer, a puritanical Wahhabi, Fahd's hedonist past meant he had to try even harder than his predecessor to support the imams. Fahd understood that religious tradition was the bedrock of Saudi life, and not all the oil money in the world could save a king who ignored it. Religious authorities and the nomadic tribes closely watched the king's early moves, especially because of their doubts over his earlier indulgent lifestyle. Balancing the desires of the young technocrats and businessmen who were more liberal-minded with those of fundamentalists who wanted to live in the ninth century was no easy task for the new king. Fahd opted for embracing Wahhabi fundamentalism to woo the hard-liners. (In 1986, he changed his official primary title from "king" to the more religiously le-gitimate "Custodian of the Two Holy Mosques.")[22] By adopting such an aggressive religious stance, Fahd deflected any questions about his own lack of Wahhabi credentials.

There was little room to maneuver within the already tough strictures of Wahhabism, but Fahd found some areas in which to reaffirm the faith's most conservative aspects. He expanded the hours of religious study inside schools. Many of the tighter standards were directed toward non-Muslims, whose very presence in the Kingdom remained a simmering point of con-tention for the religious authorities. Sheikh Abdul Aziz bin Baz was a Wah-habi fanatic who was involved in politics only to protest what he considered the decadent Westernization of Saudi Arabia. He abhorred the Miami Beach skyline that had popped up in Riyadh in a quarter century and the four-lane freeways filled with luxury cars. Bin Baz was now the Kingdom's grand mufti, the ideological watchdog for the House of Saud. To bin Baz, jihad was "the most preferable form of righteousness." But instead of seeing jihad as an internal spiritual struggle for individual Muslims, Baz lectured and wrote about how it meant a current-day holy war to fight infidels, as in Afghanistan against the Soviets, and a financial jihad, in which Saudi phi-lanthropists aggressively supported the international propagation of Wah-habism.[23] Bin Baz warned young Saudis not to travel to "heretical" places like America and Europe since such journeys could lead them to a path of evil (King Fahd would publicly endorse Baz's extreme view in 1984).[24]

Special decrees now required all foreigners in the country, whether

Aramco employees or diplomats, to "respect" the thirty days of Muslim fasting during Ramadan by "refraining from openly eating, drinking or smoking in public places, streets, or work locations." Failure to adhere to the new rules would result, said the decree, in "termination of employment and deportation from the Kingdom."[25] Another declaration warned that foreign men with long hair would be subject to arrest by the religious police, and "shorn by force." "Immodest" foreign women were ordered to cover up, and if the violation of baring too much was considered severe, they would be arrested and subject to deportation. One woman was cited for wearing a pantsuit. Before Fahd had reinvigorated the fundamentalists, women worked alongside their male counterparts at foreign firms like Aramco. That practice was now prohibited.

Tourists were chided for carrying cameras, technically forbidden by the Koran according to religious authorities. The number of articles considered offensive to the Kingdom, and stripped out of foreign periodicals before they were allowed into Saudi Arabia, was broadened. And one of the sorest subjects for the religious authorities was what they considered the flouting of the Koran's no-alcohol rule, since many foreigners smuggled liquor into the country despite customs' best efforts to find it, and then drank it in the privacy of their own compounds. Now the Saudi government ordered a new crackdown, encouraged Saudi employees in foreign firms to report any suspicion of alcohol use, and stated that "upon accusation or suspicion of intoxication, a doctor's certification must be obtained. The local Committee has the authority to incarcerate the accused pending trial and investigation." Punishment for consuming or possessing alcohol was now set at "ten lashes or imprisonment for seven days."[26] Christian religious services, to which the Wahhabi authorities had sometimes turned a blind eye if conducted quietly in private homes, were again banned completely, and ten Protestants were deported from Riyadh to set an example. Possessing crucifixes or holy water and distributing church bulletins were once more grounds for deportation.

Baldo Marinovic, Aramco's finance administrator, was detained around this time for taking a group of Aramco employees on a fishing expedition in the Gulf—too recreational for Wahhabi scholars—something he had done without incident many times before.

"The Saudis were terrified that somebody was going to be a better Muslim than they were," recalled Marinovic, "and so at that point they started clamping down to prove that they are just as good Muslims as anybody else. . . . They started tightening up."[27]

At supermarkets like A&P and Safeway in the most Westernized neighborhood in Riyadh, religious police patrolled the aisles looking for unmarried couples shopping together. When some were found, their work permits were confiscated and the men were threatened with three days in jail and eighty lashes. If they were married, the women were still often chastised for not covering their hair, or wearing knee-length skirts. Men were targeted if they wore shorts or too much jewelry. Finally, the supermarkets began stocking abayas at the front door for their customers who needed to cover themselves.[28]

The Kingdom of 1980, under the new King Fahd, was starting to look more like Ibn Saud's country of the 1930s.

CHAPTER 8

ARMING THE
HOUSE OF SAUD

By 1980, the year that America became the largest buyer of Saudi oil, the Saudis also claimed their own dubious title: the biggest buyer of American military equipment on the planet. What had started as a buildup fueled by early oil surpluses to defend the Kingdom's 4,400 miles of exposed borders, with few friendly neighbors, had by 1980 converted Saudi Arabia into the world's sixth largest army, only surpassed by those of the United States, the Soviet Union, China, Germany, and Britain. No country contributed more to the bottom line of American military sales, more than $40 billion in a decade. Some of the sales, especially for advanced weapons systems, had often become the subject of bruising political fights in the U.S., especially as the pro-Israel lobby tried hard to slow the tilt toward the Saudis promoted by their own hard lobbying.[1]

A prime fight came in 1981 with a proposed sale to the Saudis of AWACS planes. At the time, AWACS was the most advanced command-and-control radar system in the world, generations ahead of the Soviet competition. AWACS was the cornerstone of NATO's early warning system during the last decade of the Cold War. But even the NATO AWACS was kept strictly under U.S. control. What was proposed by Reagan in the early days of his new administration was not only to sell AWACS to the Saudis, but also to give the Kingdom complete control over their deployment and any intelligence they gathered. The announcement caused a chorus of protests on Capitol Hill, almost all against the sale.

This was not the first time that AWACS and Saudis had been mentioned together in a possible deal. In March 1978, Jimmy Carter had agreed to sell the House of Saud sixty advanced F-15 Eagle jet fighters.[2] It took only a couple of weeks for the pro-Israel lobby to kill the sale in the Senate. So Carter modified his offer, assuring foes that the F-15s could not be used against Israel in case of a wider Middle East war. Among the safeguards that Carter agreed to—and which the Saudis bristled at—were no auxiliary fuel tanks that would allow the fighters to reach Israel; no state-of-the-art Sidewinder missiles, capable of hitting enemy aircraft from all angles instead of just hitting the heat-emitting portion; and no sale of AWACS or "other systems that could increase the range or enhance the ground attack capability of the F-15."[3] By the terms of the deal brokered by Carter, the Saudis agreed not even to ask for any of the banned items again.

In January 1980, however, the Saudis ignored their Carter agreement and sent a request through the State Department for the very weapons previously marked "off limits." This time the Carter administration seemed more amenable to the Saudi wish list, including larger fuel tanks, tankers for refueling the fighters in midair, the advanced air-to-air Sidewinder missile, and of course, the AWACS. Once it became known that the Carter administration favored such a sale, a group of senators wrote a letter to the president reminding him of the limitations his own administration had imposed on arms sales to the Kingdom. The Senate opposition effectively squelched the deal. But the Saudis were smarting. A senior Saudi prince blamed the "Zionist lobby" for organizing congressional opposition. "We believe that with a little more courage and foresight," said the prince, "all American administrations . . . could have stood up to the Zionists' pressures."[4]

When the Reagan administration took office in January 1981, the Saudis renewed their efforts to get offensive military weapons. The House of Saud considered their fresh request an early litmus test of relations with the new president, as well as of the evolving strength of their own Wahhabi lobby, which now felt it had learned enough from its losing bouts over previous military sales to know how to maneuver in Washington to acquire coveted advanced equipment.

A month after Reagan took office, the White House surprised most observers by announcing that its first foreign policy initiative would be the sale of F-15 jet fighters to the Kingdom.[5] As in the past, the pro-Israel lobby quickly organized broad bipartisan congressional opposition. But the Reagan administration was undeterred. The following month, in fact, it formally expanded the proposed sale to include extra-capacity fuel tanks and the Sidewinder missiles.[6] To quell the outcry over how such a sale might hurt Israel's defense, Reagan agreed to sell an additional fifteen F-15s to Israel, and also to give the Jewish state an additional $600 million in military credits to offset any vulnerability. In April, the American offer to the Saudis became even bolder. While Reagan was recovering from his gunshot wound in the attempted assassination by John Hinckley, Jr., Vice President George Bush chaired a National Security Council meeting about the Saudi request. The NSC was expected to produce a compromise acceptable to both Congress and the House of Saud. Instead, the NSC approved the pending sale of all the offensive equipment asked for by the Saudis, as well as throwing AWACS into the mix, bringing the arms deal up to $8.5 billion.

Pro-Israel lobbyists worked overtime in trying to kill the deal before it even got to Congress for a vote. Dozens of representatives in both houses took the floor against the sale. By April 22, 48 senators were on the record against it. Sixty-five in total, according to unofficial polling by *Time,* were leaning to reject the package. By June 25, 54 senators sent Reagan a letter opposing the Saudi deal. That same day, 224 members of the House delivered a similar letter to the White House. Not everyone opposed to the deal was a friend of Israel. Many just thought the AWACS technology was too important to be under Saudi ownership and control. Others concluded the technology was not necessary for Saudi security.[7]

By September, Reagan was inviting senators for one-on-one meetings at the White House, using his considerable personal charm to persuade them to vote yes on the weapons package.[8] Although Reagan lobbied tirelessly (he saw forty-seven senators personally), few who heard his pitch changed their minds. Reagan then sent Secretary of State Alexander Haig to Riyadh, seeking a compromise. Might the Saudis agree to cut the size of the arms package to defuse the anger on Capitol Hill? But the royals, in a rare show of public displeasure with the United States, told Haig not to make the trip, and said that if America could not provide the weapons needed for Saudi security, the Kingdom would look elsewhere. Still fuming over what they viewed as the American abandonment of the shah in Iran, the House of Saud considered that it had no option but to stand tough with the U.S. when it came to security matters.

"If we were to accept an American presence on the planes, we accept interference with our sovereignty," one Saudi official told *Newsweek*. "If we don't accept and the deal falls through, we will be embarrassed in the Arab world. Either way, we lose." The Saudis started making backup plans to buy British-made Nimrod radar planes.[9]

Reagan decided to go for broke and submitted the entire arms package to Congress on October 1, 1981, issuing an accompanying statement that "we will not permit [Saudi Arabia] to be an Iran." That did not have much impact on Capitol Hill. Within hours of its submission, fifty senators submitted a resolution of disapproval, one short of the number required to instantly block the sale. During hearings, senators grilled Haig and Defense Secretary Caspar Weinberger. Two weeks later, the House voted 301–111 against it. The House Foreign Affairs Committee and the Senate Foreign Relations Committee also voted down the arms package.

Haig warned Prince Saud, the Saudi foreign minister, that Reagan lacked the votes to push the deal through. *Newsweek,* typical of press coverage about the sale, wrote that the AWACS vote was almost certain to "become Reagan's first major foreign policy defeat . . . [and] an imminent humiliation."[10]

Less than two weeks later, however, on October 28, in one of the most stunning reversals in post–World War II congressional history, the Senate *approved* the entire weapons package for Saudi Arabia by a 52 to 48 vote (only two days earlier, *The New York Times* had done a head count showing 53 senators against it, and only 38 in favor).[11] A grand party at the Tunisian consulate that same night brought together joyous Arab ambassadors, ecstatic corporate chiefs, and senators like John Tower, head of the Armed Services Committee, and Charles Percy of the Senate Foreign Relations Committee, who had helped successfully maneuver the bill through the Senate. There was jubilation in Saudi Arabia.

"The strength of the Zionist influence is nothing but a wooden house that can be broken when America comes first," said the lead editorial in the Saudi paper *Al-Jazira* the day after the vote. What had caused such a dramatic turnaround in only a couple of weeks?

It was solely a tribute to frenetic last-minute lobbying by the Saudis. Starting a month before the final Senate vote, five men met daily to concoct a winning strategy. Gathering at Washington's Fairfax Hotel, the group consisted of three Americans who were registered as Saudi agents (each paid more than $1 million for his work in 1981); Frederick Dutton, the Democratic party activist and ex–assistant secretary of state; Stephen Conner, a former Merrill Lynch vice president with strong ties to the Republicans; and J. Crawford Cook, the head of a South Carolina public relations and political consulting firm. Joining them were two prominent Saudis, Prince Bandar bin Sultan bin Abdul Aziz and Abdulah Dabbagh, a former commercial attaché at the Saudi embassy in Washington.

The charismatic Bandar, the son of Saudi defense minister Sultan, had been dispatched to Washington on a special assignment in the 1978 fight over Jimmy Carter's proposed sale of F-15s to the Kingdom, and now was back for the AWACS battle.[12] Bandar, and the other men, knew time was running out.[13] He assumed a marathon initiative on Capitol Hill, briefing forty senators in two weeks. Meanwhile, the registered American agents planted stories in the press that converted the AWACS sale into an issue pitting Israeli interests against American ones. "If I had my way," Dutton told *The Washington Post,* "I'd have bumper stickers plastered all over town that say 'Reagan or Begin' " (referring to the then Israeli prime minister).[14]

Off the record, the Saudi lobbyists encouraged the media to focus on the disproportionate role of the pro-Israel lobby in trying to block the sale—the American Israel Public Affairs Committee, for instance, had for five months been presenting to congressmen a detailed case against the sale. They played to senators' patriotism by suggesting that if the AWACS vote failed, Israeli prime minister Menachem Begin had exercised the equivalent of a veto over presidential decision making.

The lobbyists also served as liaisons between Saudi officials and policy makers in the White House, State Department, Defense Department, Congress, and the National Security Council. Senate majority leader Howard Baker, for instance, met with the Saudi agents and their representatives over fifty times before the final vote. Bandar once flew on his personal jet to Baker's guesthouse in Huntsville, Tennessee, for a private meeting with Baker and Undersecretary of State James L. Buckley. Baker even provided Bandar with a regular office off the Senate floor.[15] Bandar also flew to Palm Springs, where he personally lobbied former president Gerald Ford. Ford was so impressed by Bandar that he then telephoned some senators urging them to support the sale.[16]

The Kingdom's three American agents also thoroughly mined their pro-Arab contacts in the U.S. business community. With so many corporations involved in megadollar contracts in Saudi Arabia and other Arab countries, or hoping to land such business, it was not difficult to enlist the aid of several dozen leading executives, including those at Mobil, Bechtel, Westinghouse, and United Technologies, among others. For weeks before the Senate vote, different groups of American business executives were invited to Saudi embassy receptions. There, they were told about how important the weapons-package vote was to the Saudis, and that if it went against the Kingdom, it could negatively affect future business with all American companies. From October 5 to October 28, by refusing to sign pending contracts with U.S. firms, Saudi Arabia dramatically sent out the unequivocal signal that such contracts could be jeopardized without the arms sale.[17]

As a result, the chief executives of some of America's top firms enthusiastically lobbied members of Congress to vote yes. They also directed their own corporate public relations departments to go into high gear to help pass the vote. The companies deluged senators with telegrams, mass mailings, telephone calls, and other elements of a "grass roots campaign" to show public support for the AWACS sale to the Saudis. Some expressed anger at Israel or American Jews. "I'm tired of having Jews run our foreign policy," a vice president of a major international investment bank wrote to one senator, "and you should be too."[18] But most took fairly diplomatic approaches, boosting Saudi importance and loyalty to the U.S. while also emphasizing the importance of American business interests in the Kingdom and Saudi investments in the United States. Companies like Mobil ran a series of "commentaries" in national and international magazines and newspapers, hyping the "profound and rapidly growing economic partnership between the United States and Saudi Arabia."[19]

The business lobbying helped change minds as senators became convinced that prominent companies in their home states could suffer if the AWACS vote went badly.[20] Some senators who had been firmly against the sale switched their vote at the last moment. The CEO of United Technologies personally lobbied Utah's Orrin Hatch; home state firms like Valmont Industries and Union Pacific Railroad pressured Nebraska senators Edward Zorinsky and James Exon. Local defense contractors, farm manufacturing equipment firms, and even farm co-ops that did business in Saudi Arabia turned around Iowan Roger Jepsen at the last moment. David Boren of Oklahoma and Montana's John Melcher were flipped in part by tremendous pressure from oil interests in their states.

"The AWACS sale had produced the most extensive business lobbying on any foreign policy issue since World War II," concluded journalist

Steven Emerson, who studied it at length for his 1985 book *The American House of Saud*. It was little wonder there was cause for celebration among the Saudis, their registered agents, and their American corporate supporters. The Saudi lobbying had become sophisticated enough to confront head-on, and beat, the seemingly invincible pro-Israeli lobby.

CHAPTER 9

COVERT PARTNERS

During the 1980s, after the successful fight over the AWACS, not only did the Saudis feel emboldened, but the Reagan and then Bush administrations believed the House of Saud was a reliable ally that could be trusted both with advanced weapons systems and as a partner in previously off-limits covert operations. As for military equipment, Saudi Arabia was still purchasing as much as it could afford. From the $9.6 billion it had spent in 1978, it was spending more than $20 billion annually by 1980. In the 1980s, the U.S. Army Corps of Engineers oversaw five enormous military construction projects at an additional cost of $14 billion. These huge Saudi facilities were partially designed to allow for the rapid deployment of U.S. forces in case the Soviets tried to invade Iran (a fear that early on was prevalent, even if not realistic, after the Soviet invasion of Afghanistan).

In 1984, there was another watershed military transaction between the U.S. and the Saudis. This was the sale of shoulder-fired Stinger missiles to the Kingdom for the purported protection of Saudi oil tankers. Reagan withdrew the request when members of Congress, energized once again by the pro-Israel lobby, questioned not only the number of Stingers sought by the Saudis, but also why no safeguards had been built into the sale to ensure that the highly mobile rocket launchers would not fall into the hands of terrorists. But the Saudis, now veteran players in the Wash-

ington power game, were not so easily told no. The indefatigable Prince
Bandar called together the media in Washington and bluntly repeated a
threat he had used with good result before: that if they could not buy the
weapons they wanted from America, the Kingdom would go to the Soviets,
French, or British. At risk, said Bandar, were 600,000 American jobs created by American trade with the Saudis and the rest of the Arab world.

Citing a rarely used national security loophole—the Saudis needed
the weapons to protect themselves against possible Iranian air strikes (of
which there had never been a single one)—Reagan authorized the sale of
one third of the requested number of Stingers to the Saudis a month after
he withdrew the request from Congress. This bypassed the need for
approval on Capitol Hill, and while it infuriated many senators and representatives who were firmly against the deal, it again was cause for celebration in Riyadh.*

But the Stingers had become another successful test of the Saudi
relationship with America. And instead of resting, the Wahhabi lobby expanded its efforts during the 1980s to create a favorable image of the Kingdom for both the public and government officials.

The Saudis, as they had done before, hired one of the capital's most
powerful lobbying firms, Gray and Company. Founded in 1981 by Robert
Gray, a chief lobbyist for two decades for public relations giant Hill &
Knowlton, Gray's firm had extensive connections to both political parties,
but particularly the Republicans (he was cochairman of Reagan's 1980 in-
augural committee).[2] Gray shared the Saudis' view that "it is the Israeli
lobby's ability to politically reward or intimidate American politicians and
the media that has led to such intractable support for Israel among U.S.
foreign policy makers."[3] In a document in which he solicited Saudi and
other Arab business, Gray talked about the need to counter the "tens of
millions of dollars annually spent in public education and political activities by the American Israel Public Affairs Committee, B'nai B'rith, the
American Jewish Congress, Hadassah, and other pro-Israeli groups."[4] Gray

---

*Many of those Stingers ended up in Afghanistan, where they were used by Osama bin
Laden's mujahideen to fight the Soviets. After 9/11, the United States set aside $65 million
for a Stinger-buyback program and paid approximately $400,000 for every Stinger turned in
by Afghan militias.[1] Some retrieved were from the batch originally sent to the Saudis. It is
not clear whether the Reagan administration knew that the Saudis were merely conduits to
pass the Stingers to the ragtag Muslim armies fighting the Soviets. Since the U.S. used
many intermediaries for its covert financial and logistical support of the mujahideen, the
Saudis could easily have played this role on the Stinger sale.

suggested reinforcing the Wahhabi lobby with a handful of registered agents and the liberal use of petrodollars.

Among Gray's proposals was everything from coordinating coast-to-coast media campaigns, to press liaisons, a speaker's program, nonprofit front organizations, newspaper and television advertising, and even bumper stickers and posters. After the 1982 Israeli invasion of Lebanon, for instance, he organized a vast public relations campaign centered around Nouha Alhegelan, the wife of the then Saudi ambassador to the United States. She did a three-week media blitz across the U.S., and in her sixty-nine television and radio interviews and thirty-three newspaper and magazine interviews, Alhegelan pleaded with Americans to "stop the genocide" in Lebanon. Full-page newspaper ads proclaimed "Begin's Holocaust in Lebanon." As opposed to earlier lobbying efforts for the Saudis on arms fights over advanced weapons systems, this time Gray and others were on the offensive, trying to change American public perceptions about the Kingdom. They considered Israel's invasion of Lebanon an unprecedented opportunity to "alter American attitudes on the Middle East."[5]

In 1983, Gray coordinated a Saudi-American business conference in Atlanta where three hundred U.S. corporate executives paid $1,500 each to meet Saudi businessmen and government officials in the hope of landing contracts in the Kingdom. Gray also represented Prince Talal bin Abdul Aziz ibn Saud, the twenty-third son of the Kingdom's founder, in his capacity as special envoy to the humanitarian United Nations organization UNICEF. That role was considered an ideal one, through the prince's many media appearances and fund-raising events, to subtly sway American public opinion away from Israel.

Not everything the Saudis did to win their public relations war was as direct as having the wife of the ambassador make personal appeals. For instance, a group called Peace Corps for Middle East Understanding appeared in the 1980s for the first time, and sent letters to eighty thousand Peace Corps veterans asking them to lobby their congressional representatives to cut off U.S. aid to Israel. A subsequent investigation revealed that the Arab Women's Council had covertly funded it, and that the entire mailing—as evidenced by the numbers on the postage meter stamp on the envelopes—came from the Saudi embassy.

While the lobbyists tried changing the public perceptions of Saudi Arabia, the House of Saud was working hard behind the scenes to do almost anything requested of it by the Reagan administration to boost the

American government's view of its role as indispensable ally. One of the key themes of which Gray had convinced the Saudis was that "the Israeli lobby never lobbies for Israel. All of the organizations in the United States which comprise the Israeli lobby 'wrap their arguments in an American flag.' " The Saudis were persuaded that they had to make their own self-interest appear identical to American concerns. During the Carter administration, while the Saudis had personally won over the president,* their failure to support watershed events like the Camp David peace agreements had caused considerable tensions between the two governments.

Under the Reagan-Bush administration, the Saudis became full covert partners with the U.S. King Fahd and Ronald Reagan might not have had a close personal relationship, but they were right-wing political soul mates. The Soviet invasion of neighboring Afghanistan had created an opportunity. Some prominent Saudi officials, like Prince Bandar, as well as his father, defense minister Prince Sultan, saw the Soviet aggression as a chance to form a closer bond with Washington. It was a rare chance, they argued to other Saudi ministers, to replace Israel as America's strategic partner in the Middle East.[6] And as far as the Americans were concerned, the Saudis had suddenly become a friendly cash cow. "It takes King Fahd about 10 seconds to sign a check," William B. Quandt, a senior fellow at the Brookings Institution and a former Middle East specialist on the National Security Council staff, told *The New York Times*. "It takes Congress weeks to debate the smallest issue of this sort. If you can get somebody else to pay for it, it's nice and convenient."[7]

As a result, with U.S. encouragement the Saudis sent more than $500 million annually to the Afghan rebels; aided the Contras in Central America with more than $32 million in secret payments (a fact that emerged in the Iran-Contra hearings);[8] paid for American covert operations in Lebanon; gave Zaire's Mobutu Sese Seko $50 million to fight pro-Soviet rebels in Angola; handed Mohammed Siad Barre of Somalia a $200 million check to eject the Soviets from his country's Berbera seaport; bought the American weapons that assisted the conservative Yemen govern-

---

*Carter, after he left office, often fawned over Saudi leaders, telling public forums how King Fahd, Prince Abdullah, and Prince Sultan had "gone out of their way to be helpful in times of crisis and challenge and to provide me advice, counsel, and support. . . ." In raising money for his presidential library, Carter evidently had no second thoughts when arms dealer Adnan Khashoggi held a 1983 benefit for him in New York. And he appeared regularly at industry conferences, encouraging American firms to "understand" the Saudis and Arabs in order to win their business.

ment in repelling a rebel incursion; and supplied oil to white-ruled South Africa.[9]

While the relationship between the two countries had greatly improved on intelligence and military matters, the Kingdom had not become a rubber stamp for American desires. For instance, when Iraqi aircraft later attacked the frigate USS *Stark*, killing thirty-seven American soldiers, the Saudis refused a U.S. request to intercept the escaping Iraqi plane. After the attack, it also did not allow the Americans to use Saudi airbases for additional tactical support for their ships in the Persian Gulf. The Saudis did not want to get further drawn into the Iraq-Iran war, and decided the American requests were simply asking too much of them.

But whatever improvements had taken place, much of the credit could be traced back to the 1983 appointment of Prince Bandar as the Kingdom's ambassador to the United States. (The previous year he had moved to the U.S. in the role of the embassy's defense attaché.) It took the Western-educated Bandar, who knew many of the key officials in the Reagan administration, little time to ingratiate himself with Washington's elite. In his custom-tailored Savile Row suits and flashing his suave Western style and brilliant sense of humor, Bandar was quickly a fixture on the Washington social scene, the first Saudi to break into the capital's rarefied unofficial club. He played tennis, for instance, with Secretary of State George Shultz, racquetball with General David Jones, the chairman of the Joint Chiefs of Staff, and was a neighbor of Ted Kennedy's in a sprawling McLean, Virginia, house. (He would later add other homes in the U.S., including a 65,000-square-foot complex in Aspen, where he counted other members of the social and political elite as neighbors.) Bandar, within a few months of his new posting as ambassador, had become the star of the 1983 season's cocktail parties, entertaining his hosts and guests alike with self-deprecating stories about the royal family.[10]

The close covert partnership between Washington and Riyadh inspired Prince Bandar to confide to a journalist in 1981 that "if you knew what we were really doing for America, you wouldn't just give us AWACS, you would give us nuclear weapons."[11]

But not every U.S.-Saudi venture was without controversy, even under Bandar's watchful eye. In 1983, Saudi Arabia got involved, through arms merchant Adnan Khashoggi, in the scandal the press eventually dubbed Irangate. The U.S., trying to open backdoor channels to Iran, provided Tehran with Tow antitank missiles and Hawk antiaircraft missiles. Israel supplied the weapons and the Saudis paid for them. When it all unraveled, the Saudis were widely ridiculed in the Arab world for behavior that bordered on treasonous—being involved in any covert act with hated Israel.[12] The Saudis denied any official role and put all the blame on Khashoggi.[13] But the American government knew that the House of Saud had helped, at considerable risk to its own standing in Arab public opinion. To the Reagan administration, the Saudis had again shown that they were trustworthy strategic partners.[14]

The House of Saud had obviously begun to understand what its hired American lobbyists had told it for years: that it needed to adopt policies that did not anger its own citizens, but simultaneously appeared to serve American interests.

But despite the Saudis' newfound respect in Washington power circles, the powerful pro-Israel lobby could still show its muscle. The House of Saud's 1985 request for an arms package that would include more than sixty F-15s, planes Israel did not yet have, was rejected. Reagan resubmitted a new arms package for the Kingdom the following year, a tenth the size of the original deal, but it still ran into stiff pro-Israel opposition.[15] Reagan stripped the Stinger missiles from that package and then vetoed the congressional recommendation. His veto was barely sustained.

The problem for the Saudis in all of these bruising arms fights in Washington was that they felt as if they were being asked to grovel to get weapons when they thought they had earned the trust of the U.S. by helping on so many covert operations.[16] It struck at the core of Saudi honor. And to worsen matters, on issues they thought they had won—such as the 1981 fight over the AWACS—pro-Israeli lobbyists had figured out ways to put up obstacles and delay delivery. After that sale was approved, Congress imposed a condition that the administration provide evidence that the Saudis had given "substantial assistance" to forwarding the Middle East peace process before the AWACS were sent to the Kingdom. Five years later, the Saudis were still waiting for the planes.

When Vice President George Bush visited the Kingdom to mend fences in 1986, the reception from the House of Saud was noticeably cool. At a demonstration of U.S.-Saudi joint security, a fly-by was scheduled of U.S. F-5s and F-15s. But the Saudis surprised the vice president by using not American aircraft but instead their new European-made Tornado attack plane, the first of seventy-two Britain had sold to the Kingdom in a $6 billion arms deal the Saudis had signed with London the previous year when Washington had failed to provide more planes.[17]

And making matters worse, the Kingdom was under some financial pressure. By 1982, oil had dropped at least $10 a barrel from prices that had averaged $36 to $38 a barrel. An international supply glut meant the Saudis had cut production to only four million barrels daily, and still their revenue dropped nearly a third from its high of a few years earlier. The $76.4 billion Saudi national budget for 1983–84, for instance, included cuts of between 14 and 40 percent in almost every area of public government spending. The next fiscal year, revenues dropped by another $15 billion.[18] The budget deficit was $30 billion, military spending was cut back 20 percent, businesses saw their income drop, salaries were cut, and even the price of gasoline in the Kingdom doubled, to twenty-one cents a gallon. From 1982 to 1988, the country ran seven years of deficits so great that it floated government debt bonds for the first time.[19]

Still, the Saudis had kept funding their covert partnerships with the Americans, something for which they had been shown little thanks on arms packages.

The anti- and pro-American split at the highest levels of the House of Saud was as deep as ever. Those who wanted a closer relationship with the U.S. included King Fahd and Prince Sultan, but others rallied behind the pan-Arab nationalistic views of Crown Prince Abdullah and Saud al-Faisal, the foreign minister. The nationalists made a strong case that while Saudi Arabia usually helped the West by producing enough oil to keep their economies out of crisis, the U.S. had done nothing to counter the radical states like Libya and Iran, had not reined in Israel, and had frequently embarrassed the Kingdom by either denying arms it wanted to buy or making it virtually beg for them. The United States, argued the nationalists, could not be trusted to ensure the House of Saud's future. And relying on American technical superiority to protect the Kingdom had allowed the corrupting influence of U.S. values—thoroughly at odds with Wahhabi Islam—to infect wide swaths of the country. Some leading figures in Saudi Arabia decided it was time to take the protection of their ultimate asset, oil, into their own hands.

CHAPTER 10

SCORCHED EARTH

In 1986, the National Security Agency electronically intercepted a series of telephone conversations originating from the Saudi embassy in Washington. They were of such a sensitive subject matter that the NSA quickly opened a special investigative file, a copy of which is active.[1] What the NSA satellites caught were discussions between Saudi diplomats in Washington, government officials in Riyadh, and executives at construction companies in Italy and France. The dialogue was about what to do if the Saudi oil fields and infrastructure were attacked by another country—Iran being the greatest fear at the time—or taken over in a scenario in which a Shiite uprising brought down the House of Saud. In Saudi Arabia's eastern province of Hasa, Shiites make up one third of the population. Hasa has more than seven hundred oil wells, accounting for 98 percent of the country's production, which made the royals uneasy as Shiite tensions rose.[2]

Also, some American officials wondered if the Saudi leaders, who were mostly the same as those who ran the country in the 1970s, were contemplating a threat from the United States. Unknown then publicly, a joint intelligence report titled "UK Eyes Alpha," dated December 12, 1973, had been prepared for the British prime minister, Edward Heath. A committee including the chiefs of MI5 and MI6 concluded that the U.S. would rather risk military action than be held ransom by the Arabs and their oil weapon. The American defense secretary, James Schlesinger, had confided as much to the British ambassador in Washington, Lord Cromer, the documents revealed. Cromer quoted Schlesinger as saying that "it was no longer obvious to him that the United States could not use force."[3]

Contingency plans covering many possible scenarios are not uncommon among military strategists. "Eyes Alpha" suggested that the "U.S. could guarantee sufficient oil supplies for themselves and their allies by taking the oil fields in Saudi Arabia, Kuwait, and the Gulf State of Abu Dhabi. . . . preemptive action would be considered, and that two brigades could seize the Saudi oilfields." The Saudi operation was considered straightforward since the "peacetime garrison of Dhahran is one lightly armed National Guard battalion and a Hawk anti-missile battery. The initial assault could be made by a brigade tasked to knock out the Hawk, seize the airfield, and so far as possible prevent sabotage to the oilfields."[4]

Two years after "Eyes Alpha" had been prepared, the Arab boycott of Israel was flourishing and most major American companies were aggressively chasing petrodollars. In the midst of that, February 1975, the London *Sunday Times* published information from a leaked and classified U.S. Department of Defense plan code-named "Dhahran Option Four." It also revealed details for a military invasion to capture the Saudi oil reserves.

That same year, Secretary of State Henry Kissinger hinted at possible military action in an interview about oil prices with *Business Week*. "I am not saying that there's no circumstances where we would not use force. But it is one thing to use it in the case of a dispute over price, it's another where there's some actual strangulation of the industrialized world."[5]

Robert Tucker, a U.S. intelligence and military analyst, wrote an article for *Commentary* magazine, owned by the Jewish American Committee, titled "Oil: The Issue of American Intervention." Tucker contended that "without intervention there is a distinct possibility of an economic and political disaster bearing . . . resemblance to the disaster of [the] 1930s. . . . The Arab shoreline of the Gulf is a new El Dorado waiting for its conquistadors." And this was followed in February by an article called "Seizing Arab Oil" in *Harper's,* written by a Pentagon analyst using a pseudonym, Miles Ignotus. He argued that there was an urgent need to seize Saudi oil fields, installations, and airports.

Further, in August 1975, a study titled "Oil Fields as Military Objectives: A Feasibility Study," was produced for the Senate Committee on Foreign Relations. It concluded that potential targets for the U.S. included Saudi Arabia, Kuwait, Venezuela, Libya, and Nigeria. "Analysis indicates . . .

[that military forces of OPEC countries are] quantitatively and qualitatively inferior [and] could be swiftly crushed."[6]

The subject of the American contingency plans to seize the Saudi oil fields if U.S. national security were threatened had evidently long been bantered around diplomatic and military circles. "If you really want to keep something secret," a retired senior State Department official told me, "you don't have the secretary of defense tell the British ambassador that we're thinking of having a preemptive strike on the biggest oil producer in the world. That's a surefire way to make sure that the news gets broadcast, and gets back to the Saudis, which is probably what the game plan was all along."[7]

The United States was still economically pressured by the oil embargo, and the threat of military intervention put out so clumsily, together with the drumbeat of media enthusiasm for options like Dhahran Four, seemed very much a coordinated U.S. government effort to make sure the Saudis knew the extreme degree of frustration and anger in Washington. It is unlikely, from background conversations with former officials in both the Department of Defense and the State Department, that the threat of preemptive action against the oil fields was anything more than that, a mere threat. But it was one America wanted the Saudis, and other OPEC countries, to hear. There is no evidence that a single military unit was activated, or any alert level heightened, or even that exercises consistent with the operations in "Eyes Alpha" or Dhahran Option Four were ever conducted. The military scenarios never got past the talking stage. But that they were even discussed almost certainly found its way back to Riyadh. One thing the preemptive-strike talk did was to start a debate inside the Kingdom about what to do in case a superpower such as the United States decided to seize the world's largest oil fields for its own benefit, and simultaneously overthrow the House of Saud. There was no simple answer for the royal family.

In 1976, one year after *The Times* of London had disclosed the U.S. military contingency plans about seizing Saudi oil reserves, the royals struck a deal with Aramco to transfer complete control of the Kingdom's petroleum industry to the Saudis. It would take more than a decade for the workforce and administration to completely change at many of the largest refineries and ports.[8] In the meantime, King Fahd dismissed the Kingdom's powerful oil minister, Sheikh Ahmed Zaki Yamani, in 1986, blaming him at the end of his twenty-year reign for a precipitous decline in oil prices and Saudi revenues. (As was typical of Fahd's treatment of his ministers, even the top few, Yamani learned of his dismissal from an official Saudi newscast.)

It was after Yamani was dismissed and King Fahd took full control of determining oil policy that the NSA picked up its first conversations about possible fail-safe scenarios for the Kingdom's oil. It was also a time when an increasing number of Saudi ministries were being run by Fahd's sons, some of whom had no government experience and no formal education, their only qualification for their posts being their heredity. In those positions, most focused on commerce, earning money from commissions on commercial assignments and projects in their provinces, and over time the family's involvement in Saudi business was so systematic that they often competed heatedly with one another.[9] One province emir, for instance, demanded a $3 million payment from the Saudi agents of a Swedish contractor doing business in his territory, undeterred by the fact that their profit on the project would only be $2 million.[10] Even those family members who were in charge of provinces containing the largest oil reserves seemed more concerned with the commissions they received from foreign contractors than with managing the oil under their control.

When Aramco ran the industry, company officials did not think Saudi security forces were effective enough, and as a result, Aramco often utilized a private California company, Vinnell, to protect the oil fields from sabotage or foreign attack. Vinnell had hired a former U.S. army general, ex–Vietnam veterans, and an assortment of foreign mercenaries to guard the Kingdom's oil production (Vinnell was bought by Washington's powerful Carlyle Group in 1992, and then spun off later to Northrop Grumman).[11]

But once Aramco was no longer in charge—after a November 8, 1988, royal decree from King Fahd announcing the name change of Aramco to the Saudi Arabian Oil Company—the foreign security forces were dispatched home. The key installations, surrounded with high fences and elevated watchtowers, were now manned by the Saudi army. While preventing sabotage from outsiders was still a top priority,[12] a special team designated by the Saudi Interior Ministry—composed of structural engineers, explosives experts, and architects—began canvassing major installations to best determine how the smallest amounts of explosive charges could cripple the Kingdom's production capacity. They made a short list of the facilities that would be easy to derail with minimum effort.

"Infrastructure is very resilient," says John Pike, director of Global-Security.org, a private defense and security consulting firm. "But some of it is very complex, and some I understand is of scarce supply. In that case, a small number of properly placed explosive charges may have a disproportionately destructive effect. But the key is you would really have to hit panacea targets to do major, long-term damage."[3]

The Saudis, of course, know better than anyone which are their "panacea targets." The Kingdom's oil infrastructure is protected largely by the sheer vastness of its facilities, which are spread over thousands of square miles. To significantly disable it, the Saudis knew that multiple target strikes had to force the system off-line. While fires in working oil fields, including wells, can be dramatic and disruptive, they do not inflict critical or permanent damage. Unless wells are struck with explosives deep enough in the wellhead to result in lasting damage, facilities can be quickly repaired. Each modern oil rig has a self-triggering shutoff valve three hundred feet below ground that automatically closes the well when there is trouble, leaving only the top three hundred feet of oil to burn off. The valves can be shut off manually or by remote control. So in addition to the wells, the Saudis studied other targets critical to oil production, such as water injection and pumping facilities, gas-oil separators, and desalination plants—the loss of any of which would seriously interrupt production and require months to repair.

When Saddam Hussein invaded Kuwait, on August 2, 1990, the fear that Iraq could invade the Kingdom and grab its oil production was one of the primary reasons that the king, in heated debate with his aides and princes, decided personally to allow American troops to enter and protect the country. Adding to the internal rift was that Fahd supported the American-led coalition's war against Iraq by issuing almost $60 billion in debt notes to the U.S., France, Britain, Pakistan, Turkey, Syria, Egypt, and others. The Saudi economy, already weak from depressed oil prices through most of the 1980s, was set further back by the enormous expenditures for the Gulf War. By the time the brief war was over, Saudi Arabia was in the twelfth year of a budget deficit, and had burned through all the reserves it had built since the country's founding nearly sixty years earlier.

After the Gulf War, the House of Saud realized that it could not rely permanently on American troops to protect the oil fields from foreign attack or a homegrown insurgency. Once again, U.S. intelligence agencies began picking up renewed discussions about the Saudis' own contingency plans for its oil reservoirs and production facilities. But, as opposed to the preliminary discussions seven years earlier, the NSA monitoring revealed that the Saudis this time had set out to create a comprehensive and ambitious doomsday scenario.

The NSA now intercepted conversations about the feasibility of constructing an interconnected, nationwide grid whereby the major oil fields, petroleum refineries, thousands of miles of pipelines, docking and storage facilities, and pumping stations could be rigged with explosives and controlled from a central location. The Saudis were essentially exploring the possibility of a single-button self-destruct system, protected with a series of built-in fail-safes. It was evidently their way to ensure that if someone else grabbed the world's largest oil reserves and forced them to flee the country they had founded, the House of Saud could at least make certain that what they left behind was worthless. The NSA dubbed the new file "Petro SE," for "Petroleum Scorched Earth," because of its similarity to Adolf Hitler's unfulfilled World War II policy of leaving nothing but a scorched country for the Allied armies conquering Germany.

The House of Saud gave Petro SE a top priority. The destructive agent of choice for the new program was apparently unmarked Semtex, a crystalline high plastic explosive with a binding agent that makes it effective in a wide range of temperatures, including desert heat. It can easily be cut to size and molded. And what distinguishes "unmarked" from the more ordinary explosive of the same name is that it is neither detectable by machines nor by specially trained dogs. Produced in an eastern Bohemian factory called Explosia, it has been banned by treaty since the early 1990s, but the Czech army is allowed to use its old stocks until 2013. There is an estimated sixty tons of unmarked Semtex in Czech army barracks, in addition to the tons that were already sold to mining companies in other countries, and to military units, particularly in the Middle East, that had stockpiled it in the 1980s and before the treaty ban (Libya, for instance, bought almost seven hundred tons). At $2.50 a pound to licensed buyers, unmarked Semtex was one of the great bargains in the explosives world. Half a pound is enough to blow up an airliner. Fifty pounds will destroy a ten-story building.

The Saudis, according to American intelligence analyses, accumulated their Semtex prior to the international restrictions that made the unmarked variety much harder to acquire and easier to trace between seller and purchaser. Based on the time they would have acquired it, the Saudi

Semtex has a shelf life of twenty years, versus the three of today's brand. Also, new supplies have metallic codes that allow it to be traced even after an explosion, as well as the addition of an almost imperceptible odor, but one that dogs can detect. The House of Saud never made direct purchases, but always bought through third-party countries or companies, leaving a buffer between them and any direct link to large sales of explosives.

But according to the electronic intercepts of Saudi conversations about Petro SE, the House of Saud had evidently decided after Iraq's invasion of Kuwait that leveling the major oil production facilities and blasting away the core of the industry's infrastructure was not enough to deter an enemy from seizing its prized commodity. Flattened buildings, ports, pipelines, and storage facilities can be rebuilt, so the program would only be a temporary setback to whoever grabbed control of the Kingdom. As a result, the Saudis embarked on a program to mix a variety of chemicals that can create radiation dispersal devices (RDD), often called "dirty bombs," where not only is there massive explosive damage, but the blasts emit low-level radioactivity that can contaminate the sites for a decade or more.

What is known of the Saudi effort makes it both thorough and remarkably effective. Their engineers have utilized, says the NSA report, possibly three different radioactive elements. One is a highly flammable chemical, rubidium, that when combined with the Semtex can be adjusted to produce an RDD. Also, the Saudis talked frequently about employing cesium 137, a malleable, silver-white metal isotope found in atomic clocks but used most often in medical radiotherapy treatment, particularly for cervical cancer. Finally, their most extensive conversations were about strontium 90, a silvery metal that is a waste by-product of the fission of uranium and plutonium in nuclear reactors and weapons. It is also used as a radioactive tracer in medical and agricultural studies, and for long-life, lightweight power supplies used in remote locations, such as navigational beacons, weather stations, and space vehicles. Strontium 90 is also employed widely in electron tubes, industrial gauges, and for the treatment of eye diseases. Both cesium and strontium have half-lives of roughly thirty years, longer than the Semtex with which they were mixed.

Each offered the Saudis a different set of advantages, and their engineers and scientists debated the pros and cons. Cesium had the benefit of being widely dispersible once released since it has the consistency of talc. But it also emits high-energy gamma rays that can be detected with sensitive instruments like scintillation counters, so it required greater effort at commercial facilities to ensure that it was not detectable in case those installations were ever inspected by third parties. On the other hand, strontium 90, while not as dispersible, emits alpha and beta particles that are much harder to detect and occur in extremely low concentrations, better for concealment. Cesium interacts as effectively with muscle tissues as it does with soil and building materials because it has a chemical similarity to potassium, which muscles require in order to flex. But the body is accustomed to processing these kinds of chemicals, and excretes half of any cesium it absorbs in about three months. Strontium 90, on the other hand, interacts more easily with the body. Similar to calcium, it is rapidly absorbed into bones and teeth—doctors call it a "bone seeker"—by inhalation, as well as through food and water. It can take thirty years for the body to get rid of it.

Although the NSA is not certain of the radioactive elements finally used by the Saudis, they believe Petro SE successfully developed dozens of radiation dispersal devices. These RDDs that the Saudis have integrated into their oil infrastructure are far less lethal than traditional nuclear weapons. The risk is not mass fatal casualties as with a nuclear explosive, but rather increased cancer rates over many years. In the short run, the psychological fear that an area is contaminated by radiation might be so great as to make it commercially unproductive.

The Federation of American Scientists did a review of what would happen in Washington, D.C., if a small conventional bomb of only ten pounds of TNT and cesium 137 the size of a pea was detonated. "The initial passing of the radioactive cloud would be relatively harmless, and no one would have to evacuate immediately. However, residents of an area of about five city blocks . . . would have a one-in-a-thousand chance of getting cancer. A swath about one mile long covering an area of forty city blocks would exceed EPA contamination limits, with remaining residents having a one-in-ten-thousand chance of getting cancer. If decontamination were not possible, these areas would have to be abandoned for decades."

In a computer simulation of a dirty-bomb attack on New York, the detonation of seven thousand curies (units) of cesium—about 3.5 ounces—would spread radioactive fallout over 120 city blocks.

Israeli intelligence analysts share the NSA's belief that the Saudis have deployed crude RDDs throughout the Kingdom as part of Petro SE.

Mixing conventional explosives with ingredients like cesium 137, rubidium, or strontium 90 was evidently attractive to the Saudis because it was so simple. Some of the conversations the Saudis had were about the radioactive isotopes carrying electron charges that influence how they behave in the environment. By positively charging them before making them part of the explosive infrastructure, they speculated, the radioactive isotopes would stick to negatively charged soil particles, such as the clay and rock that constitute the rich Saudi oil reserves. Even without the charging process, cesium easily combines with other elements, so the isotope simply attaches to the area where it is freed. Saudi engineers calculated that the soil particulates beneath the surface of most of their three hundred known reserves are so fine that radioactive releases there would permit the contamination to spread widely through the soil subsurface, carrying the radioactivity far under the ground and into the unpumped oil. This gave Petro SE the added benefit of ensuring that even if a new power in the Kingdom could rebuild the surface infrastructure, the oil reserves themselves might be unusable for years.

Once areas are contaminated with cesium, it's almost impossible to clean off. "The Russians tried to clean it up for years, and they eventually gave up. It just wasn't economically viable," says Fritz Steinhausler, who led the International Atomic Energy Agency's environmental assessment of the disaster at Chernobyl. "People had to give up their village or city. Large areas became simply empty. It really destroys a society."

The accumulation of radioactive materials like cesium, strontium, and rubidium was not difficult. In the 1990s, the United States and other Western countries focused on unguarded Soviet stockpiles of weapons-grade uranium and plutonium as well as their vast stocks of chemical and biological weapons. Pre-9/11, the radioactive chemicals that the Saudis were accumulating were under the radar as far as international inspectors and intelligence agencies were concerned. And even if there had been recognition of the potential threat from the combination of conventional explosives and radioactive materials, the focus by the CIA, Interpol, and others would have been on preventing such devices from falling into the hands of terrorists or being exported by a country for devious purposes.

It is almost impossible to imagine that anyone could have thought a country might obtain such material under the many guises of legitimate uses available for them and then divert small amounts internally into explosive devices that could render large swaths of their own country uninhabitable for years. It is the equivalent of economic nuclear suicide for the Saudis. But it is precisely because of its ingenuity that Petro SE worked. While the rest of the world tried to stop nuclear proliferation so fewer countries developed atomic weapons, the Saudis used readily accessible radioactive materials to build an explosives grid that could potentially have more global impact than a weapons-grade nuclear device used in a limited war.

If an RDD exploded in a civilian population, people in the affected area would be relocated while the multibillion-dollar cleanup was under way. The Saudi oil reserves cannot be relocated, so the consequence of a radiological release over the oil fields is potentially more difficult to resolve.

The Saudis have evidently made their deposits of rubidium, cesium, and strontium virtually undetectable by enclosing them in small, multiple-sealed, lead-shielded cylinders. While the sealing prevents the radioactive material from being found by detection equipment, it also guarantees against leakage. Great effort has been expended on disguising the destructive network not only from casual observation but also from professional inspections. The containers, canisters, and cylinders of explosives were camouflaged to appear as though they are architectural and industrial components of the sprawling facilitates into which they are imbedded.

In Petro SE, the radioactive contamination can only be released if a series of redundant, fail-safe procedures are first satisfied, and then a series of explosions are detonated in a specific order to release the radioactive elements. The Saudis did not want a system that was remotely prone to accidental detonation. But based on intercepted conversations, there is probably enough cesium, strontium, or rubidium to contaminate small cities in several locations in Saudi Arabia.

The Kingdom has some eighty oil and gas fields, with over one thousand wells. It has not talked about sabotaging all of them, but only primary ones that would gut the core of its petroleum industry. Many analysts have long thought the Saudi oil fields were impervious to a foreign or terror attack since they lie beneath thousands of feet of sand and since critical production facilities such as control rooms, power lines, and pipeline junctions are layered in concrete. Even if dozens of wells were blown up, production would continue at the others. Oil would also keep flowing even if a major pipeline were blasted; they are rapidly repairable. That is why the Saudis realized that only by contaminating large swaths of land around

the wells and along sections of the major pipelines could they create a scenario that would turn an aggravating situation into a full-blown, long-term crisis.

Based on the electronic intercepts in the Petro SE file, the oil fields that are likely mined with radioactive dispersal devices include the world's largest, at Ghawar, particularly in the zone dubbed "Arab-D." Ghawar is 150 miles long by 25 miles wide. Other targeted fields include Marjan, Zuluf, Abu Sa'fah, Shaybah, Qatif, Berri, and Hawtah.* The enormous field at Abqaiq, which also has the world's largest oil processing complex, is mined, likely with RDDs, in at least three of its ten cylindrical towers that carry out the indispensable processing of the crude. The destruction of the several-hundred-acre facility at Abqaiq would instantly eliminate almost seven million barrels of crude oil a day from the market. That is double the amount removed from the world's supply during the Iran-Iraq war, and almost a quarter of all U.S. crude consumption. During the 1980s, according to a former American intelligence official, the U.S. government did a secret study of the vulnerability of the Abqaiq facility, and concluded that a single well-placed explosive device could cause chemical reactions that would cripple Abqaiq's gas-oil separation plant for months. (Today, there are fifty-eight such separation plants around the Kingdom.[4])

Fields like Shaybah, which also has natural gas reserves of twenty-five trillion cubic feet, located in the remote Empty Quarter of the Kingdom, border the United Arab Emirates. Nuclear contamination of the ground wells and oil reserves would almost certainly affect some of the nearby UAE production.

The oil fields themselves, the lifeline for future production, are wired under Petro SE to eliminate not only significant wells, but also trained personnel, the computerized systems that seemingly rival NASA's at times, the pipelines that carry the oil from the fields (for instance, the Shaybah complex has a 395-mile pipeline to connect it to the closest gathering center at Abqaiq), the state-of-the-art water facilities (water is injected into the field to push out oil), power operations, and even the power transmission into the region. At Ghawar, for instance, Petro SE specifically targeted the elimination of main producing structures Ain Dar, Haradh, Shedgum,

---

*Some fields were initially outfitted with conventional explosives in the late 1980s, including Khurais, Abu Hadriya, Abu Jifan, Harmaliyah, and Khursaniyah. But Petro SE files indicate that those facilities, mothballed in the 1990s, have had their destructive components completely removed.

Uthmaniyah, Udayliyah, Farzan, Al, and Hawiyah.* Safaniyah, the world's largest offshore field, with estimated reserves of thirty-five billion barrels, evidently has no radioactive dispersal device, but has conventional explosives built into core structures, ensuring its destruction but not multiyear contamination.

The Saudi work on Petro SE is ongoing and often passed off as regular upkeep and security enhancements to existing facilities. Some of the electronic intercepts by the NSA reveal that the Saudis were evidently particularly proud when in 2002 they were able to insert a smaller, more sophisticated network of high-density explosives into two gas-oil separation plants being built in the eastern part of the country, near Dhahran. The work had to be done without raising the suspicion of workers from Italy's Snamprogetti Company, which had a contract to increase oil capacity in that region.

While the destruction, or at least multiyear abandonment, of their oil fields is the primary objective of Petro SE, the Saudis also realized, according to NSA intercepts, that its pipelines and export system had to be crippled. Major platforms at Ras Tanura, the world's largest offshore oil-loading facility, are evidently set with conventional explosives and selective placement of radioactive dispersal devices. Platform 4, which accounts for 45 percent of all of Ras Tanura's output, is apparently set with an RDD that, for reasons not clear, can be operated separately from the rest of the grid.

"If a major facility was knocked out, such as the Ras Tanura export facility, and it looked like it would be out for many months," says Adrian Binks, publisher of the *Petroleum Argus* newsletter, "then the market would be absolutely frenzied and prices would rise through the sky almost."[5]

The NSA believes that a combination of RDDs and conventional explosives are at Yanbu (the largest oil terminal on the Red Sea coast), Al-Juaymah, Jizan, Ras al-Khafji, Zuluf, and Rabigh.

The twenty-mile stretch of the Persian Gulf shoreline from Al-Juaymah to Al-Khobar is the biggest concentration of the Kingdom's port facilities. Part of the self-destruction grid includes the ports' oil transshipment storage tanks: each one is two football fields wide and almost seven stories tall, holding up to thirty million barrels of oil. The explosives there are evi-

---

*Part of the explosive grid, evidently conventional only, includes the $4 billion natural gas processing plant at Hawiyah, completed only in 2002. It represents the largest Saudi natural gas project in more than a decade.

dently adequate enough to break the concrete protection walls that normally encase, and thereby limit damage in case of fire or accident to, each storage tank.

All eight of the Kingdom's refineries are part of the destruction grid. Each has at least one RDD in place.* Thirty pumping stations, on which the Kingdom's pipelines depend, have all been conventionally wired. Conventional explosive packets are at critical juncture points along the 750-mile Petroline pipeline that carries all oil from the two largest fields, Abqaiq and Ghawar, to Yanbu on the Red Sea (the Abqaiq–Yanbu liquid natural gas pipeline runs parallel to the Petroline and is also wired as part of the conventional explosive grid). Also, each of eleven pumping stations along the Petroline have plastic explosives set to incapacitate their gas turbine electric generators, their primary power source. The inclusion of the Petroline pipeline, which Saudi Arabia took over from Mobil in 1984, is an example of Petro SE's redundancy. Although the oil fields at Abqaiq and Ghawar are to be destroyed and unusable, the House of Saud still wants to ensure that should something go wrong on the successful destruction of those fields, the oil from them could not be transported anywhere because the Petroline pipeline would be useless. But by also taking out the Red Sea terminal at Yanbu, the Saudis would eliminate the normal fallback export capability in the Kingdom once the Gulf facilities were down. Yanbu also boasts the largest polyethylene plant (petrochemicals) in the world, completed in 2001 for $1 billion.

Although they are set to destroy all thirty pumping stations on which their enormous pipeline network depends, the Saudis also have plastic explosives at all six generators that could provide backup power to those stations. If the oil field destruction is complete, there will be no need to worry separately about gas-oil separator facilities, but still Petro SE includes a dozen, and also evidently has as part of the destruction grid the electric power facility near Dhahran, which controls three electrical plants, all providing power to the very same gas-oil facilities. Just as the Saudis have built a remarkably efficient energy system, complete with redundancies in case of natural disaster, man-made mistakes, or a terror attack, they have also built in the same careful redundancies to their own self-destruction network.

*These include Saudi Aramco–Rabigh, the facility at Ras Tanura, Yanbu, Riyadh, Jeddah, Saudi Aramco/Mobil-Yanbu, Petromin/Shell-al-Jubail, and the Arabian Oil Company–Ras al-Khafji.

It is all part of what the Saudis, who understandably know the inter-dependencies of their oil production network better than anyone else, have accomplished in creating a nationwide self-destruct system.

Finally, the Saudis have, according to intercepts received as late as the fall of 2004, mined a recently opened underground storage facility in Jeddah. This is the final stage of folding five such underground strategic storage facilities, the others being in Riyadh, Abha, Medina, and Qassim, into Petro SE. The five facilities evidently have conventional explosives at the pipeline connection points to ensure that even if the storage stocks were not destroyed, they could not be transported to bulk plants or refineries.

Separate from Petro SE, the House of Saud takes extensive measures to protect its oil facilities from external or terrorist attack. So long as the royals remain in control of the country, at any one time there are up to thirty thousand guards protecting the Kingdom's oil infrastructure, while high-technology surveillance, common at the most important facilities and antiaircraft installations, defends key locations. Special security units of elite troops watch over the Kingdom's vast energy infrastructure. Helicopter and jet fighter surveillance of the largest facilities is normal. With hundreds of miles of oil fields, and thousands of miles of pipeline, it is no easy task. From 2002 through 2004, the Saudi government added more than $1 billion to its $5 billion security budget specifically to fortify the oil sector from external attack. (The security budget is classified in Saudi Arabia, but Western intelligence analysts make annual estimates of its size.) While that has been reassuring to many Western oil analysts, and particularly to jittery energy markets, it has nothing to do with the real long-term threat to the Saudi oil industry, the covert Petro Scorched Earth.

Amy Jaffe of the Baker Institute, at Rice University in Texas, notes that in 1985, OPEC maintained about 15 million barrels of spare capacity, then a quarter of world demand. At the time of Iraq's invasion of Kuwait, OPEC's spare capacity had fallen to 5.5 million barrels, less than 10 percent of world demand. But still there was enough spare capacity to allow the cartel to quickly expand output to absorb several disruptions simultaneously. That is no longer true. As of early 2005, there are only about 2 million barrels on hand, less than 3 percent of international demand—and it is entirely in Saudi control.

After the 1973 oil embargo, when the West was reeling from the effects of the reduced oil shipments, it was Saudi Arabia, after the embargo ended, that almost single-handedly increased production so that the U.S. and

Europe stabilized quickly. During the Iran-Iraq war, the Saudis pumped millions of extra barrels to keep a lid on prices. And during the 1990–91 Gulf War, the Saudis again produced nearly five million extra barrels daily to make up for the loss of Iraqi and Kuwaiti oil. Even after 9/11, the Saudis put nearly nine million barrels on the market within twenty-four hours of the attack, most of it destined for the U.S., in an effort to stabilize prices. If Saudi Arabia has been the main factor in price stabilization after previous crises, it is hard to calculate the effect if the Kingdom were completely removed from the oil market because of Petro SE.

The U.S. has strategic oil reserves totaling about 600 million barrels, and another 700 million barrels are in reserves held by other nations. But they cannot be drawn down all at once. Even if all the nations agreed to withdraw only 6.5 million barrels daily, the emergency supplies would only last six months. Much more oil would be removed from the market because of the loss of all Saudi production. Once the strategic stocks proved inadequate, a nuclear environment in Saudi Arabia would create crippling oil price increases, political instability, and economic recessions unrivaled since the 1930s and the Great Depression.

What is not clear about Petro SE is whether everything American and Israeli intelligence have picked up since the late 1980s is correct, or whether the Saudis, possibly aware that they were subject to such surveillance, have carefully concocted a much more sophisticated fail-safe system just for the ears of third-party intelligence agencies. The rationale behind fabricating, or at least grandly embellishing, such a self-destruction grid is that since the U.S. and other Western powers share the intelligence about it and could not physically check its veracity by inspecting the facilities, they would have to operate on the assumption that most if not all of it was accurate. What better incentive for Western powers, particularly the United States, to come to the aid of the House of Saud if it were under external or internal attack than to think that if it fell, like the shah of Iran did a quarter century ago, they would take the energy infrastructure of Saudi Arabia with them?

However, the other explanation is that the Saudis under surveillance did not know that the NSA and Israelis were regularly intercepting their conversations and therefore Petro SE is exactly as described in the intelligence files of both countries.

Petro SE, even if built to every detail the Saudis have discussed, has approximately ten years to run. That is because the unmarked Semtex, the bulk of the conventional explosive used in the destruction grid, has a twenty-year life span. Saudi Arabia acquired most of it in 1991 and 1992 at the latest, not long after Iraq's invasion of Kuwait had pushed their dooms-day program to a high priority. The Semtex has already passed half its life span. By 2012 and 2013, the destruction grid created so carefully will be largely useless. If the House of Saud is still in power, the potential crisis posed by Petro SE will have naturally passed. Before that time, however, only by asking Saudi Arabia to permit international inspectors into its most secure energy facilities and infrastructure might it be possible to confirm whether the House of Saud has adopted its own doomsday plan, and how best to confront it.

One thing is certain. If the House of Saud ever implemented Petro SE, senior royals have ensured that they, at least, would be safe, even if they happened to be caught in the Kingdom when it happened. King Fahd has built a multimillion-dollar, state-of-the-art underground war bunker near Riyadh capable of withstanding nuclear, biological, and chemical weapons. Those involved in its construction and design probably never en-visioned that it might one day offer safety to senior royals from their own actions, not those of threatening countries.

CHAPTER 11

THE INFIDEL ARRIVES

When Saddam Hussein invaded Kuwait on August 2, 1990, he violated an unwritten rule that no Arab country should invade another. But with Kuwait falling within hours, the House of Saud feared that Iraq's million-man army might march south and take control of the Kingdom's oil fields, establishing the enormous empire about which Hussein had dreamt. Five days after the Iraqi invasion of Kuwait, Secretary of Defense Dick Cheney arrived in Jeddah to meet with the king and his senior princes and ministers. Cheney arrived with a small team of advisors, including Undersecretary of Defense Paul Wolfowitz, Central Command chief General Norman Schwarzkopf, the National Security Council's Sandy Charles, and Richard Clarke, then assistant secretary of state for politico-military affairs. Cheney also brought along U.S. spy satellite photos that showed Iraqi military units gathering along the Kuwait-Saudi border.

Cheney told the king that American troops were ready to be deployed to protect the Kingdom. President Bush had authorized Cheney to promise that the troops would leave either when the threat was over or when the king ordered them out.[1]

A raucous debate between the Saudi royals took place directly in front of the American contingent. Prince Bandar, the ambassador to the U.S., had flown in to add his support of allowing U.S. troops into the Kingdom. But others, like Crown Prince Abdullah and interior minister Prince

Nayef, opposed allowing any American soldiers on the country's holy soil. "They will never leave," said one.

Unknown then to Cheney and his small team, Osama bin Laden had met only a few days earlier with senior princes and offered his ragtag mujahideen army, fresh from a decade of fighting the Soviets in Afghanistan, to deploy along the border to protect the oil fields. Bin Laden's argument was that no Muslim army would fight the mujahideen, the holy warriors of Afghanistan. But the very fact that Iraq had already attacked a fellow Muslim nation gave the royals little faith that bin Laden's view was right. That was why Cheney was allowed to fly to the Kingdom and make the offer of American protection.

Finally, the king turned his back to his brothers and stared directly at Cheney. "I trust President Bush. Tell him to have his Army come, come with all they have, come quickly. I have his word that they will leave when this is over."[2]

The United States dispatched a much larger force to the Kingdom than the king and his advisors had envisioned. The empty desert stretching out from King Khalid Military City at Wadi al Batin was quickly packed with American troops, tanks, armored personnel carriers, and small cities of tents and prefabricated buildings. However, it was not the force's size but its mere presence that set off a firestorm among the religious fundamentalists and even Saudi nationalists.

"I guess this is the biggest mistake committed by America," says Sheikh Nasser al-Omar, a leading Wahhabi fundamentalist, "that caused it all that hate and hostility."[3]

To bin Laden and other fanatical Wahhabis, the Koran expressly prohibited the entrance of an infidel force like the Americans, and they feared it would eventually colonize the Kingdom. For nationalists, the decision to accept American military troops was a humiliating public admission that after the tens of billions of dollars the Saudis had spent with Western companies to build one of the world's best-equipped military forces it could not even be depended upon in a crisis to defend the country. What had been the purpose of the massive and often embarrassing political fights in Washington to get advanced weapons systems if, in the moment of a real threat to the nation, the Saudis had to rely on American soldiers?

Average Saudis, without the passion of the fundamentalists or the anger of the nationalists, still overwhelmingly opposed the American troops.

These were nonbelievers, Israel's most important and critical ally, and their entrance into the Kingdom could only bode ill.

The House of Saud knew its decision was controversial. It had obtained approval from some friendly religious leaders for a Koranic exception so the U.S. troops could arrive, but that did little to defuse the distaste most in the country had for the soldiers. And while the leading imams weakly said yes, other prominent clerics, like Sheikh Safar al-Hawali, were so vitriolic in their opposition that the Saudis jailed him for five years.[4]*

Still, the House of Saud did its best to make sure that the troops stayed on their isolated compounds, far away from most Saudis. And they tried to apply some of the Wahhabi restrictions that covered foreign workers to the American soldiers. Red Cross emblems on ambulances or tents were painted over with the Red Crescent. Chaplains had to remove their crosses. Scheduled USO shows with dancing girls were canceled. But the most vexing problem for the Saudis was that the Americans had integrated into their armed forces a large number of women. They acted as flight coordinators, mechanics, and supply officers, and worked side by side with their male counterparts. The Saudis were initially horrified.[5] They quickly passed their own code of conduct for the female warriors. T-shirts were banned, even in the 115-degree heat. Legs had to be covered if the women left their bases. Jogging was forbidden. Women could not drive any vehicle outside the military compounds. But certain compromises—small by Western standards but significant by Wahhabi rules—were reached. For instance, at a formerly men-only gym at a Saudi airbase, female soldiers could work out during a daily two-hour period, but only if they entered and left through the back door.[6]

The American military also passed rules to assuage the Saudi unease. Starting in 1991, the U.S. military required all female personnel based in the Kingdom to wear black head-to-foot abayas whenever leaving the base. (This made Saudi Arabia the only country where U.S. female soldiers were expected to wear a religiously mandated garment.) Further, women had to ride in the rear seat of vehicles and always be accompanied by a man when off base.[7]**

---

*In 2004, al-Hawali was one of twenty-six religious scholars and preachers who signed a declaration urging the Iraqi people to fight a jihad against U.S. forces in that country, stating that only through armed resistance would it be possible to stop "the Jews who are infiltrating into Iraq and the coalition forces which exploit differences to consolidate their domination."

**Lieutenant Colonel Martha McSally, the highest-ranking female fighter pilot in the U.S.

But despite the efforts to have the troops be invisible inside the Kingdom, their presence was something that few forgot, or allowed the royal family to forget. Thousands of U.S. troops roamed major Saudi cities like Riyadh while on leave from their bases. They shopped in local supermarkets and traveled in mixed-sex groups. The army even established a military radio station whose broadcast could be heard throughout the Kingdom. To the fundamentalists, the Americans had come under the guise of protecting the House of Saud and had turned into occupiers. For strict Wahhabis, the American military presence was the most serious threat they had ever confronted.

When President George Bush, his wife, and congressional leaders traveled to Saudi Arabia to visit with U.S. troops at Thanksgiving, before their mission to retake Kuwait began, the Saudis were particularly sensitive to any symbolism that might further upset the religious authorities. When Saudi officials learned that the president intended to say grace before dinner with the troops, they objected. Even the president, who had dispatched 400,000 troops to protect the Kingdom from its belligerent neighbor, could not say a Christian prayer on Saudi soil. Bush acquiesced, and instead of celebrating Thanksgiving at the largest military base in the Kingdom, he did it aboard the USS *Durham,* an amphibious cargo ship in international waters.[8]

In the spring of 1991, after the threat from Iraq was over but American troops were still visibly in the Kingdom (they would not leave until September 2003, after Saddam Hussein was toppled from power), 453 religious scholars, university professors, judges, and other professionals issued a strongly worded petition urging a restoration of strict Islamic values, a reaffirmation of the primacy of religious law, an end to government corruption, and a series of twelve mild political reforms. That such a document, distributed widely at religious schools and mosques throughout the Kingdom, could come from people who had long been thought of as solid supporters of the House of Saud and their policies unsettled the monarchy.

The following August, 106 religious scholars passed around an even more defiant "memorandum of advice" to King Fahd. It criticized both domestic and foreign policies, mentioned several times the stationing of

Air Force, fought those regulations as discriminatory beginning in 1995. It took her seven years, and the filing of a lawsuit against the Defense Department, before those regulations were rescinded, only a year before the army withdrew completely from the Kingdom.

American troops on holy soil, and served as the basis for an increasing number of harsh Friday sermons at mosques. The scholars were particularly incensed at what they considered the marginalization of the religious leadership in government decision making.[9]

These pressures finally forced King Fahd to institute a weakened Consultative Council. It fell well short of what had actually been promised as far back as 1970, when the House of Saud had pledged to establish a parliament with two thirds of the members elected. Even in 1975, Crown Prince Faisal had raised the concept of a Consultative Council, together with a constitution to guarantee fundamental citizen rights.[10] But nothing was done. And Fahd's creation was composed of sixty members appointed by the monarchy, and the king was the arbiter on all matters. The opposition that had been energized by the American troop deployment recognized that the reform was largely cosmetic, and was not mollified.

The Saudis arrested some sheikhs and imams for their politically angry sermons. They even offered a $500,000 reward to anyone who could find the author of a bestselling underground cassette damning the royal family.[11] By 1993, however, there were occasionally spontaneous street demonstrations in which Islamists demanded the release of those imprisoned for criticizing the government. These steady challenges to the House of Saud, and questions about how allowing U.S. troops into the Kingdom might have affected the average Saudi's view of the royal family's legitimacy as the defender of Wahhabi Islam, forced the Saudi leadership once again to adopt more austere trappings of their faith.

In 1995, Prince Salman, the powerful governor of the province including the capital of Riyadh, converted to fundamentalism. His son was Prince Ahmed bin Salman, the forty-three-year-old media tycoon who died after a top al Qaeda terrorist told American investigators that he knew about the 9/11 attack before it happened. Even prior to his fundamentalist rebirth, Salman had been a strict enforcer of Wahhabi rules. He had become famous a few years earlier in Arabia when he had a young prince named Bader publicly flogged for getting into a fistfight with the religious police who had stopped his female relative at a downtown shopping center. And in the role of supervising many of the Kingdom's major charities, Salman was the official, more than any other, who made the decisions about how millions of dollars supported Wahhabism worldwide. The elder Salman's conversion to the roots of his faith was not atypical. There seemed to be a rash of "born-again" Wahhabis among senior government ministers and members of the royal family. Some princes who had spent decadent years in the West chasing women and partying hard now renewed themselves in their ascetic faith and viewed their Western binges as a recovered drug addict or alcoholic looks back on a conquered addiction.

In order to illustrate to its conservative critics that it had not lost the right to claim the mantle for protecting Islam's holiest sites, the House of Saud made up for its acquiescence to American troops by reenergizing the Kingdom's most militant forms of Wahhabism. To strengthen its frayed relationship with the religious authorities, the monarchy ensured that Saudi schools had curriculums that promoted only the most strident Islamic views. For instance, school textbooks that were widely distributed during the 1990s invariably stressed the indisputable supremacy of Islam while denigrating nonbelievers. An eighth-grade book says that Allah cursed Jews and Christians and turned some of them into pigs and apes. Ninth graders read that Judgment Day cannot come until "the Muslims fight the Jews and kill them." A tenth-grade chapter warned Muslims against ever befriending non-Muslims. "It is compulsory for the Muslims to be loyal to each other and to consider the infidels their enemy."[12] The same harsh program of study was exported throughout the Muslim world as the Saudis funded thousands of radical madrassas, religious schools scattered around the globe. By the mid-1990s, over a million children outside the Kingdom were being steeped in Wahhabi-approved teachings that mirrored those inside Saudi Arabia.

Such teachings were typical of a Wahhabi culture that bred so much antipathy to non-Muslims that it was easily used to promote violence. "Saudi kids are just set out on a path of thinking, 'OK, those are our enemies,' and in some rare cases they take action," according to Ali al-Ahmed, the Saudi-born executive director of the Virginia-based Saudi Institute, a non-profit organization promoting human rights in the Kingdom. "The system has to be more careful with what it is teaching, who is teaching it, and how it is interpreted. The schools, and other activities like the religious summer camps the monarch sponsors, contribute to attitudes that shape young people. Bin Laden and these hijackers are the products of this."[13]

"I think the educational system in Saudi Arabia, especially since 1979—the whole culture of education in Saudi Arabia," says journalist Dr. Sulaiman al-Hattlan, "gave people dangerous tools, tools to teach people how to hate. Tools of anger. And not tools of understanding the reality of the world. Not tools of creating bridges with the West, the East, everywhere else."[14]

But not everyone in the Kingdom agrees. "We oppose the change of the curriculum because America is interfering in our religion, in our traditions and in our privacies," says prominent Wahhabi cleric Sheikh Nasser al-Omar. "America is aiming to attract Muslims to its own culture thus gaining more members. This is a fundamental issue. Muslims are willing to renounce everything but their religion. They are willing to renounce their jobs, willing to renounce their terrestrial welfare, but not their religion . . . America does not grasp our curriculum."[15]

Yet the prince responsible for Saudi education, Faisal bin Salman bin Abdul Aziz—the brother of the late Prince Ahmed who was named by a leading captured al Qaeda terrorist as his chief Saudi contact—has downplayed the importance of the radical message in the Kingdom's education. "I mean, I am a university teacher. I have trouble getting my students to remember what I told them two weeks ago, let alone asking students to remember what they might have read about five or six years ago. . . . schools do not form the people's view of the world entirely." Faisal said his own review of thousands of pages of Saudi textbooks showed less than 1 percent was "anti-non-Muslim," and criticized focusing on those pages as "selective."[16]

When confronted with the inflammatory textbooks even as late as 2002, Foreign Minister Saud al-Faisal said he would launch a review. He told 60 Minutes that the Saudis had been relieved to find that only "ten percent of what we found was questionable. Five percent was actually abhorrent to us." Saud promised to excise the offensive material from all textbooks. "We have changed," he said.[17] Repeated requests by the U.S. embassy in Riyadh for a rundown of the changes went unanswered. Although a tenth-grade text that included a chapter encouraging hostility between Muslims and nonbelievers was slated to be deleted, most of the objectionable language remained almost two years later.[18]

When Turki al-Hamad, a Saudi columnist for a London-based Arabic paper, wrote that the problem was Wahhabism itself, and that Saudis should "renounce" its violent and unyielding doctrines, the answer from several Saudi clerics was to issue a fatwa, or religious order, for his death.

———

By the fall of 1994, the House of Saud had an opportunity to demonstrate to the fundamentalists that it would not rubber-stamp every U.S. request to add troops to the Kingdom. Saddam Hussein tested the collapsing Gulf War coalition by moving twenty thousand of his Republican Guards near the Kuwaiti border and activating another fifty thousand in Basra. The Clinton administration asked the Saudis to host an additional U.S. armored brigade. The king declined. President Clinton visited the Kingdom. He tried changing Fahd's mind, and boasted about the good progress that had been made in the Middle East with the advent of the Oslo Agreement between the PLO and Israel. Clinton also asked the Saudis to stop the funds that kept flowing freely to Hamas. But the president failed on both fronts. The message was clear. In currying favor with the fundamentalists, the House of Saud could no longer embrace every American request. The hard-line interior minister Prince Nayef later commented, "Ever since the Gulf War of 1991, we are perceived in the Arab world as a pawn of the United States."[19] It was this image the Saudis wanted to change.

But the royal family, while taking steps to pacify the fundamentalists, also drew a line the militants should not cross. In September 1994, Saudi security arrested two of the most inflammatory—and prominent—clerics who castigated the monarchy for corruption and abandonment of Wahhabi ideals. It detained twenty-five more hard-liners, but released all of them after six weeks—still, the warning was clear.[20] It also revoked Osama bin Laden's Saudi citizenship in 1994, tired of his increasing verbal attacks on the royal family through long "open letters" that chastised King Fahd for not being sufficiently committed to Wahhabism and for allowing "the Crusader and the Jews, who are profaning the holy places," into the Kingdom.[21] That same year, Prince Turki bin Faisal, the chief of intelligence, made a rare public appearance at a mosque, where he pleaded for a cessation of the personal attacks on the royals.

The answer of the hard-core fundamentalists, in November 1995, was a massive bomb detonated at the Saudi National Guard barracks in Riyadh. Five Americans died and dozens were wounded. Months later, in June 1996, a suicide truck bombing at the al-Khobar military complex killed nineteen more Americans and wounded hundreds. The House of Saud was furious that the terrorists had struck inside the Kingdom, making them look weak on security. They also thought they had a truce with the fundamentalists, and to again illustrate their own Islamic loyalties, the royals did not cooperate too fully with the Americans on the investigations into the terror strikes.[22]

As for the National Guard barracks bombing, the Saudis blocked the FBI from the investigation. Justice Department officials unsuccessfully appealed to the Clinton White House to pressure the Kingdom. In five months, the Saudis caught the Americans by surprise when they announced that they had broken the case by obtaining the confessions of four local radicals. The men were beheaded six weeks after their arrest, before any American investigator was permitted to question them. When it came to the much more deadly bombing at the Khobar towers, FBI director Louis Freeh flew to Riyadh to oversee a team of nearly one hundred agents and support personnel. But Saudi officials who steadfastly refused to give the FBI any substantive role frustrated him repeatedly. Again, the Clinton White House failed to persuade the Saudis to cooperate, and the FBI agents were reduced to sitting in makeshift offices reading interrogation transcripts completed by Saudi investigators.

Meanwhile, bin Laden had accelerated his calls for American troops to be expelled from the Kingdom. In his 1996 "Declaration of War Against Americans Occupying the Land of the Two Holy Places," the document's subtitle was "Expel the Polytheists from the Arabian Peninsula." Bin Laden railed about the "Zionist and Christian Crusader Alliance," blamed the U.S. for the Saudi arrests two years earlier of prominent fundamentalist clerics, and even belittled King Fahd, saying he "wore the cross on his chest." The following year, 1997, bin Laden told *al-Huquq*, an Arabic periodical, that what mattered most in the Riyadh National Guard bombing was that "no Saudi was hurt, only Americans were killed." His message was still directed at forcing U.S. troops from Arabia, and ensuring that the royal family paid a price for having allowed them in. Bin Laden hoped that average Saudis would rally to his words. While the Saudi press censored his statements in the national media, they nevertheless were widely known to the general population, with many ordinary citizens at least agreeing that the Americans should go.

In 1998, bin Laden released his third major declaration, this time in a widely circulated newspaper, *al-Quds al-Arabi*. Now calling his group the "World Islamic Front," he urged a "jihad against Jews and Crusaders." His primary grievance was that "for over seven years the United States has been occupying the lands of Islam in the holiest of places, the Arabian peninsula."[23] He refrained this time from criticizing the Saudi royal family. Just months earlier, in the summer of 1998, intelligence chief Prince Turki bin Faisal, the chief of Saudi intelligence, had visited Kandahar, Afghanistan, and met with the Taliban—bin Laden's Afghan hosts—discussing bin Laden and his war of words on the royal family.[24] Earlier in 1998, representatives of two prominent Saudi families visited bin Laden's Afghan compound and made a "donation" of $10 million on the understanding that he direct his ire at the Americans, not the Saudis. The donations, the Saudi representatives said, had the blessing of the House of Saud.[25]

Inside the Kingdom, clerics accelerated their harsh anti-Christian and anti-Jewish rhetoric. In the central mosques of Mecca, before tens of thousands of Muslim worshippers, religious leaders called Christians the "descendants of the Spanish Inquisitors who tortured the Muslims most abominably" and of "those who led the Crusades in which thousands of Muslims were killed and their wives taken captive," as well as the "perpetrators of the collective massacres in Bosnia-Herzegovina, Kosovo, Indonesia, and Chechnya. Can we expect compassion from these murderous wolves?" As for Jews, an imam at the popular Taif mosque told worshippers that hopefully the day was approaching when it "will become possible to torture them [Jews] and kill them to the very last one."[26]

Sheikh Muhammad bin Abd al-Rahman al-'Arifi, imam of the mosque of King Fahd Defense Academy, wrote, "We will control the land of the Vatican; we will control Rome and introduce Islam in it. Yes, the Christians . . . will yet pay us the Jiziya [poll tax paid by non-Muslims under Muslim rule], in humiliation, or they will convert to Islam."[27]

The House of Saud did almost nothing to moderate the escalating radicalism in its mosques during the late 1990s. The only significant exception was the treatment of Medina's grand imam, Sheikh Abdul Rahman al-Hudaifi, who was removed after a fiery 1998 sermon. But his offense was not anti-Christian or -Jewish invective, of which there was plenty, but an attack on Shiite Muslims. The former president of Iran, Hashemi Rafsanjani, was in the mosque that day attending prayer services as a guest of Crown Prince Abdullah. The royal family decided the anti-Shiite portion of the service was an insult to both the Iranians and the House of Saud, so the imam was fired.

Only after 9/11 would it become clear that six of the fifteen Saudi hijackers went through religious recruitment while living in the Kingdom. Some were introduced to al Qaeda through militant mosques in southwest Saudi Arabia. Only two of the Saudi hijackers ever got to Afghanistan. For the rest, the indoctrination for their suicide mission and the commitment they held to al Qaeda was a result of what they learned in Saudi Arabia during the 1990s.

In its effort to counter the image in the Arab world that it was too dependent on American military interests—especially after allowing U.S. troops into the Kingdom—the House of Saud had publicly distanced itself from the U.S. on as many issues as possible, even on cooperating in the fight against terrorism. As they had done many times in their short history, when confronted with internal dissent, the Saudi rulers invariably compromised with religious authorities to strengthen Wahhabi influence in the Kingdom. The royal family had abdicated the moral pulpit to the extremists. It was a decision that not only made 9/11 inevitable, but also eventually would turn on the royals themselves.

CHAPTER 12

THE PRINCE
WHO WOULD BUY
AMERICA

While the fundamentalists might have been condemning the United States as the leader of the new Crusades, prominent Saudi businessmen were continuing to make the "Great Satan" their prime investment. There are no official figures provided by either government. The Saudis, when they started investing with their oil embargo profits in 1974, struck a deal with Treasury Secretary William Simon that the U.S. government would never disclose specific figures for the Saudi money coming into America. The House of Saud did not want to be accused of buying America, and as a result, despite repeated efforts by Congress and private groups to get the figures, the Treasury Department has relied on two laws—the Bretton Woods Agreement Act and the International Investment Survey Act—to claim it cannot release information about "individual investors," which it considers Saudi Arabia to be. Financial analysts, however, have made a concerted effort to obtain an accurate picture of how much Saudi money is in the U.S. The Securities and Exchange Commission requires that investments in public American companies be disclosed only if they exceed 5 percent of the firm's value. That means that many investments are made "under the radar," where foreign investors keep their money under the 5 percent threshold. Those are more difficult to accurately calculate.[1] Also, it is hard to determine the extent of Saudi real estate purchases, as many of those are done through an intricate layer of offshore banks and third-country corporations, represented by a combination of American and foreign law firms that are not required to disclose any details about their furtive clients. None of the real estate deals made through such complex financial arrangements are illegal or connected to money laundering, but rather are constructed for the very purpose of providing as much legally available privacy as possible. For the Saudis it has worked well, leaving most investigators only making educated guesses at the amount of America the Kingdom owns. The most common estimate is that the Saudis have about $600 billion in America.[2] That dwarfs the investment by any other country.

After 9/11, when the mood in the U.S. swung against the Saudis for their seemingly cavalier attitude toward reining in extremists and several lawsuits were filed on behalf of the victims of the terror attacks against Saudi officials and banks, some financial commentators predicted that a withdrawal of Saudi investments was imminent. A figure widely bandied about was that the Kingdom's investors would yank up to $200 billion out of the U.S., fearing that the money might be attached in some future legal proceeding and that the investment environment in America had become inhospitable.

A year after the terror attacks, the Kingdom's largest investor in the U.S., King Fahd's nephew Prince Al-Waleed bin Talal bin Abdul Aziz Al-Saud, told the British Broadcasting Corporation that senior members of the Saudi ruling family were not abandoning their American investments and in many instances were actually increasing them.

"I'm holding on to all of them [my investments] and in all honesty increasing my stakes in certain companies in the US," he said.

When asked about the rumors of large withdrawals, he said he had read the stories, found them "surprising," and that "my information tells me none of this is correct. . . . What I am telling you represents the position of the Saudi Royal Family 100%."[3]

There is no better source for such information than forty-eight-year-old Prince Al-Waleed. He is the prince who more than any other is single-handedly buying America Inc. *Time* magazine hailed him as the "Arabian Warren Buffett." *Business Week* once said Al-Waleed "is probably the most important financial kingpin that you've never heard of" and said that by 2010, he could be "the most powerful and influential businessman on earth."[4]

Al-Waleed was born in 1957 to Prince Talal bin Abdul Aziz, one of the many sons of the late King Ibn Saud, and Mona al-Solh, the daughter of

Lebanon's first postindependence prime minister, Riad al-Solh. His father emerged during the 1950s as the leading voice of a small cadre of liberal princes, known as "Free Princes," who pushed for political reform in the House of Saud. As the 1960s began, Prince Talal proposed drafting a constitution and forming an elected consultative council. Not only did King Saud reject the ideas, but religious leaders issued a fatwa condemning them as violations of Islamic law. In 1961, the House of Saud canceled Talal's passport and tried muffling him. He left for Cairo, where he declared himself a socialist and broadcast anti-Saudi radio propaganda, earning the nickname "the Red Prince."[5]

In 1964, Talal reconciled with the royal family and was allowed to return to the Kingdom so long as he did not express any more political views. He agreed, and for the next two decades focused on business, primarily construction and real estate. In those enterprises he earned a small fortune.

Talal's son Prince Al-Waleed left Saudi Arabia at nineteen (in 1976) to attend Menlo College, just outside of San Francisco. He later told *Business Week,* "From the age of 16, I realized I wanted a plane and a boat and to make money."[6] At Menlo College, the prince studied business, and upon graduating with honors, returned to Saudi Arabia in 1979 to take advantage of the postembargo petro boom that was still sweeping the Kingdom. By the time Al-Waleed went home, Saudi Arabia was already a multibillion-dollar investor in America. Four years after the embargo, Saudi Arabia had become, for instance, the largest holder of Federal National Mortgage Association (Fannie Mae) notes, and held about $40 billion separately in U.S. securities.[7]

In those early years, the Saudis picked relatively low-key companies in which to put their money, and often favored conservative ones in banking, investments, or industrial production. For instance, among initial Saudi investments were brokerage firms Smith Barney and Donaldson Lufkin Jenrette; banks like the National Bank of Georgia, the Commonwealth of Missouri, and the Main Bank of Houston; and for individual firms, North Carolina aluminum smelters Coastal and Offshore Plants Systems, Delaware truckers RLC Corp., Texas-based Sunshine Mining, and Colorado Land and Cattle Company.

But that soon changed as Saudis began investing in major corporations that were household names in most American homes. Al-Waleed would eventually lead the change. When he had returned to Saudi Arabia, he started earning his own personal fortune the same way many of his royal compatriots did—by becoming an agent for foreign companies wanting to do business in the Kingdom. In 1980, the prince mortgaged a house given to him by his father and started his own firm, Kingdom Establishment. His first deal was an $8 million contract with a South Korean company to build a bachelors' club at a military academy near Riyadh.[8]

Unlike many Saudi royals who were content just to earn fat commissions on business deals with foreigners, the twenty-three-year-old Al-Waleed had grander ambitions. A self-acknowledged workaholic, he aggressively pursued joint ventures with foreign companies, landing construction deals and lucrative military contracts. By his mid-twenties, he was raking in profits of more than $50 million annually.[9] His early investments were conservative, with most of his spare money going into real estate in and around Riyadh. It was a smart move, since he caught a wave of real estate appreciation that ballooned his personal worth over a few years.

While many Saudi princes might have stopped at that point, Al-Waleed wanted much more. So in the mid-1980s, not yet thirty, he returned to the United States to pursue a master's degree in social sciences at New York's Syracuse University. There he became convinced that the American banking system was ripe for growth. When he returned to Saudi Arabia, he did something that was then unheard of—launched a hostile takeover of one of the Kingdom's established banks, the unprofitable United Saudi Commercial Bank (USCB). Filled with fresh ideas about how to turn companies around, he slashed USCB's staff from 600 to 250 and introduced management incentives (then virtually nonexistent in Saudi Arabia), and the bank became profitable in just two years. With his new revenue, he expanded his little empire to include the Kingdom's largest supermarket chain, then branched out into such diverse fields as hospital management, livestock, and even fast-food outlets.

Satisfied that his Saudi base was now solid, Al-Waleed turned briefly to mixing philanthropy and politics, supporting the mujahideen fighters in their jihad against Soviet troops in Afghanistan. He was a major financial supporter of the Afghan Arab militias and traveled secretly to their training camps in Peshawar.[10] His last sizable donation to the mujahideen — $5.4 million—was in April 1990, shortly after the Soviets had left and the country was beginning its descent into civil war.[11]

But by that time, Al-Waleed had also turned his attention to investing some of his newfound money into America. In 1987, he had examined then ailing banks in the United States. He began acquiring shares of Chase Manhattan, Citibank, Manufacturers Hanover, and Chemical Bank. Sometimes he called in buy orders from a cellular phone while horseback riding in the desert.[12]

Within months, he had spent close to $250 million—at one point owning 2.3 percent of Chase. All the banks were having difficulties in a tough market, and their shares seemed like bargains to him. In 1990, he profitably sold his stakes in three of the banks, and funneled $207 million into Citibank, acquiring a 4.9 percent stake through stock purchases (just under the 5 percent that would have triggered public disclosure by the SEC rules). By the autumn of 1990, the bank, then America's largest, was in worse condition than when Al-Waleed originally invested.[13] The savings and loan debacle had shaken Wall Street's confidence in financial institutions. Citibank urgently needed an infusion of money, had hemorrhaged red ink on its property loans, and was widely exposed to third-world loans that seemed uncollectible. It needed $1.5 billion to survive, but was having difficulty finding investors. As fears mounted that Citibank might fail, its shares plunged by half.

"I was the only one in the world willing to talk to Citi," Al-Waleed later said.[14] He decided to invest more money, but because that would put him above the SEC's 5 percent disclosure rule, he wanted advice on the most politic and savvy way to proceed as a foreigner buying into America's largest bank. The Washington, D.C., law firm of Hogan & Hartson suggested he hire the Carlyle Group to navigate the approval process.

The Washington-based Carlyle Group is one of the world's largest private equity firms, managing about $14 billion. They have earned a reputation for forging multibillion-dollar business deals between governments and the military-industrial complex. One of the reasons the Carlyle Group is so successful is that many of its senior officers are retired Carter, Reagan, and Bush administration officials who still wield influence in both business and government circles. Included in the Carlyle Group are ex–Reagan secretary of defense Frank Carlucci, former Bush secretary of state James Baker, and Fred Malek, former Republican National Committee chairman. Ex-president George H. W. Bush joined Carlyle in 1999, and among other tasks has visited South Korea to lobby for business.[15] John Major, the former British prime minister, joined Carlyle in 1998 to run its European bureau.

The Carlyle Group has extensive business with Saudi companies.

One of the Saudi companies that later invested several million dollars into the Carlyle Group was the Bin Laden Organization. That connection became public when *The Wall Street Journal* broke the story on September 27, 2001. A month after that disclosure, an embarrassed Carlyle Group cut its ties with the bin Laden family and refunded their money.

In February 1991, Osama bin Laden was far from the minds of either the Carlyle Group or Al-Waleed. Instead, American troops stationed in the Kingdom were preparing to retake Kuwait from Iraq. And Prince Al-Waleed, guided by the Carlyle Group, spent $590 million to buy an additional 10 percent of Citibank.*

His timing was impeccable. Two weeks later, a syndicate of international investors ended Citibank's money crisis by putting another $600 million into the bank. (Al-Waleed's cash infusion had effects on the bank in ways that few could have foreseen. CEO John Reed, a Manhattan society insider, probably could never have imagined that a couple of years later, he and his son would fly to Saudi Arabia and don Bedouin robes for a late-night party at Al-Waleed's high-tech encampment thirty miles outside Riyadh—complete with roast camel, Bedouin dancers, and some target practice with machine guns.)[16]

By April 1998, after Citibank announced plans to merge with Travelers, the value of Al-Waleed's under-$1-billion stake in the company (now called Citigroup) had climbed to $7.6 billion (it's now worth over $10 billion). That deal put both Al-Waleed and the Carlyle Group on the map.**

Al-Waleed's acquisition of part of Citigroup was followed over the next decade by significant investments in other poorly performing blue-chip American and European companies. The portfolio he collected as a

*One of Citibank's many businesses was the credit card Diners Club, which it had purchased years earlier. Prince Al-Waleed distributed a number of Diners Club cards to his friends and family members as a promotion, proud of his new investment. His friends ran up $30 million in unpaid charges, and when Diners Club asked Al-Waleed to pay the debt, he simply refused. Suing the prince under Saudi law was futile. So instead, on June 4, 1992, Diners Club announced it was ceasing all operations in the Kingdom, citing financial instability as the reason behind its decision.

**Although Al-Waleed's investment style might resemble that of the conservative midwesterner Warren Buffett more than the glitzy New Yorker Donald Trump, in his personal style he outdoes even Trump. In 1991, he bought Trump's 283-foot yacht at the knockdown price of $18 million from Trump's creditors. He renamed the yacht *Kingdom*. By the time of the Citicorp deal he had 400 employees, including 160 at his main Riyadh palace, a permanent crew of 40 for his yacht, and an unknown number of gun-toting security guards who followed him around the clock. He is a regular guest in Monaco with Prince Albert, and in England enjoys polo events with the queen and Prince Charles.

bargain hunter is eclectic, typically composed of minority stakes in everything from media, telecoms, information systems, retailing, property, entertainment, hotel-management, and dot-coms.

In 1994, for instance, he made headlines by buying 24 percent of Euro
Disney for $360 million (another Carlyle Group–brokered deal).[17] That
same year, the prince made waves in Europe when an Al-Waleed-led alliance beat out Rupert Murdoch by bidding $1.2 billion for a stake in the
TV empire of the current Italian prime minister, Silvio Berlusconi.[18] In
1995, he grabbed a 50 percent stake in New York's Plaza Hotel for $160 mil-
lion and 10 percent of London's enormous Canary Wharf (the latter as part
of a consortium headed by Laurence Tisch, the late business tycoon from
New York). He also added control of the Saks Fifth Avenue upscale chain
of stores, and a significant ownership interest in the ultra-luxe hotel chain
the Four Seasons.

In February 1997 he invested in a relatively new Internet service
provider called America Online (AOL)—he eventually put more than
$2 billion into AOL.[19] The following month, he acquired a 5 percent stake
in Apple after shares had plummeted from $50 to $18, and that same
month he bought 5 percent of TWA stock.[20] Boeing was his next target. In
1999, Al-Waleed became the controlling shareholder of Compaq Computer (he was bought out when Hewlett Packard merged with it two years
later). That same year he put substantial money into Xerox. By 2000,
Al-Waleed had moved new money to other high-tech firms, such as
eBay, Amazon, Priceline.com, AT&T, WorldCom, Sun Microsystems, and
Kodak. He spent over a billion dollars acquiring high-tech shares.[21] He
rushed money in 2001 into deflated share prices at Internet ventures like
Drugstore.com, DoubleClick.com, InfoSpace, Netscape, and Internet Capital Group. In the past few years, Al-Waleed has added substantial investments into Pepsi and Procter and Gamble. Among his latest ventures, he
bought stakes in Ford Motors; the NewsCorp, the parent company of the
New York Post and the Fox News Channel (his 3 percent stake is second
only to owner Rupert Murdoch's); Time Warner; and also Motorola.[22]

Although Al-Waleed has favored high-tech firms, he has not completely avoided more traditional companies. He bought a quarter of the
Planet Hollywood restaurant chain. And among his many non-U.S. investments are such high-profile companies as England's premier advertising
firm, Saatchi & Saatchi; Korean car makers Daewoo and Hyundai; and
Norwegian Cruise Lines.

There is no doubt that Al-Waleed is energetic, articulate, and tireless.

The thrice-divorced prince has built a sterling reputation among other international business titans, and they respect his grasp of details and his hands-on approach to his investments. In his Riyadh offices, not far from his 317-room castle, he has assembled a young, aggressive team of hard-working advisors who emulate his success. Eight television monitors are tuned at all times to international business and news channels. Al-Waleed prides himself on needing only five hours of sleep nightly, and being involved in the minutiae of his empire.[23] Some financial commentators have greatly rankled him by suggesting that he could be a front man for a larger consortium of senior-level Saudi royals anxious to buy a sizable piece of America but not wanting the glare of publicity.

"Many have assumed the slim, 5-foot-8-inch, 140 pound Al-Waleed," *Business Week* wrote in a detailed 1995 profile, "is a one-man investment front for other, more publicity-shy Saudi princes. Some have whispered about contracts to build secret military bases in Saudi Arabia—or even fat commissions on oil shipments. Al-Waleed himself hasn't done much to quell the rumors."[24]

In 1999, the respected British business magazine *The Economist* concluded that the prince "has not earned enough from his investments" to pay for his massive stock purchases in the 1990s and may "have a valuable and unrevealed source of income": "Prince Alwaleed is the modern face of Saudi royalty, but his sums don't add up. . . . His business empire has a mystery at its heart."[25]

Based on an extensive investigation of Al-Waleed's SEC filings, as well as interviews with the prince and his entourage, *The Economist* raised doubts about the true extent of his success as a stock market investor and whether his Saudi real estate deals could have produced enough money to launch his 1990s American buying spree.

The Economist asked, "Where did it [his money] come from?"

The mystery starts with his first major investment, the 1997 money that went into Citibank. Al-Waleed is adamant that it came only from personal funds. He started out, he claims, with a loan of just $35,000 from his father, something that *Business Week* once dubbed "an implausible story."[26] He also mortgaged a house that his father had given him, raising about $400,000. And each month, as a grandson of the Kingdom's founder, Ibn Saud, he received a stipend of between $15,000 and $19,000. But somehow, by 1991, he was able to risk $797 million on a possibly failing American bank.

The Federal Reserve Board must approve any investor's purchase of more than 10 percent of an American bank. After Al-Waleed had raised his stake in Citibank, he filed an application at the end of 1991 asking the Fed to approve his purchase. Most applications are approved within sixty days. After fourteen months, the Fed had still not given the prince's application the green light, despite aggressive lobbying by his American lawyers. Al-Waleed says he "got the message," and saying he "had to play by the rules of America," sold just enough shares to bring his ownership to under 10 percent.[27]

The Fed is the only regulatory body ever to have publicly investigated Prince Al-Waleed. It will not officially comment on why it did not approve his application, but it appears that it was affected by breaking news that began in the spring of 1991 about the unraveling BCCI bank fraud. It involved Pakistanis, Saudis, and layers of investors hidden behind a few apparently clean front men and businesses. Since the Fed could not be absolutely certain that all of Al-Waleed's money was his own, they evidently decided it would be safer if he cut his holdings to under 10 percent.

Citibank was only the beginning. Since 1990, Al-Waleed has invested about $4.5 billion in cash into different companies around the globe. But he rarely sells any investment, and denies firmly that his money is either an inheritance or a gift. Al-Waleed has always declared on federal regulatory filings that the money is his alone. He has seldom borrowed any funds, and then it is usually when he is buying hotels, to borrow against the building he is buying, reducing his tax bill. And again in his filings with federal regulators, the prince has declared that he has not built his empire on secret debt.

The Economist was troubled by $1.5 billion of the $4.5 billion the prince had for investments. It was earned in the mid-to-late 1980s in buying and selling land in Saudi Arabia, says Al-Waleed. There are no public records of real estate deals in the Kingdom, and Al-Waleed refuses to give specific examples, saying instead that by the early 1990s he had acquired twenty-five million square feet of prime Riyadh real estate and fourteen square miles of property just outside the city, making him the largest private landowner in the Saudi capital.[28] "Yet chartered surveyors who were working in the Middle East," reported *The Economist*, "between 1986 and the Gulf war say the market was 'flat' throughout that period."

The slightest hint of corruption or malfeasance causes outrage among the prince and his family. In 1998 his father, Prince Talal, challenged "anyone to come forward and provide me with documentary proof that Prince Al-Waleed accumulated this fortune by corrupt or illegal means."

It would be almost impossible to come by such evidence even if it did exist. Prince Al-Waleed's enormous empire is anything but transparent. Most of his investments are held through a maze of companies registered in tax havens where total secrecy is guaranteed. In the Cayman Islands more than 120 firms are registered under the corporate name used by Prince Al-Waleed, Kingdom 5-KR (the prince says "KR" stands for the initials of his children's first names but refuses to say what the "5" means as it is "confidential").[29]

Whatever its intention, the effect of this complex financial structure is to obscure the trail of the prince's money outside Saudi Arabia.[30]

There is no doubt that high-ranking members of the House of Saud would not, for internal political reasons, be able to publicly undertake the types of investments that Al-Waleed pursues. Several chief executives of firms in which he has invested—such as Disney's Michael Eisner, Sanford Weill of Travelers Group, and clothing designer Donna Karan—as well as some of his business partners—like Canadian real estate developer Paul Reichmann or the late Laurence Tisch—are Jewish.

And no matter how close Al-Waleed is to the royal family, and how much he is admired as one of Saudi Arabia's greatest success stories, it has not spared him sharp criticism when the House of Saud thinks he has gone too far searching for a profit. A 1994 deal with pop star Michael Jackson to establish Kingdom Entertainment, a venture in which they promised to promote "family values" at a joint press conference, led to public rebukes from some Saudi royals. At the time, Jackson gushed about Al-Waleed, "We want to create a new multimedia empire. The prince is sweet and humble but at the same time very daring and wants to do incredible things. Just like I do." (A couple of years earlier Al-Waleed had one of his private jets bring Jackson for lunch to his ocean-liner-sized yacht, then moored off the French Riviera—associates of Jackson say he was "dazzled" by Al-Waleed's luxurious lifestyle and business acumen.)[31]

In 1997, ART satellite television, in which Al-Waleed is the largest shareholder, broadcast the "Miss Arab of Israel" contest from Haifa. It earned him similar disapproval, although it is not clear if such criticism is merely for public consumption inside the Wahhabi Kingdom and behind the scenes Al-Waleed actually has a green light for all his ventures from the House of Saud.

The prince himself is quite sensitive to charges that his investments reflect a pro-Western bias. To bolster his own Wahhabi credentials, he has regularly donated huge sums to Muslim institutions, and ensured that such gifts receive widespread news coverage inside the Kingdom and Arab world. He gives away nearly $100 million annually. Among his bequests, in December 2001, Al-Waleed announced he would finance fifty new mosques in Saudi Arabia. These were in addition to the thirty-nine mosques he had previously paid for. In May 2002, he gave $4 million to the Grand Mosque in Carthage, Tunisia, and $2 million to a Lebanese mosque. During a live 2002 telethon, he pledged $27 million to help rebuild Palestinian infrastructure destroyed by Israel and supply vehicles and clothing. He also gave $6 million to Palestinians thrown out of work by the Intifada, and helped reconstruct Lebanese power plants destroyed by the Israeli air force.[32]

On October 11, 2001, precisely a month after the 9/11 attacks, Al-Waleed and his entourage visited New York and had a walking tour of ground zero with the city's mayor, Rudy Giuliani, and other city officials. At the time he was ranked by *Forbes* magazine as the sixth wealthiest man in the world (he was fourth in the 2004 rankings, worth an estimated $21.5 billion).[33] During his visit, he gave Giuliani a $10 million donation to the September 11 relief fund. It might have been seen as a magnanimous gesture and made Al-Waleed an instant hit in America if it had not been for a written statement circulated later that same day by his publicist. In it, Al-Waleed said, "Our Palestinian brethren continue to be slaughtered at the hands of the Israelis while the world turns the other cheek . . . At times like this one, we must address some of the issues that led to such a criminal attack. I believe the government of the United States of America should re-examine its policies in the Middle East and adopt a more balanced stance toward the Palestinian cause."[34]

Suggesting that America might be to blame for bringing such a horrific terror strike upon itself as a result of its Middle East policy produced a firestorm of public and media criticism. Giuliani, who said that he thought he had noticed Al-Waleed and others in his entourage "smirking" as they walked around the massive ruins, angrily returned the donation.[35] Al-Waleed, furious at the snub, left the U.S. immediately for Saudi Arabia. Days later, in an interview with a Saudi newspaper, he blamed Giuliani's decision on "Jewish pressures."[36] He later told *Newsweek,* "Giuliani should never have politicized the matter." When asked if he had warned

Giuliani that he would make a political statement, Al-Waleed, who is obviously not accustomed to anyone rejecting his money, said, "It was none of his business. His business was to receive the check."[37]

Since the fiasco at ground zero, Al-Waleed has avoided publicly challenging the Bush administration. His only other 9/11-related activity came in March 2002, when he gave $1 million to an Arab League fund intended to repair Western perceptions of Islam following the terror attacks.

While Al-Waleed's rejected donation might be viewed in the West as a public relations debacle, in the Middle East, his confrontation with Giuliani transformed him from a superrich but politically marginal member of the Saudi royal family into one of the most respected figures in the Arab world. He again showed his credentials to the Arab street when he said after 9/11, "There's no company in Palestine I'm not involved with."[38] In 2002, he donated millions to a Saudi government–sponsored telethon to raise money for Palestinian "martyrs."[39]

This fame may eventually translate into political power. Almost overnight, Al-Waleed became a regular part of any serious discussion about possible political contenders in the third generation of Saudi royals who will one day inherit power from the aging senior princes now in line for succession to the crown.

In the meantime, the prince has adopted a patient attitude toward his U.S. investments. He is confident that the anti-Saudi mood prevalent since 9/11 is merely a passing phase.

"The U.S. right now is in a mood that is unrealistic," says Al-Waleed, "and I hope that once the dust settles the U.S. government, people and the media will go back to reality and normal."[40]

As for Al-Waleed, despite the torrent of religious leaders inside the Kingdom who condemn the United States as a crusading imperialist that must be ostracized from the Arab world, he continues to invest in America. In February 2004, Microsoft founder and chairman Bill Gates invited Al-Waleed to dinner at his home to discuss business projects, including their joint investments in the Four Seasons Hotels and Resorts (Al-Waleed had earlier owned 50 percent of the Fairmont Hotel chain). The prince offered to help Microsoft expand its operations in Saudi Arabia.[41]

That same month, Al-Waleed met in New York with Hank Greenberg, the chairman of AIG (American International Group), the world's largest insurance company. Saudi Arabia is planning to require Saudi employers to provide health insurance for all employees, and Al-Waleed is looking at whether AIG should get the contract inside the Kingdom.[42] While in America, he had private meetings with Steve Jobs, the head of Apple Computer, former president Bill Clinton at his Harlem office (their fourth get-together), Scott McNealy, CEO of Sun Microsystems, and Rick Braddock, chairman of Priceline.com.

The chill in U.S.-Saudi relations has not slowed the prince who would buy America.

CHAPTER 13

"A MAD SPENDER"

Prince Al-Waleed is unusual among Saudi princes. Many of the other male relatives in the royal family seem only to live off government stipends, or commissions they can force from business deals inside the Kingdom. Their lavish lifestyles fuel the charge by fundamentalists that the monarchy has lost its way, abandoned the strictures of Wahhabism, and fallen prey to the illicit temptations of an indulgent West. There may be no royal who better represents what the bin Ladens of the Muslim world detest than one of the favorite sons of King Fahd, fifty-four-year-old Prince Mohammad bin Fahd bin Abdul Aziz.

The American-educated Mohammad, a former minister of communications and the current governor of the Kingdom's oil-rich Eastern Province, came under public scrutiny in 1998 when British court proceedings exposed his opulent standard of living. The litigation involved secret defense contracts; a disgraced former Conservative government defense procurement secretary, Jonathan Aitken; and the prince.

The glimpse inside the prince's rarefied world came from Mohammed Said Ayas, a Lebanese business colleague of both Aitken and Mohammad. Ayas's fear that he might be sent to prison encouraged him to provide sworn details about the prince and the British minister.[1] Ayas was charged with conspiracy and "perverting the course of justice," but the prosecutors dropped the case in 1999. Aitken, who had to resign his government post after revelations of a completely unrelated sadomasochistic affair with a prostitute, eventually pleaded guilty to a perjury charge and was sentenced to eighteen months in prison. No charges were ever brought against the prince.[2]*

Ayas told investigators that Mohammad earned spectacular "commissions" on British defense contracts. He claimed that between 1972 and 1998 the prince received more than $1.2 billion in commissions, most of it hidden through front companies and bank accounts in different countries, particularly the Channel Islands, the secretive British offshore tax haven.[4]

Mohammad's main business vehicle is Al Bilad Establishment for Fair Trading and Economy of Riyadh, with offices worldwide. (Aitken was one of the directors of Al Bilad UK.) The firm owns, for example, 51 percent of the U.S./Saudi engineering and construction company Brown & Root Saudi, which managed the $1 billion refurbishment of the Ras Tanura export oil refinery in Mohammad's Eastern Province.[5] In 1977, at the age of twenty-seven, he put together his first great coup through his Al Bilad group. It was a contract for the Kingdom's first national telephone system—Mohammad was widely reported to have taken a commission of $500 million from the successful Swedish/Dutch consortium.[6]

In 1994, London's *Guardian* said Mohammad had "earned a reputation as the commission man par excellence."[7] The following year, journalist Jim Anderson, in an article speculating about the line of succession in the House of Saud after King Fahd's stroke, said that Mohammad "is regarded as able and ambitious, but his habit of demanding outrageously high 'commissions' on all foreign business deals has given him a tarnished reputation, even in a country where such kickbacks to royal persons are routine."[8]

While the size of the commissions paid to Mohammad, revealed as a by-product of the British litigation, may have dwarfed those of many other royals, what was as startling were the disclosures about his spending. In a family that has set modern-day standards for overindulgence, Mohammad seems to be the standard-bearer. Friends of his, as a London *Sunday Times*

---

*Aitken had sued the *Guardian* newspaper and Granada Television's investigative news program *World in Action* for libel in 1997, when they first reported his ties to Prince Mohammad and raised questions about payoffs for defense contracts, as well as charging that he had provided women for Mohammad and his entourage at a British spa. Not only did Aitken's lawsuits fail, but also during the proceedings he perjured himself. He ended up owing almost $4 million in legal costs. In 2000, it was disclosed that Prince Mohammad had secretly funded Aitken's libel suit.[3]

investigation discovered, estimated Mohammad had burned through a billion dollars on personal expenses in a little over a decade. Hodda Abdelrahman, who for two decades was the lady-in-waiting to Mohammad's wife, dubbed the prince "a mad spender."[9]

To the annoyance of conservative clerics in the Kingdom, Mohammad, who has repeatedly been told to adopt a lower profile, especially after 9/11, is still as likely to be found in Cannes as in Riyadh. And his indulgences in gambling, fast cars, and women are all considerable irritants to traditionalists.

"We used to visit Las Vegas a lot," says Sue Bennett, a New Zealander who had served as a flight attendant aboard Mohammad's BAC-111 jet from 1979 to 1981, when he was first making his fortune.

"I never saw him drink, and as for the stories of prostitutes, we used to hear a lot of those. I can't say myself, but he was good looking and you got that feeling he was a bit of a playboy. I think there definitely were girls from what others told me, but very expensive ones flown in, and they probably would have been insulted to be called that."

Bennett, who now runs her own recruitment company in her native New Zealand, has only fond memories of the prince, saying he's "no Donald Trump."[10]

In his South of France playground, though, few would describe Mohammad during the 1980s and 1990s as low-key. He invariably arrived in one of the family's fleet of private Boeing jets. His entourage often exceeded one hundred people, including several dozen maids, nannies, and bodyguards. In his traveling group were up to twenty-five handpicked Bedouins, barely literate, but always dressed in Western suits. Their role was to keep him entertained, which primarily meant long games of poker when he was bored.[11]

Mohammad varies where he stays when in Cannes. One of his homes—the Jardin de Nouf—sits on a hilltop called "Millionaires' Row," with a spectacular view of the bay. This palatial Renaissance villa, with twenty-five bedrooms and fifteen permanent staff, is encircled with a network of closed-circuit television cameras and security patrols. He also owns a sprawling ranch just outside Cannes. He once had an entire orchard uprooted from northern France and transplanted there so that his mother could have fresh fruit whenever she visited.[12]

Known as a collector of the finest cars, he spent more than $5 million to build an underground garage for the more than one hundred he keeps in Cannes. Although his private garage houses Rolls-Royces, Ferraris, Lamborghinis, and customized Mercedeses, the prince seldom drives them.[13]

And there are times when Mohammad arrives in Cannes and decides on a whim not to stay in one of his homes, but instead to be pampered at the luxurious Hotel Majestic, along the seaside resort's promenade. There, staff reported, he routinely ran bills of about $4 million for a summer stay for himself and his entourage.[14]

"He would put us, the staff, at the finest hotels in each city, from Marbella to London to Geneva," recalls Bennett. "I got huge sums of money for doing so little. He flew me first-class to New Zealand one Christmas so I could see my family I hadn't been with in four years. And his friends and cronies, who we used to fly around, would always tip. They'd give us five envelopes for each of the plane's crew, and each envelope would have a thousand pounds in it. He was very generous, and so were his friends." Bennett says the Saudi elite tipped the help for everything, and at least in her case, she "never wanted anything for it."

Mohammad keeps one of his yachts, the *Montkaj,* docked at Cannes. He spent nearly $2 million in the mid-1990s to build a private marina so he could have more privacy and his own jetty. It is a 220-foot yacht custombuilt in 1993 at an estimated cost of more than $65 million.[15] His other is the *Noorah of Riyadh,* a simpler yacht that cost about $35 million, and was used about one month a year before he gave it to his eldest son as a sixteenth birthday present.[16]

Besides cars and boats, Mohammad collects watches. He boasts five thousand, stacked in drawers and safes, one of them encrusted in diamonds and gold that he loves telling visitors cost $1.5 million.[17] Mohammad prides himself on giving away these watches. At his favorite jewelry shops, like Paris's Chatila & Sons, he spends over $10 million annually. And casinos around the world know him as one of their heaviest—and unluckiest—gamblers. In Las Vegas, not only does Caesars Palace give him an entire floor for his entourage, but they also assign a staff member to satisfy his every need. Business colleagues estimate that Mohammad has lost more than $500 million in casinos around the globe.[18]

Prince Mohammad has palaces in Riyadh and Jeddah for whenever he is in the Kingdom, but also spends much time in the neighboring Gulf state of Bahrain, where he keeps three homes, one of which is said to be worth more than $100 million. In Beverly Hills, he has a $30 million mansion, and on New York's East Side a $10 million apartment. Mohammad has a multimillion-dollar town house in London's exclusive Knightsbridge, a villa in Santa Barbara, California, a country estate in Virginia, and a fourteen-bedroom, $36 million château in Geneva.

Some observers of the prince's decadent lifestyle say that he has spent more than he has earned in "commissions" and is some $500 million in debt. Ayas, the prince's business colleague who became embroiled in the British defense company scandals of the late 1990s, said at that time that Mohammad squandered most of his riches on his homes, yachts, cars, and "whores, pornography . . . and such luxuries as chartered jets, ski chalets, and jewelry."[19] In a lawsuit against Ayas in 1998 in Britain, Mohammad charged that his former friend had embezzled $231 million from the prince's accounts.[20] Ayas ended up taking out full-page advertisements in British papers apologizing to the prince and denying what he had said about him in court papers.[21]

Others contend that Prince Mohammad is still among the world's richest men. An oft-repeated story—still unproven—is that after he had his 1995 stroke, King Fahd transferred up to $10 billion to Swiss bank accounts designated for his son.[22]

On the official Saudi embassy website (www.saudiembassy.net), the only reference to Mohammad is to his role as the Eastern Province governor, talking about building housing for the poor or opening a new power plant. None of the accounts of his Western lifestyle have been allowed by Saudi censors to be published in the Kingdom. Yet stories of his extravagance are still widespread.

It is a way of life that more restrained members of the House of Saud realize endangers their longevity since it could turn the average Saudi against them. Family members have encouraged Mohammad to spend more time in the Kingdom and tend to his duties as governor. In 2001, when he attended a festival in his province sponsored by the World Assembly of Muslim Youth, he noted the financial aid given by the Kingdom to help the families of Palestinian fighters and martyrs, and told the crowd, "The Islamic organizations must bare the Zionist designs to the world."[23] But besides such occasional rhetoric at public events, Mohammad's heart does not seem to be in politics and governing as much as his relatives'.

"The legitimacy of the House of Saud rests on its allegiance to the severity of Wahhabi doctrine," wrote Abdullah Ahmad in "Freeing the Prophet's Land," "which has not only encouraged militancy and fanaticism but elevated the hypocrisy of the royals, who live alternate lives in their luxury Manhattan penthouses, London townhouses and mansions in the English countryside, and fritter away millions in the casinos of Las Vegas, Monte Carlo, Cannes, St. Moritz, etc."[24]

It is precisely that view that worries some royals about the "mad spender" and those who emulate him. In their frenzy of indulgence, they give the fundamentalists the seeds for militant converts and campaigns against the monarchy.

CHAPTER 14

FUNDING TERROR

The Saudis have often tried to have it both ways when it comes to placating Western powers as well as the terrorists and extremists inside the Arab world. In the 1970s and 1980s, while officials like Prince Bandar privately reassured the United States that the Saudis were working backdoor channels to counsel the PLO to distance itself from violence, Saudi Arabia continued financing the PLO's most militant offshoots, including Hamas.[1] In 2002, Crown Prince Abdullah announced an aggressive initiative that pledged Arab normalization of relations with Israel in return for Israel's withdrawal from the occupied territories. That same year, Saudi money was exposed as subsidizing suicide bombers' families in the West Bank and the Gaza Strip.[2]

Saudi Arabia exerted tremendous influence on Egypt in the 1970s because of the billions in annual aid the Kingdom gave to Egypt's ailing economy. So when the Camp David peace accords came about in 1978, the Carter administration wanted the Saudis' support. Although Carter had sold, six months earlier and at great personal and political cost, sixty F-15 fighter jets to the Saudis, the royals vacillated when asked to publicly endorse Camp David. (Carter mistakenly thought the sale of the fighters would moderate Saudi policy toward Israel.) When implored by the U.S. administration, the Saudis finally refused. At a pan-Arab summit in December 1978, the House of Saud went so far as to offer $3.5 billion to

Sadat to renounce the peace accords. In March 1979, they severed diplomatic relations with Egypt, instituted a trade embargo, and cut off aid. The Saudi press vilified Sadat. So instead of helping the U.S. at a rare opportunity for a breakthrough in Middle East peace, the Saudis not only balked, but also did not even stay neutral. Instead, they provided the critical consensus for Arab opposition to peace with Israel.

While Saudi Arabia condemned Pakistan's efforts to get nuclear weapons, again in private meetings with U.S. officials, at the same time it helped fund its Sunni Muslim neighbor so generously that Pakistan's nuclear program resulted in successful bomb production as well as the export of nuclear technology to countries like Libya, Iran, and North Korea. After Israeli planes had destroyed Iraq's sole nuclear reactor in a June 1981 raid, the Saudis became convinced that an Islamic bomb to counter the weapons held by the Jewish state was indispensable. Its funding of Pakistan's nuclear program was an integral plank of Saudi foreign policy during the 1980s, despite their disavowal of such support to the U.S. government.[3]

Although the Saudis condemned Osama bin Laden for years, called him a renegade, and even technically issued an arrest warrant for him, they turned a blind eye as he received millions of dollars from supporters in the Kingdom, and unofficially agreed to let him stay free so long as he kept his jihad away from the Kingdom (something he did until May 2003).[4]

What is behind this apparent Saudi duplicity on so many critical matters? Some observers believe the Saudis' stance, as in the case of Sadat and Egypt, or their praise for early PLO terror attacks, is primarily for public consumption inside the Kingdom. Because the population has been raised on a steady diet of Wahhabi education, the Saudis must often adopt harsher positions than they would otherwise. But certainly some Saudi policies, like the secret funding of Pakistan's nuclear program, its scorched-earth policy for oil production, and its covert deals with bin Laden, have nothing to do with public consumption since they are never disclosed. Rather, it appears the House of Saud is driven by two major concerns that often complement each other: survival of the monarchy at all costs and a deep-seated belief that Wahhabism is the only true version of Islam.

Supporting the PLO was done because the Saudis judged rivals to Yasir Arafat—primarily pro-Marxist, secular Palestinian radicals—as a potential threat to incite insurrection in conservative Muslim theocracies.

The Saudis turned on their multibillion-dollar aid pipeline to Pakistan not just because they were Sunni Muslim brothers, but because they shared a border with Iran, and after Khomeini's ascension to power in 1979, Pakistan was a key ally in countering Iran's radical Shiite message.

In the 1990s, when conflicts in Chechnya, Bosnia, and elsewhere put Muslims at risk, Saudis generously sent hundreds of millions of dollars to finance refugee camps, schools, and other humanitarian projects. Two hundred and forty-one Saudi charity organizations are currently operating in the Kingdom and abroad. These groups receive annually between $3 billion and $4 billion, of which between 10 and 20 percent is sent abroad.[5] In the Kingdom, the government oversees charities. In 1994, a royal decree banned the collection of money for charitable causes without official permission. King Fahd established the Supreme Council of Islamic Affairs (al-Majlis al-A'la lil-Shu'un al-Islamiyya), headed by his brother Prince Sultan, to centralize, supervise, and review all aid requests from Islamic groups. The Kingdom even has a Directorate General of Zakat and Income Tax in the Saudi Ministry of Finance and National Economy. It is responsible for organizing, auditing, and collecting *zakat*—one of the five pillars of Islam, *zakat* is the giving of 2.5 percent of one's savings each year to charity.[6]

These are not charities in the sense that Americans understand the term. The Muslim World League and the International Islamic Relief Organization (IIRO), for example, are overseen by the grand mufti, the Kingdom's highest religious authority. Both the government and royals substantially fund them, and they utilize the Islamic affairs offices of Saudi embassies abroad. "The Muslim World League, which is the mother of IIRO, is a fully government-funded organization," the IIRO's Canadian chief testified in a 1999 court case. "In other words, I work for the government of Saudi Arabia."[7]

While Saudi charities help many legitimate Muslim humanitarian efforts, there is little doubt that they have also been major financiers of religious fundamentalists and terror groups. A former Treasury Department official, David Aufhauser, told a Senate investigating committee in 2004 that "north of $75 billion" has come from Saudi Arabia to export Wahhabism internationally, much of it through its charities.[8] Osama bin Laden, particularly from 1998 to 2001, called publicly on Saudis to make contributions to his and similar radical groups.[9]

In 2003, a Senate investigating committee was informed, "Saudi Arabia is present at every stage of Al-Qaeda financing, but primarily as the major source of funding. This is an indication that Osama Bin Laden has been able to leverage his family's position in the Kingdom to gain access to major sources of funding. It is also a sign that Saudi Arabia is offering several essential conduits for Al-Qaeda funding. Over the years Al-Qaeda used various conduits for moving money to its operational cells, mainly well established channels."[10]

Not only have the charities provided al Qaeda with critical funding, but also at times organizations, like the Red Crescent, have given al Qaeda operatives passports, and the IIRO funded at least half a dozen terror training camps in Afghanistan.[11] An IIRO chapter in the Philippines has been linked to one of bin Laden's sons-in-law, Jamal Mohammed Khalifa. Philippine and U.S. authorities have accused Khalifa of using the charity's funds to bankroll Abu Sayyaf, a terrorist group associated with Osama bin Laden's al Qaeda network.[12] Khalifa, believed by U.S. intelligence to manage money for his father-in-law in Malaysia, Singapore, Mauritius, and the Philippines, was arrested in the U.S. in 1994 for "providing financial, logistical and training assistance to international terrorism." The charge was later dropped because of insufficient evidence, and Khalifa was deported. He reportedly helped fund the Islamic Army of Aden, the group that claimed responsibility for the 1999 bombing of the USS *Cole* in Yemen.

Prince Al-Waleed, the world's fourth wealthiest man (see Chapter 12), acknowledges that al Qaeda and other terrorist groups benefited from Arab charities. "Clearly, there have been loose ends," he says.[13] In Saudi Arabia, where there is no income tax, people give generously. Al-Waleed, for instance, donated $100 million last year but carefully monitors where it goes. Not everyone is as meticulous in following the money once they donate it. As an August 2004 staff report of the 9/11 Commission concluded, others gave to charities and only agreed to sign the checks so long as they had guarantees that their money would flow to al Qaeda.[14] An unnamed source, described as "a former senior Clinton administration official," told *U.S. News & World Report* in 2002 that shortly after the fundamentalists had bombed the National Guard building in Riyadh in 1995, "at least two Saudi princes had been paying, on behalf of the Kingdom, what amounts to protection money to Osama bin Laden." The money was funneled through charities. The official added that Washington did not learn of the payments for two years. "There's no question they did buy protection from bin Laden," he told the magazine. "The deal was, they would turn a blind eye to what he was doing elsewhere. 'You don't conduct operations here, and we won't disrupt them elsewhere.' "[15]*

"The Saudis took little initiative with respect to their charities," concluded the 9/11 staff report on terrorist financing. "They did not make tough decisions or undertake difficult investigations of Saudi institutions to ensure that they were not being used by terrorists and their supporters."[16] The Saudi inaction is despite early warnings they received about the exploitation of their charities. In November 1994, French interior minister Charles Pasqua visited the Kingdom and met with top officials, including minister of interior Prince Nayef. He expressed concern about how charities were being misused for funding terrorist groups.[17] In 1996, a CIA report concluded that a startling one third of all Islamic charities were linked to terrorism. During this time, the Treasury Department believes a Muslim charity, Blessed Relief, that counted some of the most prominent Saudi businessmen on its board of directors, steered millions of dollars to bin Laden.[18] A year later, a joint security committee to share information on terrorism was established in the United States. It included representatives from the CIA, FBI, and NSA. In 1999 and 2000, several officials from that committee traveled to Saudi Arabia to raise similar concerns. And also in 1999, the Saudi government conducted an audit and discovered that its National Commercial Bank had transferred at least $3 million to charitable organizations believed to be bin Laden fronts.[19] Despite those warnings, and others, Saudi Arabia supported the suspect charities even after 9/11.[20]

One of the largest and most prominent Saudi charities is al Haramain, an aid organization investigated in the United States after 9/11 for suspected ties to al Qaeda and other terrorists.[21] Al Haramain, sometimes referred to as "the United Way of Saudi Arabia," has offices in fifty countries, including one in Ashland, Oregon. (That office was raided by IRS officials in February 2004, but no formal charges have been brought against any of its officers.) Some of the Kingdom's leading businessmen and members of the royal family are on al Haramain's board.

In May 2004, the Treasury Department designated the al Haramain Bosnian branch a terrorist entity.[22] The following month, the Treasury Department extended the terror designation to al Haramain branches in five

---

*Adel Al-Jubeir, a Saudi official, denied that the payments took place. "Where's the evidence? Nobody offers proof. There's no paper trail. . . . Why would they [princes] pay? These people threaten us more than they threaten you."

more countries and placed the charity's former Riyadh chief on its list of terror supporters for giving "financial, material and logistical support to the al Qaeda network."[23] Al Haramain branches in Asia and Africa were linked to the 1998 East African terror attacks that destroyed two U.S. embassies and killed more than two hundred. In 2004, instead of closing al Haramain, or changing its charter, the Saudi government announced instead that its activities would be confined merely to Saudi Arabia. The Saudis are slowly closing the offices outside of the Kingdom, but the Ashland, Oregon, bureau remains open. Recently al Haramain opened a new religious school in Jakarta, a city that is center of Islamic terror in Southeast Asia. Al Haramain is now run by Sheikh Saleh bin Abdul Aziz al-Ashaikh, Saudi minister for Islamic affairs.[24]

Even the 9/11 Commission, which drew few harsh conclusions about Saudi Arabia, found al Qaeda had relied heavily on charities to fund itself, "particularly those with lax external oversight and ineffective internal controls such as the Saudi-based al Haramain Islamic Foundation." Terrorists, concluded the 9/11 Commission, had been supported for years by "fertile fund-raising groups" in the Kingdom, "where extreme religious views are common and charitable giving was both essential to the culture and subject to very limited oversight."[25]

Saudi funding of Muslim groups in the former Soviet republics has spread the Wahhabi doctrine, especially in Uzbekistan, and helped fuel the violent insurgency in Chechnya.[26] Saudi-backed charities like the International Islamic Relief Organization and the World Assembly of Muslim Youth have sent money to extremists in such far-flung places as Kenya and Albania.[27] A year before the 9/11 attacks, Saudi Arabia agreed to give $50 million to the Al Quds Intifada Fund, established for the families of Palestinian suicide bombers, or as the fund refers to them, "martyrs."[28] (That is more money than the Saudi government pledged to the Muslim victims of the 2004 tsunami—$30 million.)

In October 2000, for instance, the Palestinian ambassador gave a check for $100,000 on behalf of Prince Salman (the father of the late Prince Ahmed, who was named by an al Qaeda leader as his primary Saudi contact), in his capacity as chairman of the board of directors of the Disabled Children Society and secretary general of the Supreme Tourism Commission, to Muhammad al-Durrah, the father of a Palestinian "martyr child." In the bequest by Prince Salman, the suicide bomber was called "the spark which made the world know about the barbaric acts being carried out by the Israeli aggressors against unarmed Palestinians."[29]

On April 11, 2002, just seven months after 9/11, King Fahd ordered a telethon to raise money for Palestinian "martyrs" that was broadcast on government-owned television. It brought in $92 million. One princess donated a Rolls-Royce and another gave her dowry. Almost one third of the money—$27 million—came from Prince Al-Waleed, whose $10 million offer for the victims of the World Trade Center had been rejected by New York mayor Rudy Giuliani.[30]

The House of Saud does not limit its flow of money to the Middle East. It was indispensable to Muslim groups that became Wahhabi acolytes during the battles for Bosnia and the Balkans. The Kingdom has sent more than $400 million there since 1993.[31] Bosnian intelligence agents concluded that the Saudi-based al Haramain charity essentially operated "as a channel for financing the activities of terrorist organizations."[32] In October 2001, a NATO force raided the offices of the Saudi High Commission for Aid to Sarajevo. Founded in 1993 by Prince Salman, the commission was supposed to help orphans. It had raised more than $600 million. But NATO found maps of Washington, D.C., with bull's-eyes drawn over government buildings, a computer program on crop duster aircraft (something Mohamed Atta, the ringleader of 9/11, had inquired about in the run-up to his operation), and photographs of previous American terror targets. Bosnian police, in 2002, also raided the office of Benevolentia, a branch of the Islamic Benevolence Committee that was headquartered in Jeddah until 1993. It was suspected of having ties to al Qaeda. During their search of Benevolentia's offices, they retrieved a computer file labeled "Tareekh Osama," or "Osama History." That file was delivered to the U.S. embassy. Dubbed the "Golden Chain" by investigators, it revealed al Qaeda's earliest Saudi financial sponsors. Included in the list of twenty names were twelve prominent businessmen, two of whom had been former government ministers, and six bankers (two on the list have not yet been identified).[33] The cumulative corporate net worth of those identified as the early Saudi sponsors of al Qaeda totaled more than $85 billion, or 42 percent of the Saudi annual gross national product. Those businessmen and bankers own or control sixteen companies ranking among the top one hundred Saudi companies.[34]

But Saudi money doesn't always support terrorists as directly as the evidence in the Golden Chain. In many instances, instead of being funneled directly to the terrorists, the money goes to Wahhabi causes that reinforce the extremist views that are the oxygen of the terror recruiters.

The House of Saud has, in the past, launched massive fund-raising campaigns for the International Islamic Relief Organization, the World Assembly of Muslim Youth, the Muslim World League, and a London-based charity, al-Muntada al-Islami.[35] Those four recently formed a U.S.-based trade group called the Friend of Charities Association, and hired a prominent Washington, D.C., firm to represent them.[36] Much of the work by these Saudi-backed charities is to propagate Wahhabi Islam. Al Haramain, for instance, annually spent more than a third of its budget on "religious propagation and education," while only a little over 10 percent went to relief work.[37] The Muslim World League considers it part of its mission to ensure that not an inch of Palestine is given up to Israel, and that "Zionist allegations" always be rebutted.[38]

Saudi money that flows to Muslim organizations always comes with the implicit understanding that the institution or mosque receiving it has to promote Wahhabism. In the Balkans, while Saudi money backed the Muslim fighters against the Serbs, half of the millions sent to Kosovo were for 388 religious "propagators" whose mission was to convert to Wahhabism those secular Muslims who had strayed. The Active Islamic Youth, a group founded with Saudi funds, distributes a popular book titled *Beliefs That We Have to Correct*.

In East Africa, for instance, where Saudi charities targeted Tanzania in particular, Wahhabi fundamentalists have taken over thirty mosques, and begun physically enforcing the rule that women only venture outside if fully covered. The Saudis send about $1 million a year to Tanzania to build new mosques and spread Wahhabism. The International Islamic Relief Organization has taken credit for funding 575 mosques in Indonesia, complete with accompanying Wahhabi literature and Korans.[39]

It is difficult, of course, to account for how all the money is used. "Say a charity builds a mosque in Bosnia that cost $800,000," said a terrorism-financing expert, who spoke on the condition of anonymity to the *Chicago Tribune* in 2004. "Did it really cost $800,000? Or did it cost $600,000, and $200,000 was siphoned off for Al Qaeda? Good luck trying to find that out."[40]

Even in countries without Muslim majorities, such as the United States and in Europe, the Saudis are actively exporting their unique version of the faith. The House of Saud has paid for 210 Islamic centers, more than 1,500 mosques, 202 colleges, and 2,000 primary schools in non-Muslim-majority nations.[41] Its $130 million printing plant near Medina, built in 1984 and devoted to producing Saudi-approved translations of the

Koran, is responsible for distributing 138 million copies worldwide (in 2004, the Saudis stopped distributing their version of the Koran in the United States).[42] According to Mohammed al-Khilewi, a Saudi diplomat who defected to the U.S. in the mid-1990s, "The Saudi government spends billions of dollars to establish cultural centers in the U.S. and all over the world. They use these centers to recruit individuals and to establish extreme organizations."[43]

In Germany, the King Fahd Academy, a Saudi-run school in a Bonn suburb, was founded in 1995 with a $20 million gift from the king. Teaching a strict Wahhabi curriculum to the children of Saudi diplomats and to German Muslims, the academy had a teacher who regularly called for jihad, schoolchildren who were taught the "determined action" of martyrdom, and a parents' group that is a who's who of suspected Islamic extremists. After 9/11, German authorities tried in vain to shut down the school. Chancellor Gerhard Schroeder, in a 2003 meeting with King Fahd in Riyadh, raised the issue. Schroeder later announced, "We discussed the issue, and it will be stopped." But it was not. The school remains open and still teaches from Wahhabi texts.[44]

In the United States, many Sunni community centers receive Saudi money. Estimates are that half the mosques and Islamic schools in America were built with Saudi funds.[45] Before the passage of the Patriot Act in the autumn of 2001, mosques were not only off-limits for law enforcement probes, but were not subject even to IRS reporting requirements. This made them ideal vehicles through which to funnel money.[46]

The largest Saudi-built American mosque is the King Fahd, a multimillion-dollar complex in Culver City, a Los Angeles suburb, financed privately by the king and one of his sons. In May 2003, the State Department refused reentry to Fahad al-Thumairy, a Saudi diplomat who also was the chief imam at that mosque. The 9/11 Commission Report says the State Department had determined al-Thumairy "might be connected with terrorist activity." Al-Thumairy ran an "extremist faction" at the mosque, and it was frequented by two of the eventual 9/11 hijackers, but the imam claimed he never met them, a denial The 9/11 Commission Report deemed "somewhat suspect."

King Fahd's own website shows sixteen Islamic and cultural centers the Saudis have underwritten from California to New York. A 2000 survey of 1,200 U.S. mosques, undertaken by four Muslim groups, found that 70 percent of imams were favorably inclined toward fundamentalist teachings, and nearly a quarter followed strict Wahhabism.[47] The Institute of Islamic and Arabic Sciences in Fairfax, Virginia, was funded largely by the Saudi embassy. It not only adhered to a fiery version of Islam in its courses, but the Institute trained at least seventy-five lay leaders to serve as chaplains in the U.S. military.[48]

Children in America receiving religious instruction in Arabic almost certainly have a Saudi textbook. A seventh-grade Saudi text, for instance, used in the U.S., explains one Koranic verse: "We have to be careful of infidels, and we can ask Allah to destroy them in our prayers."

The Michigan-based Islamic Assembly of North America (IANA), pre-9/11, got half its money from private Saudi contributors and the rest from the Saudi government. Four months before 9/11, the IANA's website justified "martyrdom operations," including crashing a plane "on a crucial enemy target." The IANA, like its brethren organization the Muslim World League, also spent considerable time proselytizing in America's prisons, where black Muslims are often receptive to the "Western non-Muslim is evil" message.[49] Radical Muslim newspapers published in the U.S., such as *Assirat al-Mustaqeem,* often talked about the duty of every Muslim to wage jihad against infidels, Zionist crusaders, and apostates. Not only was *Assirat al-Mustaqeem* Saudi funded, but the two successive editors prior to its post-9/11 closing returned to Saudi Arabia, where they received teaching positions at universities.

Some Saudi-backed charities, like the Chicago-based Islamic Benevolence Committee, were closed after 9/11. Only then did federal investigators discover the extent of the link between it and bin Laden operatives. The charity's director, although encouraged by friends to return to the safe haven of the Kingdom, did not leave before federal prosecutors indicted him in October 2002 on seven counts of conspiracy and racketeering.[50]

In December 2001, less than three months after the terror attacks on the World Trade Center and the Pentagon, Richard Newcombe, the head of foreign assets control in the U.S. Treasury Department, spent four days in Saudi Arabia trying to convince the Saudis they had to close the money pipeline to terror networks and religious extremists. The Saudis resisted freezing bank accounts merely because Washington said they were linked to terrorists. Saudi officials demanded that Newcombe produce incontrovertible proof that Saudi-funded charities were diverting money to terrorists. On December 8, the first day that Newcombe's delegation was in the Kingdom, interior minister Prince Nayef told reporters that he still did not

even believe that fifteen of the nineteen September 11 hijackers were
Saudis.

"The truth is missing so far," he said. Nayef had been opposed to U.S.
military action in Afghanistan to root out the Taliban and al Qaeda, having
told reporters in the middle of that campaign, "This is killing innocent
people. The situation does not please us at all."[51]*

It is not surprising that Newcombe and his party left the Kingdom
with only a promise that the Saudis would be helpful at the next meeting
in January.[53]

While American officials might have made little progress inside Saudi
Arabia in getting cooperation on closing the money line, they have been
more successful at closing the spigot unilaterally inside the U.S.

In 2002, federal agents raided the northern Virginia headquarters of
some of the nation's most respected Muslim leaders, searching for evidence of tax evasion and financial ties to terrorists. They filled a dozen
panel trucks with papers from offices and homes affiliated with a Herndon-
based foundation, a tight-knit cluster of prominent Muslim groups funded
by wealthy Saudis. Formerly known as the SAAR network—named for Sulaiman bin Abdul Aziz al-Rajhi, the head of the Saudi family that funded
it—the group consisted of more than one hundred Muslim think tanks,
charities, and companies, many linked by overlapping boards of directors,
shared offices, and the transfer back and forth of money. They gave generously to charities, invested in companies, and sponsored research, all with
the intent of spreading Islam. Among the findings of the federal investigators was the alleged transfer of millions of dollars from the network to two
overseas bankers who have been designated by the U.S. government as
terrorist financiers. Another is the network's history of ties to the militant
Muslim Brotherhood.[54]

In January 2004, immigration authorities arrested Omar Abdi Mohamed, a Somalian political refugee who lived in San Diego. Federal court
records show that while he is only held on immigration violations, he is
suspected of being a conduit for terrorist funds.[55] Mohamed was one of
thirty Saudi-financed preachers in the U.S., receiving $1,700 a month from

---

*The theme that Zionism or Israelis were behind al Qaeda was not just a passing thought
for the Saudi royals. Even as late as May 2004, when al Qaeda terrorists attacked a Saudi oil
facility in Yanbu and killed six Westerners, two of them Americans, Crown Prince Abdullah
said, "Zionism is behind it. It has become clear now. It has become clear to us. I don't say,
I mean . . . It is not 100 percent, but 95 percent that the Zionist hands are behind what happened." Prince Nayef said, "Al-Qaeda is backed by Israel and Zionism."[52]

Saudi authorities to teach Wahhabism at his decrepit Somali social center. The Saudi Islamic Affairs Ministry pays the salaries of 3,884 Wahhabi missionaries and preachers worldwide as of 2004, and the charity al Haramain supports a separate army of 3,000 missionaries. Mohamed also ran a charity, ostensibly to help Somalian famine victims, and over three years received $326,000 from the Global Relief Foundation, a private Illinois-based Islamic charity that after 9/11 was designated by the Treasury Department as a terrorist-financing entity that has "provided assistance to Osama bin Laden, the al Qaeda Network and other known terrorist groups" (a charge Global Relief denies and is contesting).[56]

The Saudis, under pressure from the Bush administration, have recently taken small steps toward accountability. Saudi charities must now get government approval before sending large amounts abroad. Half a dozen charities, including al Haramain, have had some restrictions placed on their fund-raising. Saudi foreign minister Prince Saud al-Faisal told *Time* in 2003, "The money aspect is now completely controlled, and your government knows it."[57]

But American officials say the cooperation is only "selective." "It is sort of like trying to stamp out crabgrass," says former U.S. ambassador to Riyadh Robert Jordan. "As soon as you stamp one of them out, something springs up somewhere else under a different name."[58]

Two years after the 9/11 attack, the FBI's acting director for counterterrorism, John Pistole, told the Senate Subcommittee on Terrorism, Technology and Homeland Security that "the jury's still out" on Saudi Arabia's efforts to stop terror financing. American counterterrorism officials complained that the Saudis still appeared to be protecting charities associated with the royal family and its friends. In one instance, the bank records of a charity suspected of being an al Qaeda front mysteriously disappeared.[59] David Aufhauser, the Treasury Department's general counsel, told the same Senate subcommittee that two years after the terror attacks, Saudi Arabia remained the "epicenter" for funding terrorism in general and al Qaeda in particular.[60]

In the summer of 2003, the FBI, in an unprecedented move that strained relations with the Kingdom, subpoenaed records for dozens of bank accounts, worth over $300 million, belonging to the Saudi embassy in Washington, part of an investigation into how much of the hundreds of millions of dollars Riyadh spends in the United States each year ends up in the hands of Muslim extremists.[61]

Although Saudi organizations and Saudi-sponsored Muslim groups had been probed in the past, this was the first investigation to directly look into Saudi government funding. The National Security Council's working group on terrorist financing approved the probe, and it concentrated on the embassy's Islamic and Cultural Affairs Office as well as the Saudi consulates around the United States.[62] The subpoenas were issued several weeks after the May 2003 deportation of Fahad al-Thumairy, who had worked since 1996 in the Los Angeles consulate's Islamic and Cultural Affairs division. Thumairy's visa was revoked, and he was deported because of suspected ties to terrorists, according to Homeland Security officials.

Saudi officials, who considered the subpoenas unnecessary grandstanding by the FBI, were outraged, but nevertheless complied by turning over embassy spending records covering millions of dollars that had flowed into America over the past twenty years.[63] In April 2004, *Newsweek* reported that federal investigators on the case had tentatively identified more than $27 million in "suspicious" transactions from Saudi embassy bank accounts—including hundreds of thousands of dollars paid to Muslim charities, clerics, and Saudi students who are being scrutinized for possible links to terrorist activity.[64]

The probe also has uncovered large wire transfers overseas by the Saudi ambassador to the United States, Prince Bandar bin Sultan. The transactions recently prompted the Saudi embassy's longtime bank, the Riggs Bank of Washington, D.C., to drop the Saudis as a client after embassy officials were "unable to provide an explanation that was satisfying," says a source familiar with the discussions. Riggs has had its own problems. In May 2004, federal regulators fined Riggs a record $25 million for a "willful, systemic" violation of anti-money-laundering law, specifically its handling of tens of millions in cash transactions in Saudi-controlled accounts under investigation for possible links to terrorism financing. By August 2004, the Justice Department had launched a criminal investigation into possible wrongdoing at the bank. Riggs pleaded guilty on January 27, 2005, to one count of violating the Bank Secrecy Act by failing to file reports to regulators on suspicious transfers and withdrawals by clients. It paid another fine of $16 million.[65] Investigators working on the case called Riggs "the Saudi Bank of America."

Some of the Saudi money found its way to at least two of the hijackers involved in 9/11, and the matter remains unresolved despite three years of official inquiries. A Saudi immigrant in California, forty-four-year-old

Omar al-Bayoumi, was a Saudi intelligence asset whose duty was to keep watch on possible dissidents in the Southern California area who could pose problems for the House of Saud.[66] He received $2,800 monthly from the Saudi Civil Aviation Authority, a job for which he never reported to work.[67] Al-Bayoumi not only "accidentally" met two of the hijackers, Khalid al-Midhar and Nawaf Alhazmi, immediately after they arrived in the United States, but he also befriended them by giving them around $40,000 to get settled in the States as a sign of "goodwill." He introduced them to another Saudi agent, Osama Bassnan, a radical who once hosted a party for Omar Abdel Rahman, the "Blind Sheikh" convicted of plotting a day of terror in New York. Bassnan had received $15,000 from the Saudi embassy in Washington, and his wife received checks—between $2,000 and $3,000 a month—from a charity list run by Princess Haifa bint Faisal, the wife of Saudi ambassador to the U.S. Prince Bandar.

Ostensibly, the charity from the Saudi government to the Bassnans was for thyroid surgery Bassnan's wife had in 1998. But the money from the Saudis continued into 2001, and starting in 2000, Bassnan's wife began signing over the checks to al-Bayoumi's wife. To many investigators, it looked like a backdoor way of funneling official Saudi money to two of the hijackers (something Prince Bandar and Princess Haifa adamantly deny, claiming their motive was only charity, "a common Saudi practice"). The money Princess Haifa gave to the Bassnans was drawn on an account she maintained in Washington at Riggs Bank.

When Crown Prince Abdullah met with President George W. Bush and his father in 2002, Osama Bassnan flew to Houston and met with a member of the crown prince's official delegation.[68] The subject of their discussion has never been disclosed. Bassnan is now back in Saudi Arabia. So is al-Bayoumi. The Saudis have adamantly denied that either is an intelligence agent. Prince Nayef, the interior minister responsible for internal security and the police, has publicly assured the pair that they will not be extradited to the United States, nor will American investigators be allowed to question them. Nayef is the leading royal who has promulgated his own conspiracy theory since 9/11. Similar to the Web-initiated free-floating conspiracy theory that Zionists somehow were behind 9/11 and that they warned four thousand Jews supposedly employed in the World Trade Center not to turn up for work that day, Nayef said, "We know that the Jews have manipulated the September 11 incidents, and turned American public opinion against Arabs and Muslims." Arab terrorist networks,

Prince Nayef elaborated, have links to foreign intelligence agencies, and "chief among them is the Israeli Mossad."[69]

Payments by the Saudi embassy or the ambassador's wife to two acquaintances of some of the 9/11 hijackers are not the only questionable ones on which federal investigators have focused. Between December 2000 and January 2003, $19,200 in checks from the Saudi embassy went to a Florida-based imam, Gulshair Muhammad al-Shukrijumah. He had been on the FBI's radar screen for testifying on behalf of convicted terrorist Clement Hampton-El. The imam's son, known as "Jafar the Pilot," is a suspected al Qaeda operative, currently the subject of a worldwide FBI manhunt. According to the Saudis, the imam was only a "missionary" whose payments ended in 2003.

Another FBI inquiry involves $70,000 in wire transfers on July 10, 2001, to two Saudis in Massachusetts. One of them wrote a $20,000 check that same day to a third Saudi at an address used by Aafia Siddiqui, a microbiologist who was the American operative for 9/11 mastermind Khalid Shaikh Mohammed. Most of that money was then wired to an account in Saudi Arabia, where the FBI lost the trail.[70] Interestingly, Prince Bandar deflects any questions about the difficulty of following money inside the Kingdom by turning the issue around. He told PBS in 2002, "Money leaves Saudi Arabia, goes to Europe, and we can follow it; goes to the United States, America, and we lose contact with it."*

Even after 9/11 the Saudis were not afraid to give money to groups and individuals the U.S. designated terrorists. In 2003, Khalid Mishaal, a senior leader of Hamas, the militant Palestinian organization that has claimed responsibility for hundreds of civilian deaths through its suicide attacks in Israel and the occupied territories, attended a charitable fundraising conference in Riyadh where he chatted at length with Crown Prince Abdullah.

According to a summary of the meeting written by a Hamas official,

---

*Other money trails found by federal probers might not have anything to do with terrorism, but could be personally embarrassing to Prince Bandar, the dean of the Saudi diplomatic corps in Washington. Records show $17.4 million in wire transfers in 2003 from the official Saudi Defense Ministry account to a man in the Kingdom identified only as the coordinator of "home improvements/construction" for Bandar. The funds were to build the prince a new palace, his eighth. A lawyer for the Saudi embassy said, "Just because it went through a government account doesn't mean it's not his personal money." Bandar is well known in Washington and Riyadh for his substantial personal expenditures. In 1997, for instance, he donated $1 million to George Herbert Walker Bush's presidential library in College Station, Texas.

Mishaal and other Hamas representatives thanked their Saudi hosts for continuing "to send aid to the people through the civilian and popular channels, despite all the American pressures exerted on them. . . . This is indeed a brave posture deserving appreciation."[71]

Mishaal is on the U.S. Treasury Department's list of terrorist financiers. At least 50 percent of Hamas's current operating budget of about $10 million a year comes from Saudi contributions, according to estimates by American law enforcement officials, diplomats in the Middle East, and Israeli officials. After 9/11, the Saudi portion of Hamas funding actually grew as donations from America, Europe, and other Persian Gulf countries dried up.[72]

Several large federal investigations continue into the Kingdom's funding of Saudis studying in the U.S., including many enrolled in flight schools. The probes are part of a larger effort by the FBI and the Treasury Department to trace as much as they can of the up to $4 billion the Saudi government spends around the world each year to spread Wahhabism and support charities. And probers are also looking at how Saudi Arabia occasionally disguises the trail of the money it spends on its causes and charities.

For instance, when radio ads critical of Israel ran in fifteen U.S. cities in the spring of 2004, the sponsor was identified as the Alliance for Peace and Justice, described by its Washington, D.C., public relations firm, Qorvis Communications, as a syndicate of Middle East policy groups based in America. But when Qorvis reported its ad work to the Justice Department in 2002, it revealed that funding for the $679,000 campaign actually came from the Saudi government (Qorvis receives more than $200,000 a month from the Saudis for its services).[73]

President Bush, in 2003, refused to allow publication of 28 pages in the 900-page Joint House-Senate intelligence report into the September 11 attacks. Bush based his decision to black out this material on the grounds that the information is part of a continuing investigation. The pages are reported to show that Saudi authorities allowed millions of dollars to flow to terrorist groups and individuals through supposed charities and other front organizations in the U.S. One man reportedly named in the blacked-out section is none other than Osama Bassnan, the Saudi who was the link between two of the 9/11 hijackers and money from Prince Bandar's wife.

Some Bush critics believe that the release of the twenty-eight now classified pages from the congressional report would not hinder or imperil any ongoing probe, but that the administration withheld the information so as not to further embarrass the Saudis and expose how they had used their money in supporting extremists.

While the Bush administration may delay the public's right to see the material Congress gathered, the public disclosure of those pages and the eventual conclusion of the federal criminal probes now under way may eventually shed some light on the extent to which Saudi government ministries, officials, and members of the royal family have knowingly donated millions of dollars that encourage extremism and terror worldwide. Six 2002 class action lawsuits filed on behalf of the 9/11 victims against eight Saudi charities and several senior officials of the royal family for funding terrorism promised to show how money destined for philanthropic purposes ended up fueling bin Laden. Six of the largest Saudi charities formed a bloc in 2003 to fight the legal charges in the United States. They each denied having knowingly sent any money to terrorists. (In January 2005, the lawsuit was dismissed against Saudi Arabia, the senior officials, and several banks, but was continued against several companies and all the charities.)[74]

According to the latest figures available, since September 11, 2001, Saudi Arabia has frozen forty-one bank accounts belonging to seven individuals for a total of $5,697,400, or 4 percent of the total amount of terrorist-related funds frozen around the world. Given its track record of being the major source of financing for terror organizations, the actions by the House of Saud are obviously inadequate.

The charities are inventive. They often deal in huge sums of cash. It is unlikely that the weak Saudi rules will do much more than force them to be more creative in sending funds to Islamic militants worldwide. Turning off the Kingdom's money spigot to terrorists will require far more than the House of Saud's window dressing, intended to placate the Bush administration since 9/11.

CHAPTER 15

THE FUTURE?

King Fahd turned eighty-two in 2005. He is grossly overweight, suffers from debilitating diabetes, and a 1995 incapacitating stroke has left him confined to a wheelchair. At that time, he ceded effective power to one of his twenty-five half brothers, Crown Prince Abdullah, who is a strong pan-Arab nationalist, not nearly as pro-American as Fahd. Abdullah had been against the deployment of American soldiers in the Kingdom after Iraq invaded Kuwait, but had been overruled by the king.[1] Abdullah, however, does not have the unequivocal support of Fahd's six full brothers and their sons, who often act as a power unto themselves inside the House of Saud. The anti-Abdullah contingent holds the prime positions of minister of defense and interior, more than half the governorships of the provinces, and key positions in the army, security force, and diplomatic corps.

Abdullah himself is eighty-one, semiliterate, and considered by many observers a poor decision maker.[2] His successor in the unofficial royal line is Prince Sultan, the defense minister, who at seventy-nine has been linked to the arms dealer Adnan Khashoggi and billions of dollars in payoffs. After those princes, there is no clear successor, although the speculation is that Prince Salman bin Abdul Aziz, the governor of Riyadh, younger brother of Prince Sultan and half brother of Abdullah, would step in. Salman, in his early sixties, is the father of Prince Ahmed, the media magnate who died after being named by al Qaeda leader Abu Zubaydah as one of his chief contacts inside the Kingdom.

The age of the line of successors is of concern to Saudi watchers. The specter of a crippling tribal feud after Fahd's death is a worry. But the country has many more immediate problems than playing the guessing game of who will next be king.

The Kingdom has run a deficit for twenty-one of the last twenty-two years. More than a third of the nation's annual budget goes to military hardware, while the money spent on education and health steadily declines. The budget deficit is approaching $200 billion. A third of the nation does not attend school. The demands of the ever-expanding royal family on the national finances are increasing. A water shortage that has been on the horizon for years has not been addressed.[3]

Islamic fundamentalists grow stronger all the time. Osama bin Laden has broken his uneasy truce with the House of Saud, and shattered whatever pretensions the two had of living in peaceful coexistence. For a country that had given so many millions to bin Laden's causes over the years, Osama's December 15, 2004, one-hour Internet diatribe against the monarchy and on the need to topple their corrupt regime must have been particularly galling. But the Saudi royals created their own problems when it came to the fundamentalists. By mismanaging most of the country's income during the boom years after the 1973 OPEC embargo, they laid the groundwork for the fundamentalists' most persuasive charge, that the House of Saud has squandered the nation's wealth and has nothing to show for it in terms of winning a Middle East peace, or more respect from the United States and other Western countries.

And the hypocrisy of the Saudi royals, their decades of flouting Islam's strictest tenets against drinking, womanizing, and gambling, is no longer ignored by a new generation of religious leaders. The Wahhabi-run Council of Ulemas, as early as 1991, issued an appeal for democratic reform inside the Kingdom and decried the extent of corruption. The Council is increasingly composed of younger clerics—dubbed "neo-fundamentalists"—who not only consider the lavish lifestyle of some princes reprehensible, but also believe the Sauds' relationship with the West, particularly America, is heretical. The neo-fundamentalists are critical of the traditional ulema, in the pay of the monarchy since the country was founded. They urge the older clerics to speak out more forcefully about abuses in the House of Saud and the grievances of average Saudis.[4]

The country's youth population has more than doubled in two decades, and the standard of living has dropped precipitously.[5] The once unshakable Saudi social network that provided everything from cradle-to-grave education, medical care, and even housing has now retrenched and is under growing financial constraints. As late as the 1980s, patients at the King Faisal Specialty Hospital were still eating their meals with gold-plated utensils.[6] That certainly seems an anachronism in a country where unemployment among those under thirty has reached 25 percent. The Kingdom's per capita income has collapsed from more than $28,000 in 1981 to less than $7,000 today.[7] Three million poorly paid foreign workers, most from Yemen, Pakistan, Lebanon, and Syria, do the jobs no one else wants, at salaries and with second-class treatment that no Saudi would accept. Higher taxes have been imposed on gasoline, electricity, and even telephones, putting pressure on ordinary Saudis. The Kingdom's once fabulous infrastructure is showing its age. Even the wealthy merchant class is ailing, with imports of luxury cars and purchases of yachts down sharply from the heyday of the 1980s. A huge drug problem, much of it involving heroin from neighboring Iran and Afghanistan, has spread, to the horror of religious authorities and the social bureaucrats who understand the long-term costs to the society.

The House of Saud seems more cut off than in earlier decades from the aspirations of common workers in the streets of Riyadh or Jeddah. The gap between the ultrarich—several thousand of the royal family still living in the extravagance of Byzantine emperors—and the pinched lifestyles of most Saudi citizens is a veritable time bomb for radical social change. Even the lowliest prince lives lavishly compared to most Saudis. The budgets of the royal household and the military remain bloated. No serious campaign at rooting out corruption and waste has been launched.

After Ibn Saud, each king has promised political and social reform but very little has been accomplished. There is no freedom of the press, and any criticism of the royal family, the government, or the leading religious figures is illegal (the government's control of the press is so tight that it took two days before it allowed newspapers to report that Iraq had invaded Kuwait in 1990).[8] Peaceful assembly is not allowed. Political parties are mostly banned—different political parties would be a violation of the Koran's bar on divisive sects, contend the Saudis—although some very minor ones are permitted to give the appearance of free discussion and debate (the Labour Socialist Party and Arab Nationalist Party are but two).

In October 2003, when there was an unprecedented gathering of several hundred young Saudis on King Fahd Street in the capital's Ulayah District to discuss the Human Rights in Peace and War Conference, Saudi police broke up the gathering as illegal. "Police quickly intervened to bring the traffic situation back to normal," said the government's official statement. Interior minister Prince Nayef commented the next day, "This is worthless barking and I don't think anyone will respond, except ignorant people. This is illegal and we hope Saudi citizens will rise above it."[9]

Some defenders of the House of Saud say that evidence of deliberate liberalization is in the Shoura (Advisory) Council to the king, composed of representatives from around the Kingdom. But women are banned, and it has no popular accountability. The Council is little more than a rubber stamp for the crown. Ultimate control resides squarely with the 75,000-man National Guard, run by the crown prince. It is as large as the army. Command positions are reserved only for members of the royal family.

Giving in to political pressures for reform after 9/11, however, the House of Saud authorized the first ever, three-stage nationwide elections for municipal councils, held in February 2005. The elections themselves show how far the Saudis have to go in terms of real reform. Women were banned from voting. And half the council members were elected through the vote, while the government appointed the other half. Moreover, since there have never been national elections, there were no registered voters. The drive to get Saudi men to register was largely a failure, with many viewing the elections as meaningless. In the capital of Riyadh, out of 600,000 potential voters, only 14 percent—86,462 men—registered.[10] This despite the official Saudi government efforts to encourage registration with prominent posters of senior princes signing up to vote. "It didn't occur to me [to register]," one twenty-nine-year-old public relations worker told the Associated Press. "How would it change my life?" asked another young Saudi, a twenty-eight-year-old electric company supervisor. "I want democracy, but making all that effort for municipal elections is not worth it."[11]

When the vote was held on February 10, fewer than 10 percent of eligible voters in Riyadh turned up at the polling stations. The seven representatives elected from the capital were all conservative Islamists backed by religious authorities. They overcame flashy campaigns run by wealthy businessmen and real estate developers. Outside of Riyadh, candidates from the largest tribes and provincial families won the seats.[12]

Besides the lack of any semblance of real democracy, there are few other social rights. Academic freedom of discussion on university campuses does not exist. There is extensive internal police surveillance on dissidents and ordinary Saudis suspected of being disloyal to the crown. Police have no standards to satisfy before they can place wiretaps on phones or initiate surveillance on citizens. A person can be arrested for merely acting "suspiciously" and there is no right to a speedy trial, counsel, or bail. Amnesty International has amply demonstrated that stomach-churning torture is almost universal when it comes to political prisoners.[13]

The number of educated people has exceeded the country's ability to absorb them, meaning that the House of Saud cannot even buy a graduate's loyalty with a good job and decent pay. The tribal system, which the monarchy exploited to its maximum advantage for decades, is slowly disappearing. Without secular opposition parties, the fundamentalists are the breeding ground for a surge of distrust and dislike of the monarchy.

Is it likely that a convergence of religious purists like bin Laden and an angry merchant class that feels the country's natural resources and wealth are being squandered by incompetent royal leadership will join forces to topple the House of Saud? Is it similar to what happened in Iran twenty-five years ago with the shah? Not necessarily. It is more likely that booming oil prices since the 2003 U.S. invasion of Iraq will extend the House of Saud's lifeline for some indeterminate time. In the 1980s, the Kingdom reaped more than $100 billion a year in profits from oil prices that averaged in the low $40-a-barrel range. But in the 1990s, Saudi Arabia was battered by prices hovering at about $17 a barrel. These low prices, on top of paying $60 billion to underwrite Desert Storm, and the billions more wasted on Saddam Hussein's efforts to win a futile war against Iran, left the country in debt. The flood of new money from prices now hovering above $50 a barrel will buoy many bad government programs of the past decade and give some life to a moribund welfare state. Also, the billions in new petro profits will mean less unemployment inside the Kingdom and more money for a wider class of workers. Good economic times often are the best antidote to extremist movements, whether religious or political. But if the House of Saud intends to build its stability on the current high price of oil, it is a poor plan indeed for the longevity of the ruling clan.

September 11 and its aftermath forced the hand of the Saudi leadership on many fronts. Reluctantly, they deemphasized their labyrinth of contacts with hard-liners in Pakistan's intelligence services, radicals in the Palestinian Authority, and rebel Muslim fundamentalists in South Asia. All communications with Osama bin Laden, even through circuitous third-party communications, have evidently ended. The mullahs have toned down their harshest rhetoric. There are now regular warnings against ultra-extremism in the propagation of the faith. In late 2003, the government suspended more than 1,300 imams and preachers.[14] Three hundred and fifty-three imams were sacked for extremist preaching, and more than 1,000 other clerics were sent for "retraining."[15]

This does not mean that Wahhabism is any less extreme than it was when the country was founded in 1932, but only that the violent anti-Western interpretations of bin Laden and other militants have been rejected as "deviationist thought." The easy ways of financing radicals worldwide through mosques and charities are in the early stages of a mild crackdown.

Since a series of militant fundamentalist attacks inside the Kingdom, which began with a May 12, 2003, suicide bombing of three Riyadh housing projects favored by foreigners, Saudi military officers and security police are dying in pitched gun battles with al Qaeda militants. After the May bombing, "the scales fell from the eyes of the Saudis," said Deputy Secretary of State Richard Armitage.[16] Al Qaeda, through bin Laden personally, now has recommitted itself to the downfall of the monarchy. On June 23, 2004, the Saudi leadership offered the fundamentalists a thirty-day peace feeler, to spare the lives of any militants who surrendered. One retired firebrand in the north of the country gave up, but it turned out he was not wanted for any crimes. The amnesty offer flopped.[17]

On August 16, 2004, senior clerics went so far as to issue a fatwa condemning the activities of Islamist militants. The Council of Senior Clerics pledged full support for the authorities' crackdown, accusing those who regarded terrorists' activities as religiously sanctioned of being "misguided and ignorant." "These acts have nothing to do with Jihad for the sake of God," said the statement.[18]

Before September 11, Crown Prince Abdullah was committed to pressuring the United States over the Israeli-Palestinian issue. In a rare public rebuke, Abdullah had canceled a state trip to visit President Bush because he was so infuriated with American support for Israeli prime minister Ariel Sharon. George H. W. Bush telephoned Abdullah in the summer of 2001 to assure the crown prince that his son had the right feelings about Saudi Arabia.[19] But Abdullah was still irritated by what he considered the Bush administration's public tilt toward Israel. He wrote a letter to the president, warning against the U.S. stance on Israel and bemoaning how far apart the Saudis and Americans had drifted. Bush replied in a day, saying that he supported two states, Israeli and Palestinian, and that the U.S. would work to halt the violence. Three days later was 9/11.

After the terror attacks, in deference to the American tragedy and the possible complicity of Saudi supporters of bin Laden in an even wider terror conspiracy, Abdullah was as polite to the U.S. as King Fahd would have been. Moreover, when fifteen of the nineteen hijackers turned out to be Saudi, and the press eventually uncovered the fact that one of the hijackers had received money from Prince Bandar's wife as part of her charity work, the Saudis were now on the defensive. In January 2002, Riyadh acknowledged that 100 of 158 alleged al Qaeda suspects being held at Guantánamo Bay were Saudi citizens.[20]

When the war in Iraq began, the Saudis allowed the U.S. the use of some key facilities from which to successfully wage the battle, but kept their role secret. Inside the Kingdom, public-opinion polls showed that 90 percent disagreed with the U.S. position regarding Iraq and the rest of the Arab world. Only Israel is more disliked among average Saudis than the United States.[21]

In February 2002, when Crown Prince Abdullah announced a new initiative that pledged Arab normalization of relations with Israel in return for Israel's withdrawal from the occupied territories, most Saudis bitterly opposed the plan. Many were equally furious when Abdullah reversed his earlier stance of not visiting Bush because of the White House's pro-Israel tilt, and instead went to Crawford, Texas, to see the president at his ranch in April.[22] The summit was a disaster by all accounts, and the Saudi contingent was incensed when Bush held Abdullah's hands and led him in Christian prayer. The reports only added to a feeling inside the Kingdom that the royal family was not standing tough against the American administration. The gap between the House of Saud's policy toward the United States and the sentiment dominant in the Saudi public seemed even wider after 9/11.[23]*

The House of Saud is caught in a dilemma. With one foot firmly en-

---

*Even on a post-9/11 trip to try to mend fences with the U.S., the royal family could not restrain itself from reverting to its traditional Wahhabi behavior. Before the crown prince and his entourage left Texas for the Kingdom, they requested there be no female airport employees on the ramp when they boarded, and that their private jet not be placed under the control of any female air traffic controllers once it took off. The Federal Aviation Administration and the State Department acquiesced. It only became public two days after the Saudis had left, when Dennis West, an air traffic controller for twenty-four years, told *The Dallas Morning News.*

trenched in Wahhabi Islam and pan-Arabism and the other set in the West in a strategic and economic partnership with the United States and Europe, it seems unsure how to best proceed. In a post-9/11 world, where extremists on each side have clearly staked out their positions and are in mortal combat, the compromises and appeasements on which the House of Saud built its survival now please virtually no one.

"You have to ask the simple question," says Prince Al-Waleed. "Why fifteen Saudis? You can't just say it happened by coincidence. Clearly, there's something wrong with the way of thinking here, with the way people are raised." For billionaire investors like Al-Waleed, while the United States should adopt a more balanced approach to Arab-Israeli issues, the answer remains largely in Saudi control: the Kingdom must accelerate social, political, and economic reforms and better confront the causes of the September 11 terrorist attacks.

"It's very important for moderate people in the Arab Islamic world to have their voice heard. We are not going to be silent anymore," he says.

As for reforms in Saudi Arabia, Al-Waleed believes the country has "reached the point of no return. We are very slow by nature and that's unfortunate."[24] Saying there is no such prohibition in the Koran, Al-Waleed is one of the few moderate voices willing to speak out for the rights of women to vote and to drive cars.

The Bush administration also believes that the answers to stopping terrorism and the Wahhabi role in encouraging it are to be found in the Kingdom. But beyond reform, the administration is looking for a partner willing to vigorously fight the financing and the terrorists on the ground. While publicly complimenting the Saudis on their antiterrorist cooperation, administration officials privately are bitter about the Saudi failure to help the Treasury Department stop terror financing, a lack of cooperation on a joint terrorism task force that was supposed to be operational by 2003, and their continuing financial support for spreading Wahhabism and its strident message at a time when moderation is needed most. Saudi Arabia, despite its best efforts, is not currently a trusted ally in Washington.

The House of Saud has tried to change that perception with an enormous public relations campaign launched in America after 9/11. The monarchy hired some of Washington's best lobbying firms, and spent millions running full-page newspaper ads and filling the airwaves with slick packages about what a great friend Saudi Arabia was to America.[25] In one two-week period after 9/11, there were 1,541 Saudi ads on American television. The crown prince's national security advisor, Adil Al-Jubayr, temporarily set up offices in Washington to manage the public relations campaign, and to personally take to the airwaves to counter the rush of negative post-9/11 media coverage the Kingdom received. But the campaign did little to change public or government opinion.

On the other hand, the Islamic extremists like bin Laden view the House of Saud as a corrupt family whose craven attitude toward the West is humiliating to Arabs everywhere.[26] Their overthrow is now as important a goal to the fundamentalists as is the expelling of the U.S. from all Muslim countries.

The House of Saud has no easy choices. Reform of an outdated monarchy will have to be quick enough to satisfy the pent-up frustration among Saudi youth who want some form of representative government that is less corrupt and more accountable. But if it moves too quickly, it will destabilize the peace within the fractious monarchy itself, especially when King Fahd dies and succession again confronts the country.

The royal family firmly controls the provincial governorships, the armed forces, the remarkably omnipresent secret police, and most completely the oil industry, the Kingdom's financial backbone. The opposition, on the other hand, is fragmented, and despite the exhortations occasionally emanating from bin Laden, leaderless.

This is not to say the House of Saud is safe. Fundamentalism still holds tremendous appeal among many social classes in the Kingdom. Strict Wahhabism promises a safer, traditional world that is insulated from the West's corrupting and false values. For many Saudis, a future of strident Islam seems more comforting and less threatening than the past decades of fitful attempts at modernization and coexistence with the West. There is a growing movement among the religious and the lower classes to enter a phase of "Western detoxification." That poses a great challenge for the royals in maintaining the necessary business and military links they need with the West while minimizing the cultural influences of their American and European partners.

Petrodollars and religion have kept the country glued together and the Sauds in power. But a prolonged oil slump, or an international marketplace where alternative energy sources reduce the demand for crude, might be the catalyst for violently changing the monarchy's repressive control.

The question that cannot be answered now is whether the House of Saud will endure by relying increasingly on its religious leaders, reaffirming the bond made over two hundred years ago between Saud and al-Wahhab and returning Arabia to a more authoritarian, isolated, and inflexible country. Or will the royals slowly relinquish enough control over the government so that vast numbers of Saudis can still support them while also feeling there is a government that is responsive to their modern needs and desires? The future of the United States in the Middle East, and the strength and durability of the American economy, depend largely on how a new generation of leaders in Riyadh answer those questions.

ACKNOWLEDGMENTS

Sometimes I feel like I am the waiter who brings a huge bill to a large group of dinner guests, and as I place it on the table, everyone runs away. When I call around near the end of book research to ask whether the dozens of people who were indispensable in helping me want a simple thank-you, most have politely declined, particularly on the last few books. I haven't started to take it personally yet; I do realize that many of those who provided critical information did so under some potential threat to themselves or their families, especially those residing in Muslim countries where the mere act of helping a Western journalist could spell trouble with extremists. I do not take lightly the personal danger risked by some of those who helped. Even when potential bodily injury was not an issue, some sources feared that their appearance in my book might mean the end of their current employment. While pleased to assist me, no one wanted that helpfulness to put them in an unemployment line.

I owe everyone who did help behind the scenes a wonderful thank-you. I will forever be indebted to your overall generosity and stand in awe of your courage and perseverance. You know who you are.

There are some, thankfully, who are willing to accept a public token of my appreciation. As on previous works, author Steve Emerson was always generous in pointing me to key sources and providing some of his own voluminous research. Daniel Pipes, director of the Middle East Forum, again tapped into his incredible database to send me to people who turned out to be very helpful in explaining the intricate politics of the House of Saud. Brendan Howley, a wonderfully effective Canadian investigative journalist, shared his expertise on the intelligence trade and helped me cut through some difficult obstacles in that area. Author and journalist John J. Sullivan shared willingly his wonderful original reporting on the issue of whether the flight of Saudi nationals from Tampa to Lexington only two days after 9/11 was not a big deal, as was concluded by the 9/11 Commission, or rather was an extraordinary event that the Commission either negligently or intentionally glossed over.

Thanks also, for an assortment of information and advice, to Stefan Tolin, military intelligence coordinator of security for the Mideast and Near Eastern divisions of the CIA; financial market statistical analyst J. Michael Oliver; John Pike, the director of GlobalSecurity.org; Sue Bennett, for sharing her recollections of having worked for Prince Mohammad bin Fahd bin Abdul Aziz; Ali Alyami, senior fellow of the Washington-based Saudi Institute; and former senator Bob Graham, for providing some key links to information about his own hard work on exposing possible Saudi links to 9/11.

My wife, Trisha, and I enjoyed the hospitality of South Carolina law firm Motley & Rice. Known as one of the nation's premier firms for complex, large-case litigation, it is the chief counsel on 9/11-related litigation against individual Saudi officials, government-sponsored charities, and suspected members of terrorist groups. Motley & Rice's investigative work in preparation for their case has been funded generously and personally by lead partner Ron Motley and has one of the largest private databases anywhere on terrorism and the Saudis. Many thanks, for what they could share, to Ron Motley, Mike Elsner, David Draper, Justin Kaplan, Carolyn James, and Robert Haefele. Their hard work is helping to shed light on some of the secrets still surrounding 9/11 and the Saudis.

A special thanks is due to Lois Ann Battuello, a California researcher and investigator specializing in politics, intelligence matters, and terrorism. Lois is one of many similar researchers who have dedicated much of their time since 9/11 to very lonely, and often unrewarding, searches for kernels of truth and new details of credible information. She was unstinting in her help, enthusiastically fielding, for almost two years, literally hundreds of requests on matters as mundane as the construction of oil pipelines to intricate issues involving terror financing and circuitous money trails through international banks. Lois may be disappointed that I could not cover in depth the many wonderfully enticing peripheral issues that she often developed in considerable detail, but I have little doubt we shall work together again in the future, and have the opportunity for more of her good research to see the light of day.

Andrew Wylie and Jeffrey Posternak do the unenviable task of being my agents. No one likes an agent, really. Publishers always think the agent made them pay too much. The author invariably thinks the agent did not get enough. In my case, I'm lucky to have found agents who break the rules. They perform with great professionalism both with the publisher and on my behalf, and they work hard to ensure that I have enough money to complete the often expensive research.

In a day when many authors apparently like to complain about little support or help from their publishers, I am very fortunate to have a great one. Including this book, my last seven have been with Random House, and we have built a solid working relationship. Random House had to turn this book around quickly once I submitted the draft, and do so while keeping the contents under wraps. They did so seamlessly. Daniel Barrett was invariably helpful on my many arcane requests. Michael J. Burke, the copy editor, performed admirably, and his efforts to keep order among the dozens of variations of spellings of many Arabic names used in the book will be forever appreciated. Beth Pearson, my dear friend who oversaw the editorial production, again put in many more late-night hours than I had any right to expect. She has a keen eye for details, which always helps in a book crammed with so much information. Managing editor Benjamin Dreyer maintained effortless control over a demanding schedule.

In an increasingly litigious society, where individuals will sometimes use lawsuits as tools of punishment rather than searches for the truth, I could not be more satisfied or feel more comfortable than to be under the careful purview of Laura Goldin. Senior editor Dana Edwin Isaacson was kind enough to read the first draft and make some suggestions that made it instantly better and tighter.

This book would never have gotten off the ground if I had not had a publisher willing to take a chance that I could pursue such a broad topic and return with a story that also broke some news. But Gina Centrello, the president and publisher of Random House, is rare in the business in that she is willing to give a reporter the chance to tackle such a story without being sure what, if anything, the book will eventually be. I am indebted to her for this vote of confidence.

Any of you who have read one of my earlier books has seen the fulsome thanks I give to my longtime editor and friend, Robert Loomis. This book is dedicated to him, and he deserves more credit than can be bestowed on him in a simple paragraph. He has a knack for bringing out the best in my work, knowing when to push me for harder reporting and how to control a book project that at times can seem to grow unwieldy and at other times venture off into areas too tangential to hold the readers' interest. The quality of this book is very much due to his innate sense of good journalism and his skillful editing.

It is getting more difficult in each book to thank my wife, Trisha, as I am running out of synonyms for "indispensable" and "fantastic." She has been my inseparable partner since my first project on Josef Mengele in the early 1980s, but her role with my books has evolved. Initially, Trisha was an indefatigable researcher, her natural inquisitiveness leading to wonderful reporting discoveries. Then, as she became more confident in her work, she helped me choose book subjects, marshal the voluminous research into cogent outlines, and eventually help with rough chapter drafts and a keen editing eye. Anyone who knows her marvels at her enthusiasm, and I get the benefit of sharing that tremendous energy with her in our work. Her passion fuels me. I must sound like a broken record when I say she deserves to have her name on the front of the book as much as mine. Trisha is a published author in her own right, and one day I may convince her to share the book byline as well as the monthly column we do for *Ocean Drive*. To her I say thanks with all my heart; my gratitude knows no bounds.

NOTES

CHAPTER 1: A FREE PASS FOR THE SAUDIS

1. David Johnston, Neil A. Lewis, and Douglas Jehl, "Security Nominee Gave Advice to the C.I.A. on Torture Laws," *New York Times,* January 29, 2005, p. A1.

2. National Thoroughbred Racing Association, online biographical information, http://www.ntra.com/bios_content.asp?searchdata=salman&searchby=owner.

3. Regarding Prince Salman generally, and for the statements in this chapter, see Richard Z. Chesnoff, "A Volatile Mixture in a Desert Kingdom," *U.S. News & World Report,* June 24, 1996, pp. 44, 46; Trevor Royle, "Deep Barrel of Crude," *Scotland on Sunday,* January 7, 1996, p. 9; Kim Murphy, "The Graying of Arab Leaders," *Los Angeles Times,* January 17, 1995, p. 1; Robert Fisk, "Saudis Attack Rulers by Tape and Fax," *The Independent* (London), June 21, 1993, p. 12; Christopher Walker, "Saudis Sack Founders of Rights Movement," *Daily Telegraph,* May 14, 1993, p. 10; Caryle Murphy, "Conservative Clergy Attack Saudi Government," *Washington Post,* September 28, 1992, p. A12; John Rossant and Stanley Reed, "A Kingdom Tested from Without—and Within," *Business Week,* November 19, 1990, p. 66; Philip Shehadi, "Saudi Capital Pampers Foreign Diplomats in Man-Made Oasis," Reuters, April 1, 1987; James Bruce, "Questions Remain over the Saudi Succession," *Jane's Intelligence Review,* February 1, 1996, vol. 3, no. 2, p. 3; Said K. Aburish, "Battle for the House of Saud," *Sunday Telegraph,* November 19, 1995, p. 29; Nora Boustany, "Traditional Saudis Take Dim View of Attempts to Modernize Islam," *Washington Post,* August 24, 1994, p. A22; Paul Lewis, "Critical of His Government, Saudi Diplomat Seeks Asylum in U.S.," *New York Times,* June 14, 1994, p. A6; Annika Savill, "Saudis Move to Take Over Critical Arab Press; Now You See It . . . Prince's Newspaper Makes Sure That Leaders' Wives Lose Their Taste for Wine," *The Independent* (London), November 27, 1993, p. 12; Kathy Evans, "Saudi Curb on Alms Targets Radicals' Cash," *The Guardian* (London), May 5, 1993, p. 11; "Filipino Missionaries to Be Expelled for Preaching," Agence France Presse, December 24, 1992; Youssef M. Ibrahim, "Saudis Pursue Media Acquisitions, Gaining Influence in

the Arab World," *New York Times,* June 29, 1992, p. D8; Michael Field, "The Wide
Influence of the Governor of Riyadh," *Financial Times,* April 22, 1985, Section III,
Financial Times Survey, Saudi Arabia, p. 7.

4. D. D. Guttenplan and Martin Bright, "The Model, the Saudi Prince and the U-Boat
    Commander: David Irving's Secret Backers," *Observer* (London), March 3, 2002, p. 8;
    author interview with Irving.

5. Unger first reported this story in *Vanity Fair,* October 2003, and expanded on it in his
    book. Also, the story of the first flight, a private plane on September 13, was broken
    by Kathy Steele, Brenna Kelly, and Elizabeth Lee Brown in the *Tampa Tribune,*
    October 2001.

6. Craig Unger, "The Great Escape," *New York Times,* June 1, 2004.

7. *The 9/11 Commission Report: Final Report of the National Commission on Terrorist
    Attacks upon the United States* (hereinafter, *9/11 Commission Report*) (New York:
    W. W. Norton, 2004), references to Abu Zubaydah in notes to chapters:

    Chapter 2, p. 468, #43, from 1992 Zubaydah diary, translated 6/9/02
    Chapter 5, p. 488, #2, Zubaydah identified as detainee
    Chapter 5, p. 490, #19, reference to Intelligence report, interrogation of Abu
        Zubaydah, 11/7/02
    Chapter 5, p. 491, #31, reference to Intelligence report, interrogation of
        Abu Zubaydah, 8/29/02
    Chapter 5, p. 491, #35, reference to Intelligence report, interrogation of Abu
        Zubaydah, 5/16/03
    Chapter 5, p. 497, #106, reference to Intelligence report, biographical information,
        Abu Zubaydah, 2/25/02
    Chapter 6, p. 500, #8, reference to Intelligence report, interrogation of Abu
        Zubaydah, 6/24/03
    Chapter 6, p. 507, #125, reference to Intelligence report, interrogation of
        Abu Zubaydah, 12/13/03
    Chapter 7, p. 524, #90, reference to Intelligence report, interrogation of Abu
        Zubaydah, 2/19/04
    Chapter 7, p. 526, #9, reference to Zubaydah guesthouse
    Chapter 7, p. 527, #108, reference to Intelligence report, interrogation of
        Abu Zubaydah, 2/18/04
    Chapter 7, p. 533, #11, reference to Clarke-to-Rice e-mail "Stopping Abu
        Zubaydah's Attacks," May 29, 2001
    Chapter 7, p. 533, #37, 4th paragraph of note, since the August 6, 2001, president's
        daily brief indicated "70 ongoing investigations by the FBI." Note, the seventy-
        full-field-investigations number was a generous calculation that included
        fund-raising investigations. It also counted each individual connected to an
        investigation as a separate full-field probe. Many of these investigations should
        not have been included, such as the one that related to a dead person, four that
        concerned people who had been in long-term custody, and eight that had been
        closed before August 6, 2001.
    Chapter 8, p. 535, #39, Intelligence report, "Consideration by Abu Zubaydah
        to Attack Targets in the United States," August 24, 2001

8. Laura Sullivan, "9/11 Commission Questions al-Qaida Leaders U.S. Holds,"
    Baltimore Sun, May 12, 2004, p. 1.

9. See generally Loretta Napoleoni, *Modern Jihad: Tracing the Dollars Behind Terror
    Networks* (London: Pluto Press, 2003).

10. "Terrorist Financing: Report of an Independent Task Force," sponsored by the

Council on Foreign Relations, October 2002, Maurice R. Greenberg, chair; William F. Wechsler and Lee S. Wolosky, project co-directors.

11. *9/11 Commission Report*, p. 329.

12. Jean Heller, "TIA Now Verifies Flight of Saudis," *Tampa Times,* June 9, 2004, p. 1.

13. FAA spokesman Chris White to the *Tampa Tribune,* October 2001.

14. Laura Brown to journalist John Jeremiah Sullivan, recounted to author in interview with Sullivan, November 15, 2004.

15. Interview with John Jeremiah Sullivan, November 15, 2004.

16. Ed Cogswell to John Jeremiah Sullivan, recounted to author in interview with Sullivan, November 15, 2004.

17. Heller, "TIA Now Verifies Flight of Saudis."

18. Craig Unger, *House of Bush, House of Saud: The Secret Relationship Between the World's Two Most Powerful Families* (New York: Scribner, 2003), p. 8.

19. Alexander Bolton, "Who Let Bin Ladens Leave U.S.?," *The Hill,* May 18, 2004, p. 1.

20. Interview with John Jeremiah Sullivan, November 15, 2004.

21. "NBC News Special Report: Attack on America," *NBC News,* September 13, 2001, NBC News Transcripts, Virginia Cha reporting.

22. Bolton, "Who Let Bin Ladens Leave U.S.?"

23. *9/11 Commission Report,* pp. 329–30.

24. Hearing of the House Financial Services Committee, "Terrorist Financing, Money Laundering, and the 9/11 Commission Report," August 23, 2004.

25. Terence J. Kivlan, "9/11 Commission Co-Chair Defends Finding on Saudis," *Staten Island Advance,* August 24, 2004, p. 1.

26. Robert Baer, a former CIA officer with the Directorate of Operations and author of *Sleeping with the Devil,* wrote in *The Wall Street Journal* on April 27, 2004, that "[t]he 9/11 Commission tiptoed around the subject of Saudi Arabia. That's like investigating Lincoln's assassination without dipping into the Civil War."

CHAPTER 2: A TRIBE CALLED SAUD

1. Saudi Arabia's proven reserves are more than 250 billion barrels. The largest reserve is at Ghawar, discovered only in 1948. A 300-mile-long sliver near the Persian Gulf, it is the world's biggest oil field, accounting for more than half of Saudi production.

2. Jeff Gerth, "Forecast of Rising Oil Demand Challenges Tired Saudi Fields," *New York Times,* February 24, 2004, p. A1; see also Anthony H. Cordesman and Nawaf Obaid, "Saudi Petroleum Security: Challenges and Responses," Center for Strategic and International Studies, Washington, D.C., November 30, 2004, p. 8.

3. Cordesman and Obaid, "Saudi Petroleum Security: Challenges and Responses," p. 7.

4. David E. Long, *The Kingdom of Saudi Arabia* (Gainesville: University Press of Florida, 1997), p. 24.

5. Dore Gold, *Hatred's Kingdom: How Saudi Arabia Supports the New Global Terrorism* (Washington, D.C.: Regnery, 2003), p. 13.

6. Stephen Schwartz, *The Two Faces of Islam: Saudi Fundamentalism and Its Role in Terrorism* (New York: Anchor Books, 2003), p. 85.

7. See generally Ayyub Sabri Pasha, "The Beginning of the Spread of Wahhabism," www.ummah.net/Aladaab/wahi-36.html.

8. For a detailed historical overview of the development of Wahhabi doctrine and policies in response to the invasions, see Abdulaziz H. Al-Fahad, "From Exclusivism to Accommodation: Doctrinal and Legal Evolution of Wahhabism," *New York University Law Review* 79/485 (2004), also available at http://www.saudi-us-relations.org/newsletter2004/saudi-relations-interest-08-07.html.

9. "House of Saud," *Frontline*, PBS documentary, February 8, 2005.

10. As Ad Abukhalil, *The Battle for Saudi Arabia: Royalty, Fundamentalism, and Global Power* (New York: Seven Stories Press, 2004), pp. 81–83; see generally Anthony Cave Brown, *Oil, God, and Gold: The Story of Aramco and the Saudi Kings* (Boston: Houghton Mifflin, 1999), p. 283.

11. "House of Saud," *Frontline*.

12. Said K. Aburish, *The Rise, Corruption and Coming Fall of the House of Saud* (New York: St. Martin's/Griffin, 2003), p. 11.

13. Abukhalil, *Battle for Saudi Arabia*, p. 86, citing Tuwayjiri, Li Surat Al-Layl Hatafa As-Sabah, p. 466.

14. Aburish, *Rise, Corruption and Coming Fall*, p. 26.

15. Interview with Mai Yamani, recorded for PBS *Frontline*, November 5, 2001, for the documentary "The Saudi Time Bomb?," original airdate November 15, 2001 (transcript available at http://www.pbs.org/wgbh/pages/frontline/shows/saudi/interviews/yamani.html).

16. Nadav Safran, *Saudi Arabia: The Ceaseless Quest for Security* (Cambridge: Harvard University Press, 1985), p. 58.

17. Brown, *Oil, God, and Gold*, pp. 22–23.

18. William Eddy to the Secretary of State, "Complaints by Certain Arabian Fanatics That King Abdul Aziz is Surrendering His Land to Unbelievers," December 4, 1944, in Ibrahim al-Rashid, *Saudi Arabia Enters the Modern World* (Salisbury: Documentary Publications, 1980), vol. IV, pp. 201–3.

19. Brown, *Oil, God, and Gold*, p. 77.

20. Long, *Kingdom of Saudi Arabia*, p. 34; see also Robert Lacey, *The Kingdom: Arabia and the House of Saud* (New York: Harcourt Brace Jovanovich, 1981), p. 263.

21. See Steven Emerson, *The American House of Saud: The Secret Petrodollar Connection* (New York: Franklin Watts, 1985), p. 24.

CHAPTER 3: LEGACY OF EXTREMISM

1. Robert Lacey, *The Kingdom: Arabia and the House of Saud* (New York: Harcourt Brace Jovanovich, 1981), p. 177.

2. Walter Henry Nelson and Terrence C. F. Prittie, *The Economic War Against the Jews* (New York: Random House, 1977), p. 72.

3. Said K. Aburish, *The Rise, Corruption and Coming Fall of the House of Saud* (New York: St. Martin's/Griffin, 2003), p. 9.

4. As Ad Abukhalil, *The Battle for Saudi Arabia: Royalty, Fundamentalism, and Global Power* (New York: Seven Stories Press, 2004), p. 86; see also Aburish, *Rise, Corruption and Coming Fall*, p. 32.

5. See generally Abukhalil, *Battle for Saudi Arabia*, p. 96.

6. Nelson and Prittie, *Economic War Against the Jews*, p. 72; Aburish, *Rise, Corruption and Coming Fall*, pp. 46–47.

7. Prince Amr ibn Muhammad al-Faisal, interviewed in "House of Saud," *Frontline*, PBS documentary, February 8, 2005.

8. Anthony Cave Brown, *Oil, God, and Gold: The Story of Aramco and the Saudi Kings* (Boston: Houghton Mifflin, 1999), p. 147.

9. See the examples of forty-year-old Zahra Al Nasser, who died in detention after being arrested for carrying a Shi'a prayer book, and Ali Salman al-Ammar, a sixteen-year-old Muslim who was detained for two years for the same offense. See generally Aburish, *Rise, Corruption and Coming Fall*, p. 74.

10. Ibid., p. 27.

11. Mike Ameen, interviewed in "House of Saud," *Frontline*.
12. Lacey, *The Kingdom*, pp. 369–70.
13. Susan Taylor Martin, "Inside Saudi Arabia," *St. Petersburg* (Fla.) *Times*, July 21, 2002, p. 1.
14. Abukhalil, *Battle for Saudi Arabia*, pp. 183–84.
15. Aburish, *Rise, Corruption and Coming Fall*, p. 224; Sandra Mackey, *The Saudis: Inside the Desert Kingdom* (New York: W. W. Norton, 2002), pp. 253, 256.
16. Martin, "Inside Saudi Arabia."
17. Ibid.; see also Anders Jerichow, *The Saudi File: People, Power, Politics* (New York: St. Martin's Press, 1998), p. 181.
18. Jerichow, *The Saudi File*, p. 242; see also Joan Ryan, "The Error of Too Much Tolerance," *San Francisco Chronicle*, August 26, 2004, p. B1.
19. Aburish, *Rise, Corruption and Coming Fall*, p. 73.
20. "House of Saud," *Frontline*.
21. Abukhalil, *Battle for Saudi Arabia*, p. 123.
22. Mackey, *The Saudis*, pp. 160–61.
23. Meg Greenfield, "Saudi Arabia: Paradox in the Desert," *Washington Post*, May 26, 1980, p. A15.
24. Brown, *Oil, God, and Gold*, pp. 146–47.
25. Abukhalil, *Battle for Saudi Arabia*, p. 150.
26. Aburish, *Rise, Corruption and Coming Fall*, p. 11.
27. Robin Allen, "Gulf Between Friends," *Financial Times* (London), November 9, 2002, p. 1; see also Aburish, *Rise, Corruption and Coming Fall*, p. 15.
28. Aburish, *Rise, Corruption and Coming Fall*, p. 31–32.
29. Mike Ameen, interviewed in "House of Saud," *Frontline*.
30. Hermann F. Eilts, interviewed in "House of Saud," *Frontline*.
31. Lacey, *The Kingdom*, pp. 363, 369.
32. Jerichow, *The Saudi File*, p. 181.
33. James M. Dorse, "Fire Sparks Rare Saudi Outcry at Regime," *Wall Street Journal*, March 19, 2002, p. A18.
34. Dore Gold, *Hatred's Kingdom: How Saudi Arabia Supports the New Global Terrorism* (Washington, D.C.: Regnery, 2003), p. 87.
35. See generally "The Saudi Syndrome," *New York Times*, Editorial, January 1, 2005.
36. Gold, *Hatred's Kingdom*, p. 90; see also Al Jazeera, news transcript, September 7, 2001.
37. Dr. Ali Muhammad Jarishan and Muhammad Sharif al-Zubayq, *The Methods of the Ideological Invasion of the Islamic World* (Cairo: Dar al-Itissam, 1978).
38. Michael Scott Doran, "Somebody Else's Civil War," *Foreign Affairs*, January/February 2002, p. 30.
39. See Gold, *Hatred's Kingdom*, pp. 92–93.
40. Ibrahim Sulaiman al-Jabhan, *The Facts That the Muslim Must Know About Christianity and Missionary Activity* (Saudi Arabia: The Directorate for Religious Research, Islamic Legal Rulings, Islamic Propagation, and Guidance, 1977), p. 19.
41. Gold, *Hatred's Kingdom*, pp. 13–14. These comments are based on sermons given and reported on the Internet and in local Saudi press on September 13, 1997, and September 2, 2000.
42. Gold, *Hatred's Kingdom*, p. 77.
43. Charles M. Sennott, "Fighting Terror: The Investigation: Clerics May Have Stoked Radical's Fire; Qaeda Said to Use Some Radical Clerics to Help Its Cause," *Boston Globe*, August 4, 2002, p. A30.

CHAPTER 4: THE EMBARGO

1. Robert Lacey, *The Kingdom: Arabia and the House of Saud* (New York: Harcourt Brace Jovanovich, 1981), pp. 267–70.

2. G. Jefferson Price III, "Saudis Remember FDR's Broken Promise," Baltimore *Sun*, September 1, 2002, p. 3F.

3. Anthony Cave Brown, *Oil, God, and Gold: The Story of Aramco and the Saudi Kings* (Boston: Houghton Mifflin, 1999), p. 136.

4. Said K. Aburish, *The Rise, Corruption and Coming Fall of the House of Saud* (New York: St. Martin's/Griffin, 2003), p. 156.

5. Steven Emerson, *The American House of Saud: The Secret Petrodollar Connection* (New York: Franklin Watts, 1985), p. 4. Taxes, Aramco, and the U.S. government continued to be a prickly issue for decades. After years of minor squabbles, in 1991, the IRS sought $8 billion in back taxes and interest from Aramco for what the IRS claimed were U.S. taxes evaded between 1979 and 1981, when the companies accepted Saudi oil at less than the market price and then, in some cases, transferred it to their foreign subsidiaries, where the price was marked up—out of reach of the IRS.

6. J. B. Kelly, *Arabia, the Gulf and the West* (New York: Basic Books, 1980), p. 61.

7. Aburish, *Rise, Corruption and Coming Fall*, p. 157.

8. Mohamed H. Heikal and Yomiuri Shimbun, "Strains Showing in House of Al-Saud," *Daily Yomiuri*, April 29, 1996, p. 6.

9. See generally Lacey, *The Kingdom*, pp. 318–22.

10. As Ad Abukhalil, *The Battle for Saudi Arabia: Royalty, Fundamentalism, and Global Power* (New York: Seven Stories Press, 2004), p. 189.

11. Aburish, *Rise, Corruption and Coming Fall*, p. 157.

12. Hermann F. Eilts, interviewed in "House of Saud," *Frontline*, Public Broadcasting Corporation documentary, February 8, 2005.

13. 19 Misc. 2d 205; 190 N.Y.S. 2d 218; 1959 N.Y. Misc.

14. See generally Daniel Pipes, "The Scandal of U.S.-Saudi Relations," *National Interest*, Winter 2002/03.

15. Abukhalil, *Battle for Saudi Arabia*, pp. 90–91.

16. Sandra Mackey, *The Saudis: Inside the Desert Kingdom* (New York: W. W. Norton, 2002), p. 198.

17. Said K. Aburish, *A Brutal Friendship: The West and the Arab Elite* (New York: St. Martin's, 1998), p. 77: "In Kuwait, the Getty Oil Company provided some royals with blondes. King Saud's preference for little boys was not a barrier (8) and the CIA and oil companies provided them." Reference 8 is to Miles Copeland, *The Game of Nations: The Amorality of Power Politics* (London: Weidenfeld & Nicolson, 1969), p. 208. "The suggestion in the book was confirmed to me by the writer in 1988," writes Aburish. Miles Copeland died in 1991 at the age of seventy-four, so Aburish's account stands as the current record on this matter.

   The Saudis, with their Wahhabi interpretation of Islam, ban homosexuality, and as in other Muslim countries, like Egypt, blatant homosexuals are sometimes arrested and jailed to set moral examples. The Koran strictly forbids homosexual acts. However, scholars on Saudi Arabia say that besides the religious police, many ordinary Saudis are willing to overlook occasional sexual acts between men so long as the conduct is kept strictly private and within the Saudi society. Many Saudis share with the Turks the belief that a dominant homosexual role is compatible with male virility, while the passive role is demeaning and is not condoned.

18. Aburish, *Rise, Corruption and Coming Fall*, p. 29.

19. Mike Ameen, interviewed in "House of Saud," *Frontline*.

20. Mackey, *The Saudis*, p. 198.

21. Brown, *Oil, God, and Gold*, pp. 272–76.

22. Lacey, *The Kingdom*, p. 340.

23. Abukhalil, *Battle for Saudi Arabia*, p. 139; Dore Gold, *Hatred's Kingdom: How Saudi Arabia Supports the New Global Terrorism* (Washington, D.C.: Regnery, 2003), p. 76.

24. Abukhalil, *Battle for Saudi Arabia*, p. 147, citing Salih Al-Wardani, *Ibn Baz: The Theologian of the House of Saud* (Cairo: Dar Husam, 1998).

25. Lacey, *The Kingdom*, p. 259.

26. Like Christians, Jews share many of Islam's prophets Jews follow similar dietary rules, males are circumcised, and the Koran refers to them as "people of the Book." But after Muhammad moved to Medina in 622, he came into conflict with the local Jewish community. Until then Muslims had prayed facing Jerusalem. After Muhammad's rift with the Jews, the prayer direction was changed to Mecca, and Islamic teachings about Jews became hostile and spiteful, the basis for several centuries of ruthless persecution. Six thousand were massacred in Fez in 1033 and another five thousand slaughtered in 1066 in Granada, then under Muslim rule. Pogroms in North Africa became commonplace over a five-hundred-year stretch, with massacres of scores in Iraq, Syria, Libya, and Yemen as late as 1947. Special taxes were levied on Jews in Arab countries, they were legally limited to ghettos—a creation of the Muslim world in eleventh-century Cairo—for work and living, had their homes sometimes confiscated, and at other times were subject to government-backed massacres.

27. Walter Henry Nelson and Terence C. F. Prittie, *The Economic War Against the Jews* (New York: Random House, 1977), p. 148.

28. Lacey, *The Kingdom*, p. 385; see also Efraim Karsh, "Intifada II: The Long Trail of Arab Anti-Semitism," *Commentary,* December 1, 2000; see generally Nelson and Prittie, *Economic War Against the Jews,* p. 149.

29. See generally Karsh, "Intifada II."

30. See also Emerson, *American House of Saud*, pp. 27–28.

31. Richard Webster, "Saddam, Arafat and the Saudis Hate the Jews and Want to See Them Destroyed," *New Statesman,* December 2, 2002.

32. Al-Soyyad, November 29, 1973, as cited by Ma'oz, *The Image of the Jew,* p. 23.

33. Susan Sachs, "Anti-Semitism Is Deepening Among Muslims; Hateful Images of Jews Are Embedded in Islamic Popular Culture," *New York Times,* April 27, 2002, p. B1.

34. Frank Jungers, interviewed in "House of Saud," *Frontline*.

35. Emerson, *American House of Saud*, p. 28.

36. Kenneth C. Crowe, *America for Sale: An Alarming Look at How Foreign Money Is Buying Our Country* (Garden City, N.Y.: Doubleday & Company, 1978), pp. 150–51.

37. Frank Jungers, interviewed in "House of Saud," *Frontline*.

38. Joseph A. Mahon Collection, Aramco History Project, Georgetown University.

39. Ibid.; see also Emerson, *American House of Saud*, p. 30.

40. Crowe, *America for Sale*, p. 151.

41. Brown, *Oil, God, and Gold*, pp. 293–95.

42. Crowe, *America for Sale*, p. 152.

43. James Schlesinger, interviewed in "House of Saud," *Frontline*.

44. Nelson and Prittie, *Economic War Against the Jews,* p. 115.

45. Emerson, *American House of Saud*, pp. 30–31.

46. The Beirut daily *Al-Liwa*, for instance, carried the following front-page headline: "Signs of Change in American Public Opinion in Favor of Arab Cause."

47. Crowe, *America for Sale*, p. 153.

48. Emerson, *American House of Saud*, p. 35.

49. For instance, in a cable marked "Confidential" and dated August 13, 1973, from Aramco's international vice president, R. W. Powers, to Aramco's American vice president, J. J. Johnson, Powers said there had been "excellent press and radio coverage in the Middle East and Saudi Arabia. . . . Complete coverage of the letter

was carried by most Arab radios and the arrest of Jewish Defense League activists in New York through August 9 was played up by radios Riyadh and Jidda, as well as by other Arab radios. . . . Miller's letter coming as it does so closely on the heels of the Mobil ad (which has been most effective) has been welcomed as a real step forward by Saudi and other Arabs we have talked to. Perhaps, more important, King Faisal, Yamani and others." In the memo's last sentence, Powers concluded that the "reaction in Saudi Arabia has been most encouraging and indicates that additional effort(s) along similar lines would be most useful."

50. Crowe, *America for Sale*, p. 153.
51. See Donald Neff, *Warriors Against Israel: How Israel Won the Battle to Become America's Ally* (Brattleboro, Vt.: Amana Books, 1988), pp. 218, 261–62.
52. Andrea Gabor, "A Super Saudi's Shifting Fortune," *U.S. News & World Report*, January 12, 1987.
53. Brown, *Oil, God, and Gold*, p. 294.
54. *New York Times*, November 10, 1973, p. 13; see also Brown, *Oil, God, and Gold*, p. 295.
55. James Schlesinger, interviewed in "House of Saud," *Frontline*.
56. Frank Jungers, interviewed in "House of Saud," *Frontline*.
57. See Emerson, *American House of Saud*, p. 39. As Emerson points out, "Even bankers in Western Europe, as reported by *Business Week*, were privately urging the United States to use military force to bring down the price of oil."
58. Lacey, *The Kingdom*, p. 399.
59. Telegram from the U.S. embassy in Saudi Arabia to the Department of State, July 20, 1968, *Foreign Relations of the United States, 1964–1968*, vol. XXI, *Near East Region*.
60. Nelson and Prittie, *Economic War Against the Jews*, p. 163; see also Marvin and Bernard Kalb, *Kissinger* (Boston: Little, Brown, 1974), p. 515; and Brown, *Oil, God and Gold*, pp. 301–2.
61. Kalb and Kalb, *Kissinger*, p. 515; Brown, *Oil, God and Gold*, p. 302.
62. Crowe, *America for Sale*, p. 18.
63. Nelson and Prittie, *Economic War Against the Jews*, p. 19.
64. Raymond Close, "If Arabs Mistrust America, There's Good Reason," *International Herald Tribune*, December 19, 2002.
65. Brown, *Oil, God, and Gold*, p. 298.

CHAPTER 5: THE BOYCOTT

1. Steven Emerson, *The American House of Saud: The Secret Petrodollar Connection* (New York: Franklin Watts, 1985), p. 25.
2. Marie Colvin, "The Squandering Sheikhs," *Sunday Times* (London), August 29, 1993, p. 1; see also Robert Lacey, *The Kingdom: Arabia and the House of Saud* (New York: Harcourt Brace Jovanovich, 1981), pp. 421–22.
3. Sandra Mackey, *The Saudis: Inside the Desert Kingdom* (New York: W. W. Norton, 2002), p. 341.
4. Douglas Martin, "Riyadh's Markets Reflect Its Past and Future," *New York Times*, February 7, 1982, Section 1, Part 1, p. 21; see also Mackey, *The Saudis*, pp. 222–24.
5. Mackey, *The Saudis*, pp. 360–61.
6. "House of Saud," *Frontline*, PBS documentary, February 8, 2005.
7. Lacey, *The Kingdom*, p. 433.
8. Said K. Aburish, *The Rise, Corruption and Coming Fall of the House of Saud* (New York: St. Martin's/Griffin, 2003), p. 47.
9. Mackey, *The Saudis*, p. 210.
10. Alec Thomas, "Struggling with Debt Problems," *Financial Times* (London), April 22, 1985.

11. Kenneth C. Crowe, *America for Sale: An Alarming Look at How Foreign Money Is Buying Our Country* (Garden City, N.Y.: Doubleday, 1978), pp. 46–47.

12. Ibid., pp. 48–49; see also "Sheikhs and Souks: Capital Market Formation in the Middle East (Continuity and Transformation: The Modern Middle East)," *Journal of International Affairs,* Columbia University School of International Public Affairs, June 22, 1995.

13. Emerson, *American House of Saud,* p. 44.

14. Mackey, *The Saudis,* p. 206.

15. Walter Henry Nelson and Terence C. F. Prittie, *The Economic War Against the Jews* (New York: Random House, 1977), p. 38.

16. Crowe, *America for Sale,* p. 94.

17. John Perkins, *Confessions of an Economic Hitman* (San Francisco: Berrett-Koehler Publishers, Inc., 2004), pp. 83–84.

18. Peter T. Leach, *New York Times,* May 28, 1975, page 1.

19. The Islamic Association (IA) later changed its name to the Islamic Association of Palestine (IAP), and then to Maktab al Khidamat when it finally moved from Tucson to New York. The arrival of these Muslim organizations in Tucson and Chicago in 1973 occurred in the same year that Adnan Khashoggi acquired a 79 percent stake in Arizona-Colorado Land and Cattle and Sheikh Khalid Abdullah purchased a 7 percent stake in First Chicago Corp.

20. William D. Smith, *New York Times,* May 28, 1975, p. 57, col. 3.

21. Peter T. Leach, *Journal of Commerce,* May 28, 1975, p. 1; see also Smith, *New York Times,* May 28, 1975, p. 57, col. 3.

22. Smith, *New York Times,* May 28, 1975, p. 57, col. 3.

23. Leach, *Journal of Commerce,* May 28, 1975, p. 1.

24. Nelson and Prittie, *Economic War Against the Jews,* p. 27, citing an Anti-Defamation League paper.

25. Emerson, *American House of Saud,* p. 65.

26. Nelson and Prittie, *Economic War Against the Jews,* p. 44.

27. Speech by Arnold Forster, General Counsel and Associate National Director, Anti-Defamation League, at Oxford University seminar, England, July 1975; Anti-Defamation League internal memorandum, May/June 1975, archives of the ADL, New York.

28. Donna Abu-Nasr, "Syria Boycott Office Remains Symbol," Associated Press, April 13, 2000; see also Nelson and Prittie, *Economic War Against the Jews,* p. 38.

29. Nelson and Prittie, *Economic War Against the Jews,* p. 64.

30. Joel Bainerman, "Closed Borders, Open Markets," *Jerusalem Post,* October 5, 1990, p. 5.

31. Nelson and Prittie, *Economic War Against the Jews,* p. 38.

32. Kim Murphy, "Cracks in a 45-Year Boycott," *Los Angeles Times,* May 22, 1991, p. A1; "Regulations for the Boycott of Israel," Saudi Arabia (undated), Articles 2, 7, and 8/D/5.

33. Nelson and Prittie, *Economic War Against the Jews,* pp. 49–50.

34. Ibid., p. xiii; see also Murphy, "Cracks in a 45-Year Boycott."

35. Mark Green and Steven Solow, "The Arab Boycott of Israel: How the U.S. and Business Cooperated," *The Nation,* October 17, 1981, p.1. The information Green and Solow used was not easy to come by. In March 1977, one of the authors joined with the Public Citizen Litigation Group and filed a Freedom of Information Act lawsuit against the Commerce Department to obtain the "exporter's reports" submitted by U.S. companies who had been asked by Arab countries to comply with the boycott. It took more than three years until the commerce secretary, Philip Klutznick, turned over ninety boxes of documents covering eleven years of the boycott (1965 to 1976). Of the 1,600 American firms that filed reports with the Commerce Department, 1,400 had complied with Arab demands.

36. Ibid. See in particular sidebar, ". . . and Corporate Liars," p. 378; Nelson and Prittie, *Economic War Against the Jews*, p. 56.

37. Nelson and Prittie, *Economic War Against the Jews*, see generally chap. 5; see also Murphy, "Cracks in a 45-Year Boycott."

38. Nelson and Prittie, *Economic War Against the Jews*, pp. 178–79.

39. See generally Crowe, *America for Sale*, pp. 58–59. The University of Houston says that its selection of the two professors was solely on merit and that religion and marital status were not determining factors.

40. Mackey, *The Saudis*, p. 186.

41. Linda Robinson et al., "Princely Payments," *U.S. News & World Report*, January 14, 2002; see also Mackey, *The Saudis*, p. 212.

42. Mackey, *The Saudis*, p. 211.

43. Anthony Cave Brown, *Oil, God, and Gold: The Story of Aramco and the Saudi Kings* (Boston: Houghton Mifflin, 1999), p. 232.

44. Robinson et al., "Princely Payments."

45. Lacey, *The Kingdom*, p. 470.

46. "Customers Bear Most Lockheed Bribe Costs," *Aviation Week & Space Technology*, September 1, 1975, p. 19; see also Crowe, *America for Sale*, p. 72.

47. Christopher Rhoads, "Lucent Faces Bribery Allegations in Giant Saudi Telecom Project," *Wall Street Journal*, November 16, 2004, p. A1.

48. Prince Bandar, interviewed on PBS *Frontline*; Lowell Bergman and Tim Weiner, "A Nation Challenged," *New York Times*, October 9, 2001, p. A4.

49. Brown, *Oil, God, and Gold*, pp. 235–36; see also Liz Smith, "A Dame's Best Friend," *Newsday* (New York), March 27, 2002.

50. Author interview with manager of Budget Rental, Santa Monica Boulevard, Beverly Hills, California, January 2002.

51. Felicity Barringer, "Bureaucrats Instruct the Saudis; Nation Pays to Learn American Techniques," *Washington Post*, November 14, 1983, p. A15.

52. Emerson, *American House of Saud*, p. 66.

53. Green and Solow, "The Arab Boycott of Israel," p. 377.

54. Ibid., pp. 377–78.

55. Much of the information about the role of the U.S. government in helping the Arab boycott, and the participation of the Army Corps of Engineers, came from a 1975 hearing before the U.S. Senate, Report by the Senate Subcommittee on Multinationals January 2, 1975 (Part 3) and hearings, Parts 6 and 7. See also Green and Solow, "The Arab Boycott of Israel," p. 378; and Nelson and Prittie, *Economic War Against the Jews*, pp. 70–74.

56. Edward Cowan, *New York Times*, February 27, 1975, p. 1.

57. House of Representatives, Committee on Government Operations, April 9, 1975; see also Nelson and Prittie, *Economic War Against the Jews*, p. 74.

58. "Arabs Meet on Boycott of Israel," *Facts on File World News Digest*, Middle East Section, March 1, 1975, p. 114 C1.

59. *New York Post*, April 10, 1975, p. 1, quoting an unidentified source inside Senator Frank Church's investigating committee: "They [the Saudis] are afraid of Black Muslims getting into the country. They consider them schismatics—a threat to their faith. After all, they [the Saudis] are white Muslims."

60. Nelson and Prittie, *Economic War Against the Jews*, p. 83; see also *New York Post*, February 12, 1976, p. 1.

61. Nelson and Prittie, *Economic War Against the Jews*, p. 73.

62. John F. Ahearne, deputy assistant secretary of defense, quoted in an Anti-Defamation League report, "Interim Status," authored by L. Peiretz, May 9, 1975. See also Nelson and Prittie, *Economic War Against the Jews*, pp. 74–75.

63. Crowe, *America for Sale*, p. 52.

64. Ibid., pp. 56–57; see also Glenn Plaskin, "The Shrinking Billionaire Adnan Khashoggi

Bears Up Under Financial and Legal Problems," *St. Petersburg* (Fla.) *Times*, April 8, 1990, p. 1D.

65. Robert Pear, "Payment by Raytheon Alleged," *New York Times*, October 15, 1980, Section D, p. 5; Crowe, *America for Sale*, p. 52; see also Robinson et al., "Princely Payments" and Marilyn Berger, "Entangled Saudi Who Lives Like King," *New York Times*, December 8, 1996, p. A16.

66. Robinson et al., "Princely Payments."

CHAPTER 6: FIGHTING THE "JEWISH LOBBY"

1. Raymond Carroll, "Odyssey of an Assassin," *Newsweek*, April 7, 1975, p. 23.

2. David Holden, Richard Johns, and James Buchan, *House of Saud: The Rise and Rule of the Most Powerful Dynasty in the Arab World* (New York: Henry Holt & Company, 1982), p. 380; see also Anthony Cave Brown, *Oil, God, and Gold: The Story of Aramco and the Saudi Kings* (Boston: Houghton Mifflin, 1999), pp. 284, 305–6; and Robert Lacey, *The Kingdom: Arabia and the House of Saud* (New York: Harcourt Brace Jovanovich, 1981), p. 431.

3. Said K. Aburish, *The Rise, Corruption and Coming Fall of the House of Saud* (New York: St. Martin's/Griffin, 2003), p. 166.

4. As Ad Abukhalil, *The Battle for Saudi Arabia: Royalty, Fundamentalism, and Global Power* (New York: Seven Stories Press, 2004), p. 105.

5. "Saudi Arabia: Death in the Afternoon," *Newsweek*, June 30, 1975, p. 31.

6. Lacey, *The Kingdom*, pp. 429–30; see also Aburish, *Rise, Corruption and Coming Fall*, p. 78.

7. Henry Kissinger, *Years of Upheaval* (New York: Little, Brown, 1982), pp. 665, 994–95.

8. Holden et al., *House of Saud*, p. 267.

9. Sandra Mackey, *The Saudis: Inside the Desert Kingdom* (New York: W. W. Norton, 2002), p. 378.

10. Aburish, *Rise, Corruption and Coming Fall*, p. 56.

11. Abukhalil, *Battle for Saudi Arabia*, p. 112; see also Aburish, *Rise, Corruption and Coming Fall*, p. 54.

12. Aburish, *Rise, Corruption and Coming Fall*, p. 56.

13. Brown, *Oil, God, and Gold*, p. 307.

14. Walter Henry Nelson and Terence C. F. Prittie, *The Economic War Against the Jews* (New York: Random House, 1977), p. 184.

15. Brown, *Oil, God, and Gold*, p. 311.

16. Frank Willie quoted in Kenneth C. Crowe, *America for Sale: An Alarming Look at How Foreign Money Is Buying Our Country* (Garden City, N.Y.: Doubleday, 1978), p. 82.

17. Crowe, *America for Sale*, p. 84.

18. Max Fisher, quoted in ibid., pp. 84–85.

19. Aburish, *Rise, Corruption and Coming Fall*, p. 248.

20. Crowe, *America for Sale*, p. 42.

21. Ibid., p. 74; see also Andrea Gabor, "A Super Saudi's Shifting Fortunes," *U.S. News & World Report*, January 12, 1987.

22. "An Inside Story," *U.S. News & World Report*, June 20, 1977, p. 64.

23. Anti-Defamation League press release, March 11, 1976, archives of ADL, New York; see also Nelson and Prittie, *Economic War Against the Jews*, p. 117.

24. See generally Josh Pollack, "Saudi Arabia and the United States, 1931–2002," *Middle East Review of International Affairs*, vol. 6, no. 3 (September 2002), pp. 77, 82.

25. London *Times*, April 4, 1977, p. 1.

26. *Jordan Times*, April 14, 1976.

27. Aburish, *Rise, Corruption and Coming Fall*, p. 166.

28. Charles Mohr, *New York Times,* August 2, 1976, p. 10.

29. David Johnston, "U.S. Prosecutor Met Sheik Involved in the B.C.C.I. Case," *New York Times,* October 29, 1991, p. D1.

30. Based also on author interviews with two ex–CIA officers, both from the Directorate of Operations, the Agency's covert division. "Adham was as friendly and cooperative an Arab intelligence chief as we are likely ever to have in that part of the world," one officer, who had dealt with him in the 1970s, said. See also Crowe, *America for Sale,* p. 76.

31. Crowe, *America for Sale,* p. 88.

32. Jim Hoagland, "Hussein Payments Only a Part; CIA Operations in Mideast Held Wide-Ranging Effective," *Washington Post,* February 22, 1977, p. A1.

33. Crowe, *America for Sale,* p. 89; see also Johnston, "U.S. Prosecutor Met Sheik Involved in the B.C.C.I Case."

34. There was speculation in some quarters that one of the things the new Saudi effort might have encompassed was murder. In December 1977, fifty-three-year-old David Holden, the chief foreign correspondent of London's *Sunday Times,* was killed in Cairo, execution style, by a single close-range bullet to the back of his head. His body, dumped in a ditch on the outskirts of the Egyptian capital, was stripped of all identification and robbery was not a motive. What fueled the conjecture about a Saudi link in the still unsolved murder is that Holden was working on a book titled *House of Saud.* Some suggested that Holden was about to break a major story and the Saudis silenced him. Anthony Cave Brown, author of several books on British intelligence, Saudi Arabia, and Aramco, wrote that he had "little doubt that Holden had received important assistance from a person or persons in Saudi Arabia. . . . It might well have been that an individual may had cause to prevent Holden from completing his book." In 1982, however, Holden's book was published posthumously. He had completed the first ten chapters, and colleagues finished the remainder after his death. There was nothing in his research that indicated he had uncovered anything that would have even put him on the Saudi radar. *Newsweek,* in its review of *House of Saud,* concluded that it was "dull" and that Holden's "unsolved murder in Cairo in 1977 seems to have been unrelated to his work on this book." Based on my own reporting, which was extensive, on this unresolved mystery, I have found no evidence of Saudi involvement, official, covert, or through an intermediary third party like Palestinian militants, in Holden's death. This despite the fact that in 1979, two years after the Holden murder, Saudi intelligence agents kidnapped a Saudi dissident writer, Nasser Al Said, from Beirut and took him to the Kingdom, where his fate is unknown still. In 1984, an American mercenary was arrested in London on a mission to kill a Saudi opposition leader. Arrested by British authorities, and deported to the U.S., the mercenary admitted being on the Saudi payroll. He was sentenced to twenty-one years in prison.

35. John Berry and Art Harris, "Saudi to Acquire Lance Stock; Lance to Sell NBG Stock to Saudi at $20 a Share," *Washington Post,* December 21, 1977, p. A1.

36. Crowe, *America for Sale,* p. 93; see also *Business Week,* January 23, 1978, p. 22.

37. Jerry Knight, "Arab Financier Offering Bank Stock to Connally," *Washington Post,* July 22, 1978, p. D7.

38. Dan Balz, "The Saudi Connection: The Next Best Thing to Mecca Is Houston; Houston as the Mecca for the Saudis," *Washington Post,* April 19, 1981, Outlook, p. C1.

39. *Newsweek,* June 13, 1977, p. 18.

40. Steven Emerson, *The American House of Saud: The Secret Petrodollar Connection* (New York: Franklin Watts, 1985), p. 110.

41. *Today* show, interview with Spiro Agnew, NBC, May 11, 1976.

42. Emerson, *American House of Saud*, p. 121; see generally Victor David Hanson, "Our Enemies, the Saudis," *Commentary*, July 1, 2002.

43. "Famous U.S. Middlemen for Arab Money," *Industrial Edition*, January 23, 1978, p. 85.

44. William G. Shepherd, "Investor: A Saudi's Stake in U.S. Banking," *New York Times*, October 19, 1980, Section 3, p. 8.

45. See generally Patrick E. Tyler, "Double Exposure: Saudi Arabia's Man in Washington," *New York Times Magazine*, June 7, 1992, p. 34; see also "Lobbyists Are Well Paid," *New York Times*, July 20, 1980, Section 1, Part 2, p. 28; Robert G. Kaiser, "Saudis Retain U.S. Firm to Lobby for Warplanes," *Washington Post*, March 29, 1978, p. A2.

46. Crowe, *America for Sale*, p. 147; see also Stuart Auerbach, "Law Firms Give Extra Service to Foreign Clients; Foreign Clients Pay Lawyers Well for Variety of Services," *Washington Post*, October 3, 1977, p. A1.

47. Auerbach, "Law Firms Give Extra Service to Foreign Clients."

48. Emerson, *American House of Saud*, pp. 113–14; see also Tamar Lewin, "Growth of a Coast Law Firm," *New York Times*, September 14, 1982, p. D1.

49. "Retired CIA Station Chief Now Acts as Adviser to Saudi Intelligence Head," *Washington Post*, December 20, 1977, p. A14.

50. Crowe, *America for Sale*, p. 118; see also Elizabeth Hays, "Firm's Silver-and-Gold Lining," *Daily News* (New York), March 24, 2003, p. 25.

51. "Ambassadorships Shouldn't Be Rewards," *Milwaukee Journal Sentinel*, December 12, 1997, p. 15; see Emerson, *American House of Saud*, pp. 369–71.

52. Emerson, *American House of Saud*, p. 248.

53. Crowe, *America for Sale*, p. 149; see also Jonathan Beaty, "The Dirtiest Bank of All," *Time*, June 29, 1991.

54. Jim McGee, "Who Controls First American Bankshares?" *Washington Post*, February 3, 1991, p. A1.

55. Crowe, *America for Sale*, p. 121.

56. Ibid., p. 133.

57. "Famous U.S. Middlemen for Arab Money."

58. "It Happened In August; Fulbright Called for U.S. Defense Pact with Israel but Was Labeled Anti-Semite," *Washington Report on Middle East Affairs*, September 30, 1997, vol. XVI, no. 2, p. 96.

59. *Washington Post*, February 11, 2002.

60. Anthony Sampson, *The Seven Sisters: The Great Oil Companies and the World They Made* (London: Hodder and Stoughton, 1976), p. 273.

61. See generally Emerson, *American House of Saud*, pp. 291–96.

62. Brown, *Oil, God, and Gold*, pp. 318–20.

63. *Wall Street Journal*, December 10, 1979, p. 17; see also Brown, *Oil, God, and Gold*, p. 320.

64. Brown, *Oil, God, and Gold*, p. 320; see also Lindsay Vincent, "Sharp End: Oracle of the Oil World Sheikh Yamani," *The Observer* (London), January 27, 1991, p. 41.

65. Jim Hoagland and J. P. Smith, "U.S. Moving to Repair Saudi Ties; U.S. Is Moving to Repair Relations with Saudis," *Washington Post*, June 12, 1979, p. A1.

66. Peter Osnos and David B. Ottaway, "Yamani Links F15s to Oil, Dollar Help; Saudi Ties F15s to Oil Policies, Dollar Support," *Washington Post*, May 2, 1978, p. A1.

67. Emerson, *American House of Saud*, p. 294.

68. Ibid., p. 422; see also J. P. Smith, "Oil Supply Hinges On Saudi Reaction," *Washington Post*, November 26, 1979, p. A1.

69. Emerson, *American House of Saud*, p. 157. This was not the first time the well-respected Senator Percy had come vocally to the aid of the Saudis on a controversial

position. In 1975, he had helped halt a Senate probe into the size and influence of Arab bank deposits in the U.S. and what the effect of a sudden withdrawal might mean for American financial stability. "If Saudi Arabia and Kuwait withdraw their bank deposits," he said at the time, "the biggest single loser would be the city of New York and I would say the American Jewish community, centered in New York, would be the largest loser."

70. Moorer interview with Emerson, cited in Emerson, *American House of Saud*, p. 158.
71. Emerson, *American House of Saud*, p. 167.
72. Hoagland and Smith, "U.S. Moving to Repair Saudi Ties."
73. Ibid.
74. Morton Mintz, "Arabs' Holdings in U.S. Are Understated by Treasury, Probe Told," *Washington Post*, September 23, 1981, p. A7; Tad Szulc, "Recycling Petrodollars: The $100 Billion Understanding," *New York Times Magazine*, September 20, 1981, p. 142; Hoagland and Smith, "U.S. Moving to Repair Saudi Ties."

CHAPTER 7: INSURRECTION AND IRAN

1. Robert Lacey, *The Kingdom: Arabia and the House of Saud* (New York: Harcourt Brace Jovanovich, 1981), pp. 451–52; see also Said K. Aburish, *The Rise, Corruption and Coming Fall of the House of Saud* (New York: St. Martin's/Griffin, 2003), p. 137.
2. Sandra Mackey, *The Saudis: Inside the Desert Kingdom* (New York: W. W. Norton, 2002), p. 314.
3. Aburish, *Rise, Corruption and Coming Fall*, p. 168; see Robert Lacey, "How Stable Are the Saudis?," *New York Times Magazine*, November 8, 1981, p. 35.
4. Anthony Cave Brown, *Oil, God, and Gold: The Story of Aramco and the Saudi Kings* (Boston: Houghton Mifflin, 1999), p. 344.
5. Peter A. Iseman, "Iran's War of Words Against Saudi Arabia," *The Nation*, April 19, 1980, pp. 463–66; Brown, *Oil, God, and Gold*, p. 344; see also Lacey, "How Stable Are the Saudis?"
6. Mackey, *The Saudis*, p. 230.
7. Lacey, *The Kingdom*, pp. 478–79.
8. Edward Cody, "Saudis Press to End Siege at Mecca," *Washington Post*, November 22, 1979, p. A1.
9. Mackey, *The Saudis*, pp. 230–32.
10. Edward Cody, "Saudis Raid Mosque to End Siege; Saudi Troops Raid Great Mosque to End Siege by Gunmen," *Washington Post*, November 25, 1979, p. A1; see also Lacey, *The Kingdom*, pp. 485–86.
11. Brown, *Oil, God, and Gold*, pp. 348–49.
12. Sulaiman al-Hattlan, interviewed in "House of Saud," *Frontline*, Public Broadcasting Corporation documentary, February 8, 2005.
13. Sulaiman al-Hattlan, "In Saudi Arabia, an Extreme Problem," *Washington Post*, May 8, 2002, p. 12.
14. David B. Ottaway, "U.S. Eyes Money Trails of Saudi-Backed Charities," *Washington Post*, August 19, 2004, p. A1.
15. Mr. Lester W. Grau and Dr. William A. Jorgensen, "Handling the Wounded in a Counter-Guerrilla War: The Soviet/Russian Experience in Afghanistan and Chechnya," *U.S. Army Medical Department Journal*, January/February 1998.
16. Aburish, *Rise, Corruption and Coming Fall*, p. 139.
17. Daniel Yergin, with Joseph Stanislaw, *Prize: The Epic Quest for Oil, Money and Power* (New York: Simon & Schuster, 1992), p. 717.
18. Lacey, *The Kingdom*, pp. 453–55.
19. Aburish, *Rise, Corruption and Coming Fall*, p. 1.

20. Al Webb, "What U.S. Has Riding on Saudi Royal Family," *U.S. News & World Report,* January 25, 1992, p. 30.

21. As Ad Abukhalil, *The Battle for Saudi Arabia: Royalty, Fundamentalism, and Global Power* (New York: Seven Stories Press, 2004), p. 124.

22. "House of Saud Comes Under Fire," *Daily Telegraph* (London), April 17, 1997, p. B1; see also Abukhalil, *Battle for Saudi Arabia,* p. 121.

23. See generally Sheikh Abdul Aziz bin Baz, "The Value of the Jihad and the Mujahidin," www.binbaz.org.sa; see also Dore Gold, *Hatred's Kingdom: How Saudi Arabia Supports the New Global Terrorism* (Washington, D.C.: Regnery, 2003), pp. 110–111.

24. Gold, *Hatred's Kingdom,* p. 122.

25. Brown, *Oil, God, and Gold,* pp. 349–50.

26. Ibid., p. 350.

27. Baldo Marinovic quoted in ibid., p. 353.

28. Mackey, *The Saudis,* p. 277.

CHAPTER 8: ARMING THE HOUSE OF SAUD

1. Josh Pollack, "Saudi Arabia and the United States, 1931–2002," *Middle East Review of International Affairs,* vol. 6, no. 3 (September 2002), pp. 77, 83.

2. Robert Hotz, "Carter's Jet Sales," *Aviation Week & Space Technology,* May 22, 1978, p. 11.

3. Charles Mohr, "Sale of F-15s Gear to Saudis Studied," *New York Times,* September 8, 1981, p. A8; see also Steven Emerson, *The American House of Saud: The Secret Petrodollar Connection* (New York: Franklin Watts, 1985), p. 174.

4. "Saudis Claim U.S. Pledge of Arms Sale," *Washington Star,* July 18, 1980, p. 1.

5. Barry Schweid, "U.S. to Sell Command Planes to Saudis," Associated Press, March 11, 1981, Wednesday, A.M. cycle, Section: Washington Dateline.

6. Terry Atlas, "$350 Million Saudi Missile Proposal Faces Long Road," *Chicago Tribune,* March 12, 1986, p. C5.

7. George J. Church, "Flying into Trouble; Selling AWACS: Dubious Militarily and Dangerous Politically," *Time,* May 4, 1981, p. 14; see also Richard E. Cohen, "Even If He Wins on Saudi Arms Sale, Reagan May Find It a Hollow Victory," *National Journal,* September 12, 1981, Section: Congress, vol. 13, no. 37, p. 1,621.

8. John M. Goshko, "Reagan Lobbies 27 Senators on Sale of AWACS to Saudi Arabia," *Washington Post,* September 15, 1981, p. A16.

9. Melinda Beck, with John J. Lindsay, John Walcott, Eleanor Clift, and Scott Sullivan, "The Battle over AWACS," *Newsweek,* October 12, 1981, p. 37.

10. Ibid.

11. David S. Broder, "Senate Backs Reagan on AWACS Sale," *Washington Post,* October 29, 1981, p. A1.

12. Patrick E. Tyler, "Double Exposure: Saudi Arabia's Man in Washington," *New York Times Magazine,* June 7, 1992, p. 34.

13. Paul Taylor, "Contrasting Approaches Are Taken by Saudi and Israeli Supporters; Lobbying on AWACS," *Washington Post,* September 28, 1981, p. A4.

14. Emerson, *The American House of Saud,* pp. 187-88; see also Paul Taylor, " 'Israeli Lobby' Voices Concern on U.S. Shift—Assesses the Damage," *Washington Post,* October 30, 1981, p. A1.

15. Emerson, *The American House of Saud,* p. 187; see also Taylor, "Contrasting Approaches Are Taken by Saudi and Israeli Supporters."

16. Tyler, "Double Exposure."

17. Emerson, *The American House of Saud,* p. 191.

18. Ibid., p. 211.

19. Sidney Blumenthal, "Whose Side Is Business On, Anyway?," *New York Times Magazine,* October 25, 1981, p. 29.

20. Steven V. Roberts, "Pressure on AWACS Comes with Winks and Nods," *New York Times,* October 16, 1981, p. A18.

CHAPTER 9: COVERT PARTNERS

1. "Insider Notes from United Press International," September 21, 2001, Section: General News.

2. Phil McCombs, "The Connection Makers; Robert Gray's Lobbying Army, Pressing on the Front Lines," *Washington Post,* June 29, 1984, p. B1.

3. Steven Emerson, *The American House of Saud: The Secret Petrodollar Connection* (New York: Franklin Watts, 1985), p. 345.

4. Ibid., p. 346; see generally Susan B. Trento, "Lord of the Lies; How Hill and Knowlton's Robert Gray Pulls Washington's Strings," *Washington Monthly,* vol. 24, no. 9 (September 1992), p. 12.

5. Emerson, *American House of Saud,* p. 343.

6. As Ad Abukhalil, *The Battle for Saudi Arabia: Royalty, Fundamentalism, and Global Power* (New York: Seven Stories Press, 2004), p. 195.

7. Steven V. Roberts, Stephen Engelberg, and Jeff Gerth, "Prop for U.S. Policy: Secret Saudi Funds," *New York Times,* June 21, 1987, p. A1.

8. "Congress to Hear F-15 Sale Plan; Reagan Bid to Sell Jets to Saudis Likely to Spark Debate," *Chicago Tribune,* May 16, 1987, p. C3. For a thorough overview of Prince Bandar's role in overseeing Saudi aid to the Contras, see Bob Woodward, *Veil: The Secret Wars of the CIA, 1981–1987* (New York: Simon & Schuster, 1987), pp. 401–4, 454–56, 459–60.

9. Roberts et al., "Prop for U.S. Policy"; see also Said K. Aburish, *The Rise, Corruption and Coming Fall of the House of Saud* (New York: St. Martin's/Griffin, 2003), p. 167; see generally Woodward, *Veil.*

10. Elsa Walsh, "The Prince: How the Saudi Ambassador Became Washington's Indispensable Operator," *New Yorker,* March 24, 2003, p. 48; see also Patrick E. Tyler, "Double Exposure: Saudi Arabia's Man in Washington," *New York Times Magazine,* June 7, 1992, p. 34.

11. Rachel Bronson, "The U.S.-Saudi Love Affair Predates Bush," *Los Angeles Times,* July 9, 2004, p. 13.

12. Michael White, "Contra Aid Net Cast in 6 States / New Revelations on Covert US Support," *The Guardian* (London), January 24, 1987, p. 4; see also *BBC Summary of World Broadcasts,* text of article by Konstantin Geyvandov, "Riyadh Colluding with the Arabs' Arch-Enemies," December 13, 1986, Part 1; and Aburish, *Rise, Corruption and Coming Fall,* p. 269.

13. "Irangate," *Izvestia,* January 2, 1987, p. 1.

14. Jonathan Broder, "Cast as Scapegoat, Israel Feels U.S. Ties Slipping," *Chicago Tribune,* January 15, 1987, p. C1.

15. "Congress to Hear F-15 Sale Plan."

16. See David B. Ottaway, "Saudis Use Bush Visit to Signal Displeasure; 'Special Relationship' Becoming Frayed," *Washington Post,* April 21, 1986, p. A4.

17. Ibid.

18. Sandra Mackey, *The Saudis: Inside the Desert Kingdom* (New York: W. W. Norton, 2002), pp. 347–48.

19. Aburish, *Rise, Corruption and Coming Fall,* p. 171.

CHAPTER 10: SCORCHED EARTH

1. Based on a conversation with a retired Mossad officer, whose liaison role was with the NSA and the Israeli equivalent of satellite eavesdropping. The Israelis were brought in by the NSA, according to him, because of their superior ability to penetrate Saudi diplomatic and business conversations in Europe and the Middle East. The Israelis have what they call a "shadow file," a close copy of the NSA folder, missing some materials the Americans likely held back for security and clearance purposes. The Israeli file, upon which this account is based, is not as complete therefore as the NSA file, but the core disclosures are covered in both. I have seen documents from the Israeli file, and the specifics discussed in this chapter are from notes taken while reviewing those papers. I also have had background conversations with a ranking retired American intelligence officer who had personal knowledge of the NSA's file and its general contents. While not able to confirm the details in the file, he was able to confirm the nature of the electronic intercepts, the status of the file, and the nature of the Saudi program.

    Also, as part of the research for this book, I obtained confirmation of some of the intelligence file's details from an eyewitness who had spent considerable time in Saudi Arabia. A European executive involved in the construction business for oil infrastructure facilities, this man had been in Saudi Arabia overseeing several large projects in the early and mid-1990s. He had personally observed what he considered visual confirmation of Petro SE's placement in the facilities on which he and his team had worked. Since he had access to the complete architectural schematics for the sites he was at, he noticed variances between what was supposed to be constructed and what actually was, with the changes, omissions, and additions fitting into part of what is the Saudi destruction grid. At the time of my conversations with this eyewitness, I told my Random House editor about the interviews and my enthusiasm to have someone ready to go on the record about such serious charges. However, to my disappointment, in December 2004, he telephoned to say not only that he had changed his mind about going on the record about what he had seen in Saudi Arabia but that I could not use the specific details of what he had witnessed because to do so would narrow down very quickly for the Saudis who he is. That was something he did not want after further thought. I have even honored here his request to avoid his nationality, precise dates of work in Saudi Arabia, and any reference to his age or official position. I do hope that one day in the near future, he, and others similarly placed who might be able to confirm some of the Petro SE details, might have the courage to step forward and put their recollections on the historical record.

2. "Commentary: The Saudi Oil Industry and Terrorism," United Press International, November 17, 2003.

3. In 2003, files released to the British National Archives (the former Public Record Office) after their thirty-year classified status had expired revealed that British intelligence agencies believed the United States was ready to take military action in 1973 to prevent further disruption to international oil supplies. See Lizette Alvarez, "War for Arab Oil in '73? U.S. Pondered an Attack, Papers Show," *International Herald Tribune*, January 1, 2004.

4. The American occupation would need as long as ten years, warned "Eyes Alpha," while the West developed alternative energy sources. Such an extended occupation would result in the "total alienation" of the Arab world, as well as kicking off "domestic dissension" in the U.S. But despite the risks, the British spymasters thought that the Nixon administration could be tempted to take preemptive action if

faced with the "dark scenario . . . in which the US and its allies were in effect at the mercy of a small group of unreasonable countries." As recounted by Ambassador Cromer, Defense Secretary Schlesinger was explicit that the United States was unwilling to stand for threats by "underdeveloped, underpopulated" countries.

In contrast to what actually happened eighteen years later during the first Gulf War, British intelligence thought that if the Americans seized Kuwait, Iraq might try to mount a counterinvasion to expel them since it had long had a territorial claim to that country. "The greatest risk in the Gulf would probably arise in Kuwait, where the Iraqis, with Soviet backing, might be tempted to intervene," the "Eyes Alpha" report concluded.

And foreshadowing what would take place in the Iraq invasion of 2003, the report warned that American military intervention could create strains among the Western allies. "Since the United States would probably claim to be acting for the benefit of the West as a whole and would expect the full support of allies, deep US-European rifts could ensue," it said.

5. "Kissinger on Oil, Food, and Trade," *Business Week,* January 13, 1975, p. 66.
6. Tanya Hsu, "U.S. Plans for Occupation of Saudi Arabia—Michael Moore, Richard Perle join forces," Institute for Research and Middle Eastern Policy, Inc., July 12, 2004.
7. Author interview, September 2004.
8. David B. Ottaway, "Aramco, Using Ties to West, Helps Saudi Arabia to Industrialize," *Washington Post,* January 9, 1982, p. A14.
9. Linda Robinson et al., "Princely Payments," *U.S. News & World Report,* January 14, 2002.
10. Said K. Aburish, *The Rise, Corruption and Coming Fall of the House of Saud* (New York: St. Martin's/Griffin, 2003), p. 83.
11. Robin Allen and Guy Dinmore, "Riyadh Fears Switch Towards Iraq," *Financial Times* (London), May 14, 2003, p. 10.
12. Jeff Gerth, "Threats and Responses: Desert Targets," *New York Times,* February 13, 2003, p. A18. See generally John C. K. Daly, "The Saudi Oil Industry and Terrorism," United Press International, November 17, 2003; and "What If? Terrorists Are Now Targeting Saudi Arabia's Oil Infrastructure. How Bad Could Things Get?," *The Economist,* May 27, 2004.
13. Author interview.
14. Gerth, "Threats and Responses: Desert Targets."
15. "How Secure Is Saudi Oil? New questions on the Vulnerability of the Country's Vast Facilities and How Markets Would React," CNN, November 24, 2004, CNN Senior Investigative Producer Henry Schuster and Senior International Correspondent Nic Robertson.

CHAPTER 11: THE INFIDEL ARRIVES

1. Richard A. Clarke, *Against All Enemies: Inside America's War on Terror* (New York: Free Press, 2004), p. 58.
2. Josh Pollack, "Saudi Arabia and the United States, 1931–2002," *Middle East Review of International Affairs,* vol. 6, no. 3 (September 2002), pp. 77, 83; Clarke, *Against All Enemies,* pp. 58–59.
3. Sheikh Nasser al-Omar, interviewed in "House of Saud," *Frontline,* PBS documentary, February 8, 2005.
4. Donna Abu-Nasr, "Saudi Religious Scholars Support Holy War," Associated Press, November 6, 2004.

5. Sandra Mackey, *The Saudis: Inside the Desert Kingdom* (New York: W. W. Norton, 2002), pp. 406–7.

6. Ibid., p. 407.

7. Daniel Pipes, "The Scandal of U.S.-Saudi Relations," *National Interest,* Winter 2002/03.

8. Ibid.

9. Dilip Hiro, "Saudi Dissenters Go Public," *The Nation,* June 28, 1993, pp. 906–7.

10. Dilip Hiro, "Too Little and 32 Years Late," *The Nation,* April 13, 1992, p. 486.

11. Ibid., p. 487.

12. Lisa Beyer with Scott MacLeod, "Inside the Kingdom: Saudi Arabia—A Special Report," *Time,* September 15, 2003. Below are two excerpts from Ministry of Education textbooks used by middle school students in Saudi Arabia. These books were published in 2000. PBS's *Frontline* program confirmed that these textbooks are part of the official curriculum for Saudi students. Compulsory religious studies account for 35 percent of all classes.

    The first extract, "The Victory of Muslims over Jews," is the last two pages from the prophet Muhammad's sayings (Hadith narrated by Abi Hurira):

    > "The last hour won't come before the Muslims would fight the Jews and the Muslims will kill them so Jews would hide behind rocks and trees. Then the rocks and tree would call: oh Muslim, oh servant of God! There is a Jew behind me, come and kill him."
    >
    >   Among the teachings of the Hadith:
    > 1. Allah has decided that the Muslims and Jews will fight till the end of the world.
    > 2. The Hadith predicts for the Muslims God's victory over the Jews.
    > 3. Jews and Christians are the enemies of believers, they will never approve of the Muslims, beware of them.

    The second extract, from explanations of the Koran, also deals with Muslims and Jews and presents an interpretation which says murder is a form of punishment for those who acted in opposition to Allah: "It's allowed to demolish, burn or destroy the bastions of the Kufar [infidels]—and all what constitutes their shield from Muslims if that was for the sake of victory for the Muslims and the defeat for the Kufar."

13. Ali al-Ahmed quoted by Charles M. Sennott, "Driving a Wedge/Bin Laden, the US, and Saudi Arabia: Saudi Schools Fuel Anti-US Anger—System Is Fertile Ground for Militancy, Some Say," *Boston Globe,* March 4, 2002, p. A1.

14. Sulaiman al-Hattlan, interviewed in "House of Saud," *Frontline.*

15. Sheikh Nasser al-Omar, interviewed in "House of Saud," *Frontline.*

16. Interview with Prince Faisal bin Salman, by Elizabeth Farnsworth, PBS, *The News Hour,* January 23, 2002.

17. Prince Saud al-Faisal, interviewed by Lesley Stahl, "Saudi Arabia; Relationship Between the United States and Saudi Arabia Since the September 11th Attacks," CBS, *60 Minutes,* September 8, 2002.

18. Lisa Beyer, with Scott MacLeod, "Inside the Kingdom: Saudi Arabia—A Special Report," *Time,* September 15, 2003.

19. Eric Rouleau, "Trouble in the Kingdom," *Foreign Affairs,* vol. 81, no. 4 (July/August 2002), p. 77.

20. Dore Gold, *Hatred's Kingdom: How Saudi Arabia Supports the New Global Terrorism* (Washington, D.C.: Regnery, 2003), p. 165.

21. Document 2, Communiqué No. 17, August 3, 1995, in Rohand Jacquard, Samia Serageldin, and George Holoch, *In the Name of Osama bin Laden: Global Terrorism*

and the Bin Laden Brotherhood (Chapel Hill, N.C.: Duke University Press, 2002), p. 172.

22.   Pollack, "Saudi Arabia and the United States, 1931–2002."

23.   Bernard Lewis, "License to Kill," *Foreign Affairs,* November–December 1998, p. 14.

24.   This is reported in my 2003 book, *Why America Slept: The Failure to Prevent 9/11* (New York: Random House, 2003), pp. 133, 190–91.

25.   Ibid.

26.   Gold, *Hatred's Kingdom,* pp. 174–75.

27.   Josh Chafetz, "Shills: Dishonest Analysis on Saudi Arabia from Former U.S. Ambassadors to the Kingdom," *Weekly Standard,* January 13, 2003, vol. 8, no. 17; hundreds of other recent examples of Wahhabi intolerance are available at www.memri.org, the website of the Middle East Media Research Institute, which translates Arabic media and sermons into English.

CHAPTER 12: THE PRINCE WHO WOULD BUY AMERICA

1.   Until the fall of 2004, when the SEC finally corrected it, there was another way investors could hide their ownership interests in private companies that went public on the stock exchange. The investors wishing to remain secret formed a shell company, and then the firm in the U.S. did a "reverse-merger," becoming part of the shell corporation. Historically, companies that merged into shells were not required to make detailed material disclosures about their business history, management, and controlling shareholders. They did not have to file registration statements detailing the history of their business, the background of their management team, and the identity of each controlling shareholder.

2.   "Saudi Prince Denies U.S. Asset Flight," BBC News World Edition, August 22, 2002, http://news.bbc.co.uk/2/hi/business/2209503.stm.

3.   Ibid.

4.   John Rossant, "The Prince," *Business Week,* September 25, 1995, p. 88.

5.   Gary C. Gambill and Ziad K. Abdelnour, "Dossier: Prince Al-Walid bin Talal," *Middle East Intelligence Bulletin,* vol. 4, no. 9 (September 2002).

6.   Rossant, "The Prince."

7.   Steven Emerson, *The American House of Saud: The Secret Petrodollar Connection* (New York: Franklin Watts, 1985), p. 330.

8.   Rossant, "The Prince."

9.   Gambill and Abdelnour, "Dossier: Prince Al-Walid bin Talal."

10.   Ibid.

11.   John Rossant, "A Prince with Divided Loyalties," *Business Week,* October 15, 2001.

12.   Rossant, "The Prince."

13.   Kathleen Day and Robert J. McCartney, "Saudi Invests $590 Million in Citicorp; Deal Could Eventually Mean Majority Stake in Banking Giant," *Washington Post,* February 22, 1991, p. A1.

14.   Rossant, "The Prince."

15.   Lisa Beyer, with Scott MacLeod, "Inside the Kingdom: Saudi Arabia—A Special Report," *Time,* September 15, 2003, p. 42.

16.   Rossant, "The Prince."

17.   Dan Briody, *The Iron Triangle: Inside the Secret World of the Carlyle Group* (New York: John Wiley & Sons, 2003), p. 76.

18.   Rossant, "The Prince."

19.   Robert Blincoe, "HP and Compaq Get Thumbs up from Saudi Billionaire Prince," http://www.theregister.co.uk/content/archive/22480.html.

20.   "The Mystery of the World's Second-Richest Businessman," *The Economist,* February 27, 1999, p. 67.

21. "Saudi Prince Takes Huge Stake in Internet Capital," *Philadelphia Business Journal,* May 16, 2000.

22. *The Guardian* (London), August 9, 2003.

23. Richard Verrier, "Disney's Saudi Adventurer," *Los Angeles Times,* January 6, 2004, p. A1.

24. Rossant, "The Prince."

25. "The Mystery of the World's Second-Richest Businessman."

26. "Saudi Prince Buys Shares in Amazon.com, InfoSpace," *Bloomberg News,* May 17, 2000; Rossant, "The Prince"; see also Briody, *The Iron Triangle,* p. 52.

27. "The Mystery of the World's Second-Richest Businessman."

28. Rossant, "The Prince."

29. Kingdom 5-KR is a Cayman Islands, British West Indies corporation, which itself is wholly owned by Coutts (Cayman) Limited, as trustee of The Kingdom One Trust, a trust created by HRH under the laws of the Cayman Islands.

30. "East Meets West," *The Economist,* February 27, 1999, p. 68.

31. Rossant, "The Prince."

32. Rossant, "A Prince with Divided Loyalties."

33. Forbes.com website at www.forbes.com/finance/lists/10/2004/LIR.jhtml?passListId= 10&passYear=2004&passListType=Person&uniqueId=0RD0&datatype=Person.

34. John J. Goldman and Marisa Schultz, "Giuliani Refuses Saudi's Check," *Los Angeles Times,* October 12, 2001, p. 3.

35. Dore Gold, *Hatred's Kingdom: How Saudi Arabia Supports the New Global Terrorism* (Washington, D.C.: Regnery, 2003), p. 193.

36. Associated Press, October 13, 2001.

37. Christopher Dickey interview with Prince Al-Waleed, "A Friend of America: An Interview with Saudi Prince Alwaleed bin Talal on American Bias and the Plight of the Palestinians," *Newsweek,* October 21, 2001.

38. Ibid.

39. Donna Abu-Nasr, "Saudis Raise $92M for Palestinians," Associated Press, April 12, 2002; see also "Saudi Telethon Raises $145 Million (Canadian) for 'Martyrs': Government Ordered Palestinian Fund Raiser," *Vancouver Sun,* April 13, 2002.

40. "Saudi Prince Denies U.S. Asset Flight."

41. Al-Bawaba,"Bill Gates Holds Investment Meeting with Saudi Prince Al-Waleed," Albawaba.com, February 12, 2004.

42. "Prince Al-Waleed Bin Talal Considers Investing in Insurance Sector," *Financial Times,* Global News Wire–Asia Africa Intelligence Wire, February 16, 2004.

CHAPTER 13: "A MAD SPENDER"

1. Ian Mather, "Question: Which of These Three Men Rules a 'Kernal of Evil'?" *Scotland on Sunday,* August 11, 2002, p. 14.

2. John Mason, " 'Web of Deceit' That Destroyed a Tory High-Flier," *Financial Times* (London), June 9, 1999, p. 10.

3. "Saudi Prince 'Gave Aitken Pounds 2.7M Bung,' " *Scottish Daily Record & Sunday Mail Ltd.,* June 1, 2000, p. 2.

4. "Scandal over Ex-Minister Reveals Saudi Royal Family Fortune of Bribes," Agence France Presse, March 5, 1999.

5. David Pallister, "How Aitken Courted Saudi Royal Family: Criticism of Pro-Israel Reporting of 1967 War Led to 25-Year Relationship with Arab Kingdom," *The Guardian* (London), October 31, 1994, p. 5.

6. Ibid.

7. Ibid.

8. Jim Anderson, "Fahd Reported to Be Improving, but Succession Questions Remain," Deutsche Presse-Agentur, December 5, 1995.

9. Chris Hastings, David Leppard, Jonathon Carr-Brown, and Wayne Bodkin, "The Prince Who Blew a Billion," *Sunday Times* (London), July 5, 1998, p. 1.

10. Author interview.

11. Hastings et al., "The Prince Who Blew a Billion."

12. Ibid.

13. Ibid.

14. Ibid.

15. Lela Mrakovic and James Roumeliotis, "Megayachts: Arabian Knights and Their Floating Palaces," *International Yacht Vacations and Charters*, vol. 1, issue 2 (2004); "Scandal over Ex-Minister Reveals Saudi Royal Family Fortune of Bribes."

16. Hastings et al., "The Prince Who Blew a Billion."

17. Ibid.

18. Ibid.

19. "Scandal over Ex-Minister Reveals Saudi Royal Family Fortune of Bribes."

20. Luke Harding, Owen Bowcott, David Pallister, Jamie Wilson, Clare Longrigg, and Christopher Elliot, "Saudi Scandal: On the Trail of a Prince's Missing Millions," *The Guardian* (London), January 10, 1998, p. 3.

21. "Ayas apology," *Times* (London), May 21, 1999.

22. Hastings et al., "The Prince Who Blew a Billion."

23. "At the Festival Organized in Solidarity with Al Aqsa Intifada in Al Dammam. The Governor of the Eastern Region: The Atrocities Committed Against Unarmed Palestinians Are Once Again a Proof of Israel's Barbarity," *Ain-Al-Yaqeen,* July 27, 2001.

24. Abdullah Ahmad, "Freeing the Prophet's Land," *New Straits Times* (Malaysia), November 12, 2003, p. 12.

CHAPTER 14: FUNDING TERROR

1. Steven Emerson, *The American House of Saud: The Secret Petrodollar Connection* (New York: Franklin Watts, 1985), p. 362.

2. Stephen Schwartz, *The Two Faces of Islam: Saudi Fundamentalism and Its Role in Terrorism* (New York: Anchor Books, 2003), p. 239.

3. "The Saudi Syndrome," *New York Times,* January 1, 2005, p. A12; Robert Lacey, *The Kingdom: Arabia and the House of Saud* (New York: Harcourt Brace Jovanovich, 1981), pp. 455–56.

4. See generally Thomas E. Burnett, Sr., et al. v. Arab Bank, PLC, et al., USDC Case no. 1-02CV01616, 2002.

5. Statement of Mr. Jean-Charles Brisard, CEO, JCB Consulting, on terrorism financing, before the Committee on Senate Banking, Housing and Urban Affairs, October 22, 2003; see also Brian Murphy and Mike Casey, "Saudi Charity's Aid Work Scrutinized," *Miami Herald,* February 7, 2005, p. 21A.

6. Authority of the Department is based on the Royal Decree No. 3321, Issued 21/01/1370HD and the Ministerial Resolution No. 393, Issued 06/08/1370H.

7. David E. Kaplan and Monica Ekma, with Aamir Latif, "The Saudi Connection," *U.S. News & World Report,* December 15, 2003, p. 18.

8. David B. Ottaway, "U.S. Eyes Money Trails of Saudi-Backed Charities," *Washington Post,* August 19, 2004, p. A1.

9. Statement of Mr. Jean-Charles Brisard; see also Kaplan et al., "The Saudi Connection."

10. Statement of Mr. Jean-Charles Brisard.

11.   Ibid.
12.   Jonathan Wells, Jack Meyers, and Maggie Mulvihill, "Saudi Elite Tied to Money
      Groups Linked to bin Laden," *Boston Herald*, October 14, 2001.
           Kaplan et al., in "The Saudi Connection," reveal that offices of these three leading
      Saudi charities played key roles in moving millions of dollars to terrorists or
      insurgents in some twenty countries:

      1. MUSLIM WORLD LEAGUE
         Headquarters: Mecca.
         Estimated annual budget: $45 million
         Branch offices: 36
         Terror ties: Early '90s, Manila branch sends cash to Islamic guerrillas in
         Philippines; 2001–02, MWL's Rabita trust affiliate designated as terrorist group by
         U.S. for al Qaeda ties; 2002, federal agents raid U.S. offices of MWL in terrorist
         financing case.
      2. AL HARAMAIN FOUNDATION
         Headquarters: Riyadh.
         Estimated annual budget: $53 million
         Branch offices: 50
         Terror ties: 1996, CIA links group to Egyptian extremists and Bosnian
         jihadists; 1999, Moscow says group transferred money and arms to Chechen
         rebels; 2002, staffer caught at Manila airport with explosives; 2003, U.S. says
         branches in 10 countries provide arms or cash to terrorists.
      3. INTERNATIONAL ISLAMIC RELIEF ORGANIZATION (IIRO)
         Headquarters: Jeddah.
         Estimated annual budget: $46 million
         Branch offices: 80
         Terror ties: Early '90s, Manila branch funnels cash to Abu Sayyaf and Moro
         Islamic Liberation Front; 1996, CIA reports funding of jihadists in Balkans and
         Afghanistan, and ties to Algerian and Egyptian extremists, al Qaeda, and Hamas;
         1998, FBI traces suspected Hamas money in Chicago to IIRO; 1999, staffer
         suspected in bomb plot admits IIRO funds Afghan terror training camps.

13.   John Rossant, "A Prince with Divided Loyalties," *Business Week*, October 15,
      2001.
14.   National Commission on Terrorist Attacks upon the United States, Staff Report to
      the Commission (John Roth, Douglas Greenburg, Serene Wille), August 2004.
15.   Linda Robinson et al., "Princely Payments," *U.S. News & World Report*, January 14,
      2002.
16.   National Commission on Terrorist Attacks upon the United States, Staff report to
      the Commission, p. 3.
17.   Kaplan et al., "The Saudi Connection."
18.   Wells et al., "Saudi Elite Tied to Money Groups Linked to bin Laden."
19.   Ibid.
20.   Statement of Mr. Jean-Charles Brisard; see also Press Release of Senator Charles
      Schumer, (D-N.Y.) as part of the Senate Judiciary Subcommittee on Terrorism,
      Technology and Homeland Security on "Terrorism: Two Years After 9/11, Connecting
      the Dots," September 10, 2003, available in its entirety at http://www.senate.gov/
      ~schumer/SchumerWebsite/pressroom/press_releases/PR02009.html.
21.   As Ad Abukhalil, *The Battle for Saudi Arabia: Royalty, Fundamentalism, and Global
      Power* (New York: Seven Stories Press, 2004), p. 142.
22.   Glenn Simpson, "U.S. Treasury Ties Bosnian Arm of Saudi Charity to Terror Funds,"
      Wall Street Journal, May 11, 2004, p. A6.

23. Ottaway, "U.S. Eyes Money Trails of Saudi-Backed Charities"; see also Dave Montgomery and Warren Strobel, "Two U.S. Soldiers Attacked; Saudi Charity Being Frozen," *Miami Herald,* June 3, 2004, p. 18A; and Timothy L. O'Brien, "Charity Said to Have Paid Terrorists Is Under Investigation by the Saudis," *New York Times,* September 26, 2003, p. A11.

24. Loretta Napoleoni, "Ten Things You Didn't Know About Terrorism," *The Progress Report,* 2004; see also Loretta Napoleoni, *Modern Jihad: Tracing the Dollars Behind the Terror Networks* (London: Pluto Press, 2003), p. 122.

25. Ottaway, "U.S. Eyes Money Trails of Saudi-Backed Charities."

26. See Dore Gold, *Hatred's Kingdom: How Saudi Arabia Supports the New Global Terrorism* (Washington, D.C.: Regnery, 2003), pp. 134–43.

27. Ibid., pp. 152–55.

28. "Crisis in Palestine; Ties May Be Cut, Arabs Warn Israel," *Gulf News,* October 23, 2000. This involved an emergency meeting of the Arab League to address a dramatic flare-up in violence between Israel and the Palestinian Authority. Among other actions taken in the two-day meeting, the Arab leaders established two funds, in response to a Saudi proposal. The Al Aqsa Fund, for which $800 million was allocated, is to finance projects to enable the Palestinians to be independent from the Israeli economy. The "Al Quds Intifada Fund" was given $200 million to be spent on the families of Palestinian "martyrs." Saudi Arabia agreed to pay 25 percent of the money allocated for both funds.

29. Khaled Abdullah Al-Fayez, "$100,000 Given to Father of Martyr Child," *Saudi Gazette,* Okaz Staff, October 20, 2000.

30. Donna Abu-Nasr, "Saudis Raise $92M for Palestinians," Associated Press, April 12, 2002; see also "Saudi Telethon Raises $145 Million (Canadian) for 'Martyrs': Government Ordered Palestinian Fund Raiser," *Vancouver Sun,* April 13, 2002.

31. Lisa Beyer with Scott MacLeod, "Inside the Kingdom: Saudi Arabia—A Special Report," *Time,* September 15, 2003, p. 47.

32. Gold, *Hatred's Kingdom,* pp. 146–47.

33. Tony Barthleme, "Seized Bosnian Documents Link Sauds to Terror Funding, Lawyers Say," *Post and Courier* (Charleston, S.C.), June 22, 2003; see also Glenn Simpson, "List of Early al Qaeda Donors Points to Saudi Elite, Charities," *Wall Street Journal,* March 18, 2003.

34. The Golden Chain list (or list of wealthy Saudi sponsors) was presented by the U.S. government as Exhibit 5 in the Department of Justice's "Government's Evidentiary Proffer Supporting the Admissibility of Coconspirator Statements" in the case of *USA v. Arnaout* (USDC, Northern District of Illinois, Eastern Division), filed on January 29, 2003. The list was also mentioned in the *Indictment of Enaam Arnaout* on October 9, 2002 (02 CR 892). According to the U.S. government, the document is "a list of people referred to within Al Qaida as the 'Golden Chain,' wealthy donors to mujahideen efforts."

   The complete list of Saudi donors and Al-Qaida recipients (twenty-five names) includes eight individuals already named in the complaint. The most virulent Saudi statements against the lawsuit were issued by those listed in the "Golden Chain," especially Saleh Abdullah Kamel.

   Among the most notable claims:

   • confirmation that the bin Laden family has been a major contributor to Osama, despite its statements denying such support
   • involvement of bankers representing the three largest Saudi banks (National Commercial Bank, Riyad Bank, Al Rajhi Banking and Investment Corp.)
   • involvement of former oil ministers Sheikh Yamani and Taher
   • involvement of most of them in charity organizations as founders or board members

AL QAIDA DONORS

Suleiman Al-Rashid
  Al-Rashid Trading & Contracting (Riyadh, Saudi Arabia)
Abdel Qader Bakri (Abdulkader [al] Bakri)
  CEO, Bakri Group of Cos
  CEO, Al Bakri International Power Co. Ltd (Jeddah, Saudi Arabia)
  CEO, Al-Bakri Shipping Group (Jeddah, Saudi Arabia)
  CEO, Alkhomasia Shipping and Maintenance Company Ltd (Jeddah, Saudi
    Arabia)
  CEO, Red Sea Marine Services (Jeddah, Saudi Arabia)
  CEO, Diners Club International (Jeddah, Saudi Arabia)
  Bakri Group formed in April 2002 a JV with the Malaysian International
    Shipping Corporation (MISC) to operate in Middle-East countries,
    including Yemen. MISC leased supertanker MT *Limburg* when it
    was attacked on October 6, 2002, coming from Ra's Tannura (Saudi
    Arabia).
Bin Laden Brothers
  Saudi Binladin Group (SBG)
  Bakr Bin Laden
Yousif Jameel (Youssef [Yousef] Jameel)
  CEO, Abdul Lateef Jameel Group (donated SR8 million to support Saudi
    Red Crescent Society's relief work in Kosovo in 1999)
  Former board member, major shareholder, Global Natural Resources Inc.
    (Houston, Texas)
Ibrahim Afandi (Ibrahim Muhammad Afandi)
  Board member, Ibn Baz Foundation (President: Prince Salman, VP:
    Abdulaziz bin Fahd)
  Board member, IIRO
  Chairman, Al Afandi Establishment (Jeddah, Saudi Arabia)
  CEO, Al Afandi Germany (Frankenberg)
  CEO, Sky Muzn Holding Co. BV (Netherlands)
  CEO, Saudi Industrial Services Company (Sisco) with partners Xenel
    Industries and Dallah Al Baraka
  Founder, Great Saudi Development & Investment Co. (GSDIC)
  Founder, Arabian Company for Development and Investment Limited
    (ACDIL)
  Chairman, National Committee of Saudi Contractors
  Partner, African Company (Sudan), with Al Rajhi Bank and Dallah Al
    Baraka
  Former general manager and shareholder of Al Amoudi Group
  Owner, Gang Ranch (Canada), second largest ranch in North America
  Owner, Skylight Corp, Georgia, USA
  Owner, BSA Investments (complaint from LTV Steel Company, Inc)
  US address: 6914 Los Verdes Dr Apt 6, Rch Palos Vrd, CA 90275
Saleh Kamel (Saleh Abdullah Kamel)
  Born in 1941, Mecca, Saudi Arabia
  CEO, Dallah Al Baraka (Jeddah, Saudi Arabia)—3rd largest Saudi company
  Chairman Arab Radio & Television (ART)
  Founding member and shareholder, Al Shamal Islamic Bank (Khartoum,
    Sudan)
  Partner, Tamlik Company Ltd (with Mohamed Binladen Co., Saleh Bin
    Laden)
  Shareholder, Jordan Islamic Bank

Vice Chairman Bank Al Jazira
Founder, Iqraa International Foundation

Al-Rajhi (Suleiman Abdulaziz Al Rajhi)
Board member, IIRO
Board member, Ibn Baz Foundation
CEO, Al Rajhi Banking and Investment Company (Riyadh, Saudi Arabia)—
9th largest Saudi company, 4th largest Saudi commercial bank

Al-Jumaih (Mohammad bin Abdullah Al-Jomaih)
Board member IIRO
Board member, Ibn Baz Foundation
Member of the committee for collection of donations for supporting the
Intifada (Chairman Prince Salman)
Chairman First Islamic Investment Bank
+300 companies
Al Birr donor
Bosnia donor

Al-Sharbatly (Abdulrahman Hassan [Abbas] Sharbatly)
Founder and board member, Riyad Bank (Riyadh, Saudi Arabia)—7th
largest Saudi company and 2nd largest Saudi commercial bank
(Abdulrahman A. Al-Amoudi, Senior Executive Vice President)
Offices in Houston, Texas (Riyad Bank Houston Agency, 700 Louisiana,
Suite 4770, Houston, TX 77002, USA)
Board member, Beirut Ryad Bank SAL (with Prince Khaled bin Turki and
Abdullah Taha Bakhsh)
Board member, Saudi Arabian Refinery Company (Chairman Prince Khaled
bin Turki, directors include Kaaki bin Mahfouz and Al Rajhi)
Shareholder, Middle East Capital Group (shareholders include Abdullah
Taha Bakhsh, Henry Sarkissian—President Saudi Binladin Group
International, Sami Baarma—National Commercial Bank)
CEO, Saudi Arabian Marketing Agencies and Company Ltd (Shareholder:
Salem Mohammad Bin Laden) Ferrari, Porsche, Audi and Volkswagen
dealer
Shareholder, Egyptian Gulf Bank
Shareholder, Golden Pyramids Plaza Co.
Shareholder, Savola Snack Food Co. Ltd (with Saleh bin Mahfouz and
Abdullah Taha Bakhsh)

Al Naghi (Ahmed Mohamed Naghi)
Al Naghi Brothers Co (Jeddah, Saudi Arabia)

Bin Mahfoodh (Khalid bin Mahfouz)
Former COO, BCCI
Former CEO, National Commercial Bank, 1st Saudi commercial bank
Founder, Muwafaq Foundation
Founder, International Development Foundation

Abdel Qader Faqeeh (Adel Faqih)
Board member, Ibn Baz Foundation
Chairman, Bank Al Jazira
Chairman, Savola Group (Sharbatly), merged with Azizia Panda (Walid bin
Talal)—13th largest Saudi company
Chairman, Makkah Construction & Development Company

Salah Al-Din Abdel Jawad (Salahuddin Abduljawad)
CEO, General Machinery Agencies (Jeddah, Saudi Arabia) Agent for
General Motors, Wacker Corp, Mannesmann, Renault (RVI), Opel
Board member, United Gulf Industries Corp, Manama, Bahrain (with Khalil
Bin Laden)

Ahmad Turki Yamani (Ahmed Zaki Yamani)
> Born in 1930, Mecca, Saudi Arabia
> Son of former Saudi Chief Justice
> Former Saudi minister of petroleum and mineral resources
> Former director, ARAMCO
> Founder, Investcorp (board members include Abdullah Taha Bakhsh)
> Founder of several scholarship funds (Berkeley, Oxford—including the
>   Salahuddin Abduljawad Fellowship in Islamic Art History) through
>   Barakat Trust (UK) and Barakat Foundation (USA) with Xenel
>   Industries Ltd and Khalid Alireza

Abdel Hadi Taher (Abdul Hadi Taher)
> CEO, Taher Group of Companies, 52nd largest Saudi company
> Owner, Marketing General Trading Corp (Jeddah, Saudi Arabia)
> Shareholder, Arab Company for Hotels & Contracting Ltd (with Ahmed
>   Zaki Yamani)
> Former Minister of State
> Former Governor of the Saudi state oil company Petromin, under
>   responsibility of Ahmed Zaki Yamani
> Former director, Saudi European Bank (Paris), held 25% of the bank shares
>   along with Ahmed Zaki Yamani

Mohammed Omar—not identified

Al Kuwait—not identified

Ahmad Al Harbi
> CEO, Ahmad Al Harbi Group
> (L'Houssaine Kherchtou testified on February 21, 2001, during the trial of
>   suspected al-Qaida militants in connection with the bombings of the
>   American embassies in Kenya and Tanzania on August 7, 1998, that he
>   was welcomed at Miram Shah guest house in Pakistan before joining Al-
>   Qaida by "Abu Ahmed al Harbi.")

Al Issaei (Mohammed Al-Issai)
> Board member, Saudi Research & Marketing Company (with Mohammed
>   Hussein al-Amoudi, Saleh Abdullah Kamel, Abdullah Bin Khalid Bin
>   Mahfouz, Dallah Albaraka Group)—20th largest Saudi company
> CEO, Al Issai Trade Company (Daimler-Chrysler representative)
> Deputy Chairman, Arab Cement Company (shareholders include Binladin
>   Group, Bin Mahfouz, Al Rajhi—Chairman: Turki Bin Abdulaziz Al
>   Saud)

Hamad Al Husaini (Hamad Al Hussaini)
> CEO, Akel Trading Company
> CEO, Akel Agricultural Investment Company LLC
> CEO, Al Hussaini and Company
> Board member of Al Waqf Al Islami Foundation (Netherlands)
> Brother of Abdullah Osman Abdulrahman Al Hussaini, General Director of
>   Al Waqf Al Islami Foundation, owner of Al Furqan Mosque in
>   Netherlands (linked to MWL [Muslim World League], Mounir El
>   Motassadeq and Marwan El Shehhi
> Family members include Walid Al Hussaini, representative of Abdullah Al
>   Turki (former minister of Islamic Affairs, Secretary General of MWL,
>   linked to Mohammad Zouaydi—Spanish procedure)

AL-QAIDA RECIPIENTS

Major recipients appear to be Usama Bin Laden and Adel Abdul Jalil Batterjee. They
receive donations from thirteen donors.

Usama (Usama Bin Laden)
Receives donations from the most prominent in the list: Bin Laden Brothers, Al
  Rajhi, Sharbatly, Al Naghi, Bin Mahfouz, Adel Faqih, Al Kuwait
Wail (Wael Hamza Julaidan)
Former Secretary General of the Muslim World League and Rabita Trust in Pakistan,
  designated by the United States Treasury as SGDT [Specially Designated Global
  Terrorist]
Receives donations from Suleiman Al Rashid, Abdulkader Bakri, Salahuddin
  Abduljawad, Abdul Tahi Taher
Baterji (Adel Abdul Jalil Batterjee)
Chairman Al Shamal Islamic Bank (Khartoum, Sudan)
Founder, Al-Birr Society, Benevolence International Foundation
Former Secretary General, World Assembly of Muslim Youth (WAMY)
Receives donations from Yousef Jameel, Ibrahim Afandi, Saleh Abdullah Kamel,
  Mohammad Bin Abdullah Al Jomaih, Ahmed Zaki Yamani and Mohammed Omar
Abu Mazin (??? Mazin M. Bahareth)
Son of Mohammed Saleh Bahareth (brother of Usama Bin Laden father's wife and
  tutor of the Bin Laden family after patriarch Mohammad Bin Laden's death in
  1968)
CEO, Bahareth Organization (Jeddah, Saudi Arabia)
Shareholder, Triple B Trading GmbH (Germany)—with Hassan Bahfzallah and
  Shahir A. I. Batterjee, Secretary: Abdul-Martin Tatari
Receives donations from Hamad Al Hussaini
Salem Taher
Receives donations from Ahmad Al Harbi and Mohammed Al Issai

35. Gold, *Hatred's Kingdom*, p. 126.
36. Ottaway, "U.S. Eyes Money Trails of Saudi-Backed Charities."
37. Abukhalil, *Battle for Saudi Arabia*, p. 143.
38. "Conference in Mecca of Ministers of Waqfs and Islamic Affairs," *BBC Summary of World Broadcasts*, based on a story filed from the Saudi News Agency, March 24, 1979.
39. Kaplan et al., "The Saudi Connection." Even Saudi Arabia's relief work done for the tsunami victims in ravaged areas of Indonesia came under criticism because of the presence of the IIRO. Indonesia is trying hard to contain Islamic militancy, and there was fear among some observers that the IIRO could export Wahhabism together with its tsunami relief. See generally Murphy and Casey, "Saudi Charity's Aid Work Scrutinized."
40. John Crewdson, "9/11 Study: Saudis Long Ignored Al Qaeda Funding," *Chicago Tribune*, August 27, 2004, p. 1.
41. *Ain-Al-Yaqeen*, March 2002, p. 1.
42. Ottaway, "U.S. Eyes Money Trails of Saudi-Backed Charities."
43. Beyer, with MacLeod, "Inside the Kingdom: Saudi Arabia—A Special Report."
44. David Crawford, "West's Relations with Saudis Face Growing Strains," *Wall Street Journal*, December 7, 2004, p. A12; see also Michael Isikoff and Mark Hosenball, "Terror 101: Are the Saudis Funding Schools Devoted to Fomenting Radical Islamic Ideology?," *Newsweek Online*, http://www.msnbc.com/news/1000946.asp?ocv=KB10, December 7, 2003
45. Blaine Harden, "Saudis Seek to Add U.S. Muslims to Their Sect," *New York Times*, October 20, 2001, p. A1.
46. Michael Waller, " 'Wahhabi Lobby' Takes the Offensive," *Insight*, August 5, 2002.
47. Ottaway, "U.S. Eyes Money Trails of Saudi-Backed Charities."
48. Glenn Simpson, "Saudis Cut Back Diplomatic Visas Amid Policy Shift," *Wall Street Journal*, December 8, 2003, p. B2.
49. Gold, *Hatred's Kingdom*, p. 149.

50. In February 2003, the former Benevolence director, Enaam Arnaout, pleaded guilty to a single racketeering charge, for using charitable funds partially to support fighters in Chechnya and Bosnia. In his plea agreement, Arnaout admitted to having spent some of that money of material support of fighters in Bosnia and Chechnya without the knowledge of the Muslims who generously donated to the organization. In his statement, he acknowledged illegally giving money to buy boots, uniforms, tents, and an ambulance in those regions. His lawyers indicated that the amount totaled no more than $300,000 to $400,000 out of $20 million in donations. He still denied links to al Qaeda.

51. Matthew Engel, "Muslim Allies Break Ranks with U.S.: Muslim Allies Saudi Arabia and Pakistan Break Ranks with U.S. over Bombing," *The Guardian* (London), October 16, 2001.

52. "Saudi Prince: Zionism to Blame for Terror Attack," NBC News, *World News Tonight,* reported by Lisa Meyers, June 15, 2004.

53. Robinson et al., "Princely Payments."

54. The leaders of the network in Herndon, Virginia, have all denied any wrongdoing. Douglas Farah and John Mintz, "U.S. Trails Va. Muslim Money, Ties; Clues Raise Questions About Terror Funding," *Washington Post,* October 7, 2002, p. A1; see also Rebecca Carr and Eunice Moscoso, "Charities Deny Bankrolling Terror; Feds Allege Money Laundering Plot," *Atlanta Journal-Constitution,* November 16, 2003, p. 1C.

55. Ottaway, "U.S. Eyes Money Trails of Saudi-Backed Charities."

56. Ibid.

57. Beyer, with MacLeod, "Inside the Kingdom: Saudi Arabia—A Special Report."

58. Ibid.

59. Ibid.

60. See Testimony of John Pistole and David Aufhauser, August 5, 2003, before the Senate Subcommittee on Terrorism, Technology and Homeland Security, Judiciary Committee; see also "Our Friends the Saudis," *Wall Street Journal,* August 8, 2003.

61. Douglas Farah, "Bank Data for Saudi Embassy Subpoenaed; FBI Investigating Riyadh's Spending for Terrorist Ties," *Washington Post,* November 23, 2003, Final Edition, p. A22.

62. Ibid.

63. Roland Watson, "FBI's $300m Inquiry Enrages Saudis," *The Times* (London), November 24, 2003, p. 14.

64. Michael Isikoff, "New Questions About Saudi Money—and Bandar," *Newsweek,* April 12, 2004.

65. Kathleen Day, "Criminal Probe of Riggs Bank Underway: Justice Department Is Looking into Officers, Directors," *Washington Post,* August 21, 2004, p. E1; see also "Riggs Bank Guilty, Fined $16M," *Miami Herald,* January 28, 2005, p. C1.

66. Bob Graham, *Intelligence Matters: The CIA, the FBI, Saudi Arabia, and the Failure of America's War on Terror* (New York: Random House, 2004), pp. 11, 223–25.

67. Ibid., p. 24.

68. Joe Trento, "The Real Intelligence Cover-Up: America's Unholy Alliance," Home of the National Security and Natural Resources News Services, Public Education Center, August 6, 2003.

69. David Pryce-Jones, "The New Fellow-Traveling: In the Present Crisis, a Sickening Familiarity—Increased Number of Islamist Extremists," *National Review,* June 30, 2003, vol. LV, no. 12.

70. Isikoff, "New Questions About Saudi Money—and Bandar."

71. Dan Van Natta, Jr., with Timothy L. O'Brien, "Half of Hamas Budget Funded by Donations from Saudis," *Pittsburgh Post-Gazette,* September 17, 2003, p. A4.

72. Ibid.

73. Michael Weisskopf and Timothy J. Burger, "The Saudis' Secret Ads (against Israel)," *Time,* January 20, 2003.

74. On January 18, 2005, U.S. District Judge Richard Casey issued a sixty-two-page
     order dismissing six civil lawsuits brought against Saudi Arabia, three Saudi princes,
     and several Saudi financial institutions, accusing them of providing support to al
     Qaeda before 9/11. The cases had been brought by more than 6,500 survivors of the
     2001 attacks, family members, representatives of victims, and insurance carriers.
     The lawsuits alleged that more than two hundred defendants provided material
     support for terrorism. The defendants included al Qaeda, its members and
     associates, charities, banks, front organizations, terrorist organizations, and
     financiers.

     Judge Casey said Congress had decided that the president, not the courts, has
     the authority to label a foreign nation a terrorist. The judge dismissed Saudi Arabia
     as a defendant because the plaintiffs had not provided sufficient facts to overcome
     the Kingdom's immunity. He said Saudi Arabia maintains it has worked with the
     United States to share information in the fight against terrorism. He also noted that
     the U.S. State Department has not designated the Kingdom a state sponsor of
     terrorism and that the 9/11 Commission found no evidence that Saudi Arabia funded
     or supported the 9/11 terrorists.

     The judge also dismissed as defendants Saudi defense minister Prince Sultan,
     Saudi ambassador to London Prince Turki, and Prince Mohamed Al-Faisal Al-Saud,
     among others.

     The plaintiffs had alleged that Prince Sultan and Prince Turki met with Osama
     bin Laden and made charitable contributions that helped al Qaeda. Attorneys for
     both princes had argued that any meetings were in official capacities and that the
     plaintiffs were ignoring the fact that bin Laden had targeted Saudi royalty as well as
     the U.S.

     Judge Casey said the plaintiffs had not provided facts to support a suggestion
     that the princes were close to the terrorists' illegal activities or knew they were
     making contributions to terrorists. "The court has reviewed the complaints in their
     entirety and finds no allegations from which it can infer that the princes knew the
     charities to which they donated were fronts for al-Qaeda," Casey wrote.

     The judge also dismissed the case against Prince Mohamed because the
     plaintiffs failed to show the court would have jurisdiction over him since his contacts
     with the U.S. during the past decade had consisted of only one speech and a handful
     of investments.

     Among financial institutions dismissed as defendants were Al Rajhi Bank,
     which has nearly four hundred branch offices throughout Saudi Arabia; Saudi
     American Bank, the second largest bank in the Kingdom; and Egyptian-based Arab
     Bank, which has branch offices worldwide. Casey said he found no basis for a bank's
     liability for injuries resulting from attacks funded by money passing through it on
     routine banking business. However, while the judge removed some high-profile
     defendants, he ruled that litigation can proceed against National Commercial Bank,
     Saudi Binladen Group, an engineering conglomerate run by relatives of Osama bin
     Laden, and several other Islamic charities and companies. The plaintiffs' primary
     lawyers, Motley Rice, promised to appeal the dismissal.

     Press Statement of Prince Bandar bin Sultan bin Abdul Aziz, posted on
     www.saudiembassy.net, regarding the January 19, 2005, dismissal by a New York
     federal district court of the class action proceedings brought against the Saudi
     government, senior officials, and financial institutions, by the 9/11 victims'
     families:

     [Washington D.C.]—Saudi Ambassador to the United States, Prince Bandar bin
     Sultan, issued the following statement:
         "The Kingdom of Saudi Arabia is very gratified with the decision by the United

States District Court of New York to dismiss lawsuits against the Saudi government, government officials, leading financial institutions and prominent businessmen, who were charged with financing the 9/11 attacks.

"The decision of the court is consistent with the findings of the 9/11 Commission, which concluded after exhaustive investigation that there is no evidence of involvement in or financial support for terrorism by the Saudi government or the Royal family.

"The court has dismissed claims against two government officials: Saudi Minister of Defense HRH Prince Sultan bin Abdulaziz and Saudi Ambassador to the United Kingdom, HRH Prince Turki Al-Faisal.

"The cases were also dismissed against a number of other parties including HRH Prince Mohamed Al-Faisal, CEO of three financial institutions in Saudi Arabia; Bakr, Omar, Tariq Binladin, current managers of the large engineering and construction company Saudi Binladin Group; Mohammad Abdullah Aljomaih's Estate, Saleh Abdullah Kamel, Abdulrahman bin Mahfouz, all prominent Saudi businessmen.

"The court also granted the motions to dismiss of three Saudi financial institutions: Al Rajhi Bank, Saudi American Bank and Al Baraka Investment Company.

"In the aftermath of 9/11, the Kingdom of Saudi Arabia has been confronted with many false charges. As the real facts emerge, we hope we can all move forward in the spirit of cooperation and mutual support, which is so critical to winning the war on terrorism. The people of Saudi Arabia sympathize with all victims of terrorism, and Saudi Arabia will continue to lead efforts to eliminate terrorism worldwide."

(The ambassador and his wife, HRH Princess Haifa bint Faisal, were voluntarily dismissed by the plaintiffs from these lawsuits in 2004.)

CHAPTER 15: THE FUTURE?

1. Jim Anderson, "Fahd Reported to Be Improving, but Succession Questions Remain," *Deutsche Presse-Agentur*, December 5, 1995.
2. As Ad Abukhalil, *The Battle for Saudi Arabia: Royalty, Fundamentalism, and Global Power* (New York: Seven Stories Press, 2004), p. 129.
3. Nimrod Raphaeli, "Saudi Arabia: A Brief Guide to Its Politics and Problems," *MERIA Journal*, vol. 7, no. 3 (September 2003).
4. Dilip Hiro, "Saudi Dissenters Go Public," *The Nation*, June 28, 1993, p. 906.
5. Sandra Mackey, *The Saudis: Inside the Desert Kingdom* (New York: W. W. Norton, 2002), p. 404.
6. Robert Lacey, *The Kingdom: Arabia and the House of Saud* (New York: Harcourt Brace Jovanovich, 1981), p. 473.
7. Scott MacLeod, "Inside Saudi Arabia: The Oil-Rich Kingdom Fanned al-Qaeda's Hateful Cause—and Still Harbors a Populace that Fervently Supports It," *Time*, October 15, 2001, p. 60; see also Doug Bandow, "Befriending Saudi Princes: A High Price for a Dubious Alliance," *USA Today Magazine*, July 1, 2002.
8. Said K. Aburish, *The Rise, Corruption and Coming Fall of the House of Saud* (New York: St. Martin's/Griffin, 2003), p. 73.
9. "Saudi Interior Minister Says Riyadh Protest 'Worthless Barking,' " reported by BBC News Worldwide, from Arab News website, Jeddah, in English, October 15, 2003.
10. Donna Abu-Nasr, "Saudis Aim Toward Democracy with Vote," *Miami Herald*,

February 11, 2005, p. 17A; see also Donna Abu-Nasr, "Islamists Win First Regular Saudi Vote," *Miami Herald,* February 12, 2005, p. 24A.

11.   "Many Saudis Ignoring Their Chance to Vote," *Miami Herald,* December 21, 2004, p. 19A.

12.   Abu-Nasr, "Islamists Win First Regular Saudi Vote."

13.   Aburish, *Rise, Corruption and Coming Fall,* p. 111.

14.   "House of Saud," *Frontline,* Public Broadcasting Corporation documentary, February 8, 2005.

15.   *Arab Times,* no. 415 (2003), p. 10.

16.   Lisa Beyer, with Scott MacLeod, "Inside the Kingdom: Saudi Arabia—A Special Report," *Time,* September 15, 2003.

17.   Hugh Pope, "A Saudi Leadership Adrift," *Wall Street Journal,* June 30, 2004, p. A7.

18.   "Saudi Arabia: Political Outlook," *MEED Quarterly Report—Saudi Arabia,* December 4, 2003, Section: Comment & Analysis; Forecast; Country Profile, p. 5.

19.   Jane Perlez, "Bush Senior, on His Son's Behalf, Reassures Saudi Leader," *New York Times,* July 15, 2001, p. 6.

20.   Bandow, "Befriending Saudi Princes: A High Price for a Dubious Alliance."

21.   Abukhalil, *The Battle for Saudi Arabia,* p. 200.

22.   Howard LaFranchi, "Bush-Saudi Talks Reassure Arab Nations of US Resolve," *Christian Science Monitor,* April 29, 2002, p. 1.

23.   Josh Pollack, "Saudi Arabia and the United States, 1931–2002," *Middle East Review of International Affairs,* vol. 6, no. 3 (September 2002), pp. 77, 83, 89.

24.   Richard Verrier, "Saudi Arabia Needs to Confront Its Role in Sept. 11, Prince Says," *Los Angeles Times,* November 18, 2003, Part 1, p. 4.

25.   *New York Post,* May 1, 2002.

26.   See generally Dave Montgomery, "Al Qaeda Cell Reloads with New Saudi Chief," *Miami Herald,* June 22, 2004, p. 10A.

BIBLIOGRAPHY

BOOKS

Abukhalil, As Ad. *The Battle for Saudi Arabia: Royalty, Fundamentalism, and Global Power.*
New York: Seven Stories Press, 2004.

Aburish, Said K. *The Rise, Corruption and Coming Fall of the House of Saud.* New York:
St. Martin's Griffin, 2003.

Al-Jabhan, Ibrahim Sulaiman. *The Facts That the Muslim Must Know About Christianity
and Missionary Activity.* Saudi Arabia: The Directorate for Religious Research,
Islamic Legal Rulings, Islamic Propagation, and Guidance, 1977.

Al-Rasheed, Madawi. *A History of Saudi Arabia.* Cambridge: Cambridge University Press,
2002.

Al-Rashid, Ibrahim. *Saudi Arabia Enters the Modern World.* Salisbury: Documentary
Publications, 1980, vol. IV.

Algar, Hamid. *Wahhabism; A Critical Essay.* North Haledon, N.J.: Islamic Publications
International, 2002.

Armstrong, H. C. *Lord of Arabia: Ibn Saud, An Intimate Study of a King.* Beirut: Khayats,
1966.

Baer, Robert. *Sleeping with the Devil: How Washington Sold Our Soul for Saudi Crude.*
New York: Crown Publishers, 2003.

Bahti, James H. *The Arab Economic Boycott of Israel.* Washington, D.C.: The Brooking
Institution, 1967.

Beling, Willard A. *King Faisal and the Modernization of Saudi Arabia.* London: Croom
Helm, 1980.

Briody, Dan. *The Iron Triangle: Inside the Secret World of the Carlyle Group.* New York:
John Wiley & Sons, 2003.

Brown, Anthony Cave. *Oil, God, and Gold: The Story of Aramco and the Saudi Kings.*
Boston: Houghton Mifflin, 1999.

Clarke, Richard A. *Against All Enemies: Inside America's War on Terror.* New York: Free
Press, 2004.

Cordesman, Anthony. *Saudi Arabia: Guarding the Desert Kingdom*. Boulder, Colo.:
Westview, 1997.

Crowe, Kenneth C. *America for Sale: An Alarming Look at How Foreign Money Is Buying
Our Country.* Garden City, N.Y.: Doubleday & Company, 1978.

De Gaury, Gerald. *Faisal: King of Saudi Arabia*. London: Arthur Barker, 1966.

Emerson, Steven. *The American House of Saud: The Secret Petrodollar Connection*. New
York: Franklin Watts, 1985.

Fandy, Mamoun. *Saudi Arabia and the Politics of Dissent*. London: Palgrave Macmillan,
2001.

Field, Michael. *A Hundred Million Dollars a Day*. London: Sidgwick and Jackson, 1975.

———. *The Merchants: The Big Business Families of Saudi Arabia and the Gulf States*.
Woodstock, N.Y.: Overlook Press, 1985.

Gold, Dore. *Hatred's Kingdom: How Saudi Arabia Supports the New Global Terrorism*.
Washington, D.C.: Regnery, 2003.

Graham, Bob. *Intelligence Matters: The CIA, the FBI, Saudi Arabia, and the Failure of
America's War on Terror*. New York: Random House, 2004.

Holden, David, Richard Johns, and James Buchan. *House of Saud: The Rise and Rule of
the Most Powerful Dynasty in the Arab World*. New York: Henry Holt & Company,
1982.

Howarth, David. *The Desert King: A Life of Ibn Saud*. Beirut: Continental Publications,
1964.

Jarishan, Dr. Ali Muhammad, and Muhammad Sharif al-Zubayq. *The Methods of the
Ideological Invasion of the Islamic World*. Cairo: Dar al-Itissam, 1978.

Jerichow, Anders. *The Saudi File: People, Power, Politics*. New York: St. Martin's Press,
1998.

Kalb, Marvin, and Bernard Kalb. *Kissinger*. Boston: Little, Brown, 1974.

Kessler, Ronald. *The Richest Man in the World: The Story of Adnan Khashoggi*. New York:
Warner Books, 1986.

Kissinger, Henry. *Years of Upheaval*. New York: Little, Brown, 1982.

Knauerhase, Ramon. *The Saudi Arabian Economy*. New York: Praeger, 1977.

Lacey, Robert. *The Kingdom: Arabia and the House of Saud*. New York: Harcourt Brace
Jovanovich, 1981.

Lewis, Bernard. *Middle East: A Brief History of the Last 2,000 Years*. New York: Simon &
Schuster, 1997.

———. *The Crisis of Islam: Holy War and Unholy Terror*. New York: Modern Library, 2004.

Long, David E. *The United States and Saudi Arabia: Ambivalent Allies*. Boulder, Colo.:
Westview Press, 1985.

Mackey, Sandra. *The Saudis: Inside the Desert Kingdom*. New York: W. W. Norton, 2002.

Miller, Judith. *God Has Ninety-nine Names: Reporting from a Militant Middle East*. New
York: Simon & Schuster, 1997.

Mosley, Leonard. *Power Play: Oil in the Middle East*. New York: Random House, 1973.

Napoleoni, Loretta. *Modern Jihad: Tracing the Dollars Behind Terror Networks*. London:
Pluto Press, 2003.

Nelson, Walter Henry, and Terence C. F. Prittie. *The Economic War Against the Jews*. New
York: Random House, 1977.

*The 9/11 Commission Report: Final Report of the National Commission on Terrorist Attacks
upon the United States* (hereinafter, *9/11 Commission Report*) (New York:
W. W. Norton, 2004).

Perkins, John. *Confessions of an Economic Hitman*. San Francisco: Berrett-Koehler
Publishers, 2004.

Quandt, William B. *Saudi Arabia's Oil Policy.* Washington, D.C.: Brookings Institute, 1982.

Qutb, Sayyid, and William E. Shepard (translator). *Sayyid Qutb and Islamic Activism: A*

Translation and Critical Analysis of Social Justice in Islam. Boston: Brill Academic Publishers, 1996.

Safran, Nadav. *Saudi Arabia: The Ceaseless Quest for Security*. Cambridge: Harvard University Press, 1985.

Sampson, Anthony. *The Seven Sisters: The Great Oil Companies and the World They Made*. London: Hodder and Stoughton, 1976.

Schwartz, Stephen. *The Two Faces of Islam: Saudi Fundamentalism and Its Role in Terrorism*. New York: Anchor Books, 2003.

Sheean, Vincent. *Faisal: The King and His Kingdom*. Tavistock, England: University Press of Arabia, 1975.

Sheehan, Edward R. F. *The Arabs, Israelis and Kissinger: A Secret History of American Diplomacy in the Middle East*. New York: Reader's Digest Press, 1976.

Sullivan, John Jeremiah. *Blood Horses: Notes of a Sportswriter's Son*. New York: Farrar, Straus and Giroux, 2004.

Tibi, Bassam. *The Challenge of Fundamentalism, Political Islam and the New World Disorder*. Berkeley: University of California Press, 1998.

Tivnan, Edward. *The Lobby: Jewish Political Power and American Foreign Policy*. New York: Simon & Schuster, 1987.

Unger, Craig. *House of Bush, House of Saud: The Secret Relationship Between the World's Two Most Powerful Families*. New York: Scribner, 2003.

Woodward, Bob. *Veil: The Secret Wars of the CIA, 1981–1987*. New York: Simon & Schuster, 1987.

Yergin, Daniel, with Joseph Stanislaw. *Prize: The Epic Quest for Oil, Money and Power*. New York: Simon & Schuster, 1992.

SELECTED ARTICLES AND PERIODICALS

Al-Hattlan, Sulaiman. "In Saudi Arabia, an Extreme Problem." *Washington Post*, May 8, 2002, p. 12.

Alexiev, Alex. "The Pakistani Time Bomb." *Commentary*, March 2003.

Alford, Jane. "Saudi Banks Experiment with Branches for Women." *Atlanta Constitution*, November 6, 1983.

Allen, Robin. "Gulf Between Friends." *Financial Times* (London), November 9, 2002.

Alvarez, Lizette. "War for Arab Oil in '73? U.S. Pondered an Attack, Papers Show." *International Herald Tribune*, January 1, 2004.

"Arabs Meet on Boycott of Israel." *Facts on File World News Digest*, Middle East Section, March 1, 1975.

Atlas, Terry, and James O'Shea. "Saudis in Covert-Aid Web; Probe Reveals Role in Arming Afghan Rebels." *Chicago Tribune*, December 7, 1986, p. C1.

Auerbach, Stuart. "Law Firms Give Extra Service to Foreign Clients; Foreign Clients Pay Lawyers Well for Variety of Services." *Washington Post*, October 3, 1977, p. A1.

Baer, Robert. "The Fall of the House of Saud." *Atlantic Monthly*, May 2002, p. 55.

Balz, Dan. "The Saudi Connection: The Next Best Thing to Mecca Is Houston; Houston as the Mecca for the Saudis." *Washington Post*, April 19, 1981.

Bandow, Doug. "Befriending Saudi Princes: A High Price for a Dubious Alliance." *USA Today Magazine*, July 1, 2002.

Barringer, Felicity. "Bureaucrats Instruct the Saudis; Nation Pays to Learn American Techniques." *Washington Post*, November 14, 1983.

Barthleme, Tony. "Seized Bosnian Documents Link Sauds to Terror Funding, Lawyers Say." *Post and Courier* (Charleston, S.C.), June 22, 2003.

Beaty, Jonathan. "The Dirtiest Bank of All." *Time*, June 29, 1991.

Beck, Melinda, with John J. Lindsay, John Walcott, Eleanor Clift, and Scott Sullivan. "The Battle Over AWACS." *Newsweek,* October 12, 1981, p. 37.

Beyer, Lisa, with Scott MacLeod. "Inside the Kingdom: Saudi Arabia—A Special Report." *Time,* September 15, 2003, p. 38.

Blumenthal, Sidney. "Whose Side Is Business On, Anyway?" *New York Times Magazine,* October 25, 1981.

Bradley, John. "Are the Saudis Sunk?" *American Prospect,* September 2003.

Brennan, Charlie. "A Prince to Aspen: Despite Recent Rumors, One Hears Only Praise for Saudi Royal." *Rocky Mountain News,* December 28, 2002.

Brill, Steven. "Connally, Coming on Tough." *New York Times Magazine,* November 18, 1979.

Broder, Jonathan, and Ray Moseley. "Fundamentalism's New Fervor Revolution Reaches All of Moslem World, and Beyond." *Chicago Tribune,* November 8, 1987, p. 1.

Byron, Christopher. "A Mighty Indicator Is the Saudi Prince Who's Always Wrong." *New York Observer,* December 31, 2003.

Carbonara, Peter. "Dirty Money." *Money,* January 2002, p. 91.

Carr, Rebecca, and Eunice Moscoso. "Charities Deny Bankrolling Terror; Feds Allege Money Laundering Plot." *Atlanta Journal Constitution,* November 16, 2003, p. 1C.

Chandler, Clay. "Desert Shock: Saudis Are Cash-Poor." *Washington Post,* October 28, 1994.

Church, George J. "Flying into Trouble; Selling AWACS: Dubious Militarily and Dangerous Politically." *Time,* May 4, 1981.

Cohen, Richard E. "Even If He Wins on Saudi Arms Sale, Reagan May Find It a Hollow Victory." *National Journal,* September 12, 1981, section: Congress, vol. 13, no. 37.

Colvin, Marie. "The Squandering Sheikhs." *Sunday Times* (London), August 29, 1993.

Cordesman, Anthony H., and Nawaf Obaid. "Saudi Petroleum Security: Challenges and Responses." Center for Strategic and International Studies, Washington, D.C., November 30, 2004.

Cordon, Gavin. "U.S. 'Ready to Invade' in 1973." *Birmingham Post* (United Kingdom), January 1, 2004, p. 1.

Corn, David. "South Africa Link; Funding for the Nicaraguan Contras." *The Nation,* September 12, 1987.

Crawford, David, and Ian Johnson. "Saudi Funds Tied to Extremism in Europe." *Wall Street Journal,* December 30, 2003, p. A8.

———. "West's Relations with Saudis Face Growing Strains." *Wall Street Journal,* December 7, 2004, p. A12.

Crewdson, John. "9/11 Study: Saudis Long Ignored Al Qaeda Funding." *Chicago Tribune,* August 27, 2004.

Crowe, Kenneth C. "The Dichotomy of Saudi Arabia." New York: The Alicia Patterson Foundation, May 26, 1976.

Curtis, Tom. "Allah in the Family." *Texas Monthly,* April 1977.

Dekmejian, R. Hrair. "The Rise of Political Islamism in Saudi Arabia." *Middle East Journal,* vol. 48, no. 4, Autumn 1994.

Doran, Michael Scott. "Somebody Else's Civil War." *Foreign Affairs,* January/February 2002.

Dorse, James M. "Fire Sparks Rare Saudi Outcry at Regime." *Wall Street Journal,* March 19, 2002.

Emerson, Steven. "The Arabians' Knight: The Transformation of Fred Dutton from Liberal Warrior to Foreign Agent." *Common Cause,* January/February 1986.

Farah, Douglas. "Bank Data for Saudi Embassy Subpoenaed; FBI Investigating Riyadh's Spending for Terrorist Ties." *Washington Post,* November 23, 2003, Final Edition, p. A22.

Farah, Douglas, with John Mintz. "U.S. Trails Va. Muslim Money, Ties; Clues Raise Questions About Terror Funding." *Washington Post,* October 7, 2002, p. A1.

Frank, Steve. "Prince Alaweed's Road to Riches." *Wall Street Journal,* May 16, 2001.

Friedman, Thomas L. "The Saudi Challenge." *New York Times,* February 20, 2002.

Gabor, Andrea. "A Super Saudi's Shifting Fortunes." *U.S. News & World Report,* January 12, 1987.

Gambill, Gary C., and Ziad K. Abdelnour. "Dossier: Prince Al-Walid bin Talal." *Middle East Intelligence Bulletin,* vol. 4, no. 9, September 2002.

Gerth, Jeff. "Former Intelligence Aides Profiting from Old Ties." *New York Times,* December 6, 1981, Section 1, Part 2, p. 1.

Gerth, Jeff, and Judith Miller. "Saudi Arabia Is Called Slow in Helping Stem the Flow of Cash to Militants." *New York Times,* December 1, 2002, p. A32.

Gewirtz, Carl. "Arabs Begin Blacklisting Some Banks." *International Herald Tribune,* February 8, 1975.

Green, Mark, and Steven Solow. "The Arab Boycott of Israel: How the U.S. and Business Cooperated." *The Nation,* October 17, 1981, p. 1.

Greenfield, Meg. "Saudi Arabia: Paradox in the Desert." *Washington Post,* May 26, 1980.

Hastings, Chris, David Leppard, Jonathon Carr-Brown, and Wayne Bodkin. "The Prince Who Blew a Billion." *Sunday Times* (London), July 5, 1998, p. 1.

Heikal, Mohamed H., and Yomiuri Shimbun. "Strains Showing in House of Al-Saud." *Daily Yomiuri,* April 29, 1996.

Henderson, Simon. "After King Fahd, Succession in Saudi Arabia." *The Washington Institute Policy Papers,* no. 37, 1994.

Higgins, Andrew. "In His Desert Tent, Wired Saudi Prince Monitors U.S. Vote." *Wall Street Journal,* November 8, 2002, p. A1.

Hiro, Dilip. "Saudi Dissenters Go Public." *The Nation,* June 28, 1993, p. 906–7.

———. "Too Little and 32 Years Late." *The Nation,* April 13, 1992, p. 484.

Hoagland, Jim. "Hussein Payments Only a Part; CIA Operations in Mideast Held Wide-Ranging Effective." *Washington Post,* February 22, 1977, p. A1.

Hoagland, Jim, and J. P. Smith. "U.S. Moving to Repair Saudi Ties; U.S. Is Moving to Repair Relations with Saudis." *Washington Post,* June 12, 1979.

Ignatius, David. "Royal Payoffs." *Wall Street Journal,* May 1, 1981.

Ignotus, Miles (pseud). "Seizing Arab Oil." *Harper's Magazine,* March 1975.

"In the Name of God: A Survey of Islam and the West." *The Economist,* September 13, 2003, special 16-page insert.

Iseman, Peter A. "Iran's War of Words Against Saudi Arabia." *The Nation,* April 19, 1980, p. 463.

Isikoff, Michael, with Evan Thomas. "The Saudi Money Trail." *Newsweek,* December 2, 2002, p. 28.

———. "New Questions About Saudi Money—and Bandar." *Newsweek,* April 12, 2004.

"It Happened in August; Fulbright Called for U.S. Defense Pact with Israel but Was Labeled Anti-Semite." *Washington Report on Middle East Affairs,* September 30, 1997, vol. XVI, no. 2, p. 96.

Jehl, Douglas. "Holy War Lured Saudis as Rulers Looked Away." *New York Times,* December 27, 2001, p. A1.

Jervey, Gay, and Stuart Taylor, Jr. "From Statesman to Frontman: How Clark Clifford's Career Crashed." *American Lawyer,* November 1992.

Johnston, David, with Neil A. Lewis and Douglas Jehl. "Security Nominee Gave Advice to the C.I.A. on Torture Laws." *New York Times,* January 29, 2005, p. A1.

Kaiser, Robert G. "Enormous Wealth Spilled into American Coffers." *Washington Post,* February 11, 2002, p. A17.

Kaplan, David E., and Monica Ekma, with Aamir Latif. "The Saudi Connection." *U.S. News & World Report,* December 15, 2003, vol. 135, no. 21, p. 18.

Karsh, Efraim. "Intifada II: The Long Trail of Arab Anti-Semitism." *Commentary,* December 1, 2000.

King, Wayne, with Jeff Gerth. "Private Pipeline to the Contras: A Vast Network." *New York Times,* October 22, 1986, p. A1.

Kondracke, Morton. "The Saudi Oil Offensive." *New Republic,* August 4 and 11, 1979.

Kraft, Joseph. "Letters from Saudi Arabia." *The New Yorker,* October 20, 1975.

———. "Letter from Riyadh." *The New Yorker,* June 26, 1978.

———. "Letter from Saudi Arabia." *The New Yorker,* July 4, 1983.

Kuniholm, Bruce. "What the Saudis Really Want: A Primer for the Reagan Administration." *Orbis* 25 (Spring 1981).

Lacey, Robert. "How Stable Are the Saudis?" *New York Times Magazine,* November 8, 1981.

MacLeod, Scott. "Inside Saudi Arabia: The Oil-Rich Kingdom Fanned al-Qaeda's Hateful Cause—and Still Harbors a Populace That Fervently Supports It." *Time,* October 15, 2001.

Mansur, Abdul Kasim (pseud). "The American Threat to Saudi Arabia." *Armed Forces Journal International,* September 1980, pp. 47–60.

Marks, Laurence, and Barry Hugill. "The BCCI Scandal." *Observer* (London), July 21, 1991.

Marquis, Christopher. "Worried Saudis Try to Improve Image in the U.S." *New York Times,* August 28, 2002, p. 1.

Martin, Susan Taylor. "Inside Saudi Arabia." *St. Petersburg Times* (Fla.), July 21, 2002.

———. "Hanging Out at the Mall, Saudi Style." *St. Petersburg Times* (Fla.), July 24, 2002.

McGee, Jim. "Who Controls First American Bankshares?" *Washington Post,* February 3, 1991.

Miller, Judith. "The Struggle Within." *New York Times,* March 10, 1991, Section 6; Column 2; Magazine Desk, p. 27.

Mowbray, Joel. "Blind Eye to the Saudis: Petro-Dollars Fuel Palestinian Terrorism, Yet State Sits Still." *National Review Online,* July 1, 2002.

Murphy, Kim. "Cracks in a 45-Year Boycott." *Los Angeles Times,* May 22, 1991, p. A1.

Obaid, Nawaf E. "The Power of Saudi Arabia's Islamic Leaders." *Middle East Quarterly,* September 1999.

O'Brien, Timothy L. "A Washington Bank, a Global Mess." *New York Times,* April 11, 2004, Section 3, p. 1.

O'Hara, Terence. "At Riggs, Problems Passed on with Legacy." *Washington Post,* April 18, 2004.

Ottaway, David B. "U.S. Eyes Money Trails of Saudi-Backed Charities." *Washington Post,* August 19, 2004.

———. "Aramco, Using Ties to West, Helps Saudi Arabia to Industrialize." *Washington Post,* January 9, 1982.

———. "Saudis Use Bush Visit to Signal Displeasure; 'Special Relationship' Becoming Frayed." *Washington Post,* April 21, 1986, p. A4.

"Our Friends the Saudis." *Wall Street Journal,* August 8, 2003.

Pallister, David. "How Aitken Courted Saudi Royal Family: Criticism of Pro-Israel Reporting of 1967 War Led to 25-Year Relationship with Arab Kingdom." *The Guardian* (London), October 31, 1994, p. 5.

Perlez, Jane. "Bush Senior, on His Son's Behalf, Reassures Saudi Leader." *New York Times,* July 15, 2001, p. 6.

Pipes, Daniel. "The Scandal of U.S.-Saudi Relations." *National Interest,* Winter 2002/03.

Pollack, Josh. "Saudi Arabia and the United States, 1931–2002." *Middle East Review of International Affairs,* vol. 6, no. 3 (September 2002), p. 77.

Pope, Hugh. "A Saudi Leadership Adrift." *Wall Street Journal,* June 30, 2004, p. A7.

Price, G. Jefferson III. "Saudis Remember FDR's Broken Promise." Baltimore *Sun,* September 1, 2002.

Quinn, Sally. "The Astrology of Oil and the Art of Survival; Ahmed Yamani, Saudi Arabia's Prince of Petrol." *Washington Post,* October 22, 1979, p. B1.

Rhoads, Christopher. "Lucent Faces Bribery Allegations in Giant Saudi Telecom Project." *Wall Street Journal,* November 16, 2004, p. A1.

Roberts, Steven V., Stephen Engelberg, and Jeff Gerth. "Prop for U.S. Policy: Secret Saudi Funds." *New York Times,* June 21, 1987.

Robinson, Linda, et al. "Princely Payments." *U.S. News & World Report,* January 14, 2002.

Rossant, John. "A Prince with Divided Loyalties." *Business Week,* October 15, 2001.

———. "The Prince." *Business Week,* September 25, 1995.

Rouleau, Eric. "Trouble in the Kingdom." *Foreign Affairs,* vol. 81, no. 4 (July/August 2002).

Sachs, Susan. "Anti-Semitism Is Deepening Among Muslims; Hateful Images of Jews Are Embedded in Islamic Popular Culture." *New York Times,* April 27, 2002, p. B1.

"Saudi Arabia: An Inside View of an Economic Power in the Making." *Business International,* 1981.

"Saudi School in Virginia Disparages Christianity and Judaism." Saudi Institute report, July 13, 2004.

Sennott, Charles M. "Fighting Terror: The Investigation: Clerics May Have Stoked Radical's Fire; Qaeda Said to Use Some Radical Clerics to Help Its Cause." *Boston Globe,* August 4, 2002, p. A30.

———. "Driving a Wedge/Bin Laden, the US, and Saudi Arabia: Saudi Schools Fuel Anti-US Anger—System Is Fertile Ground for Militancy, Some Say." *Boston Globe,* March 4, 2002, p. A1.

"Sheikhs and Souks: Capital Market Formation in the Middle East (Continuity and Transformation: The Modern Middle East)." *Journal of International Affairs,* Columbia University School of International Public Affairs, July 22, 1995.

Shepherd, William G. "Investor: A Saudi's Stake in U.S. Banking." *New York Times,* October 19, 1980, Section 3, p. 13.

Silverstein, Ken. "Saudis and Americans: Friends in Need." *The Nation,* December 3, 2001, p. 15.

Simpson, Glenn. "List of Early al Qaeda Donors Points to Saudi Elite, Charities." *Wall Street Journal,* March 18, 2003.

———. "Unraveling Terror's Finances." *Wall Street Journal,* October 24, 2003, p. A2.

———. "U.S. Treasury Ties Bosnian Arm of Saudi Charity to Terror Funds." *Wall Street Journal,* May 11, 2004, p. A6.

———. "A Sprawling Probe of Terror Funding in Centers in Virginia." *Wall Street Journal,* June 21, 2004, p. A1.

Steele, Kathy, Brenna Kelly, and Elizabeth Lee Brown. "Phantom Flight from Florida." *Tampa Tribune,* October 5, 2001.

Sullivan, Laura. "9/11 Commission Questions al-Qaida Leaders U.S. Holds." Baltimore *Sun,* May 12, 2004.

Szulc, Tad. "Recycling Petrodollars: The $100 Billion Understanding." *New York Times Magazine,* September 20, 1981.

"Target U.S.A.—The Arab Propaganda Offensive." Anti-Defamation League of B'nai B'rith, 1975.

Taylor, Paul. "Contrasting Approaches Are Taken by Saudi and Israeli Supporters; Lobbying on AWACS." *Washington Post,* September 28, 1981, p. A4.

Tell, David. "The Saudi-Terror Subsidy." *Weekly Standard* (London), May 20, 2002.

Tinnin, David B. "The Saudis Awaken to Their Vulnerability." *Fortune,* March 10, 1980, p. 48.

Trento, Joe. "The Real Intelligence Cover-Up: America's Unholy Alliance." Home of the National Security and Natural Resources News Services, Public Education Center, August 6, 2003.

Turner, Louis, and James Bedore. "Saudi Arabia: The Power of the Purse Strings." *International Affairs* 54 (July 1978).

Tyler, Patrick E. "Double Exposure: Saudi Arabia's Man in Washington." *New York Times Magazine,* June 7, 1992, p. 34.

Verrier, Richard. "Disney's Saudi Adventurer." *Los Angeles Times,* January 6, 2004.

———. "Saudi Arabia Needs to Confront Its Role in Sept. 11, Prince Says." *Los Angeles Times,* November 18, 2003.

Vincent, Lindsay. "Sharp End: Oracle of the Oil World Sheikh Yamani." *Observer* (London), January 27, 1991.

Walsh, Elsa. "The Prince: How the Saudi Ambassador Became Washington's Indispensable Operator." *The New Yorker,* March 24, 2003.

Walters, Robert. "Big-Name Americans Who Work for Foreign Countries." *Parade,* June 20, 1976.

Webb, Al. "What U.S. Has Riding on Saudi Royal Family." *U.S. News & World Report,* January 25, 1992.

Wells, Jonathan, Jack Meyers, and Maggie Mulvihill. "Saudi Elite Tied to Money Groups Linked to bin Laden." *Boston Herald,* October 14, 2001.

GOVERNMENT PUBLICATIONS

"Adequacy of the Federal Response to Foreign Investment in the United States." Twentieth Report by the Committee on Government Operations, August 1, 1980 (Government Printing Office).

Arab Boycott and American Business. Report by the Subcommittee on Oversight and Investigations of the Committee on Interstate and Foreign Commerce, U.S. House of Representatives, September 1976.

"Country Reports on Human Rights Practices, 2002, 2003, Saudi Arabia," U.S. Department of State.

Foreign Direct Investment in the United States, vol. 1. Report of the Secretary of Commerce to the Congress (Washington, D.C.: U.S. Department of Commerce, April 1976).

———. Appendix G: *Investment Motivation.*

Foreign Relations of the United States, 1964–1968, vol. XXI, *Near East Region.* Department of State, July 20, 1968.

Future of Saudi Arabian Oil Production. Staff report to the Subcommittee on International Economic Policy of the Senate Foreign Relations Committee, April 1979.

GAO Report. "Financial Services: Post-hearing Questions Regarding Recovering Foreign Regimes' Assets." GAO-04-831R, May 27, 2004.

———. "Investigating Money Laundering and Terrorist Financing: Federal Law Enforcement Agencies Face Continuing Coordination Challenges." GAO-04-710T, May 11, 2004.

———. "Combating Terrorism: Federal Agencies Face Continuing Challenges in Addressing Terrorist Financing and Money Laundering." GAO-04-501T, March 4, 2004.

———. "Investigations of Terrorist Financing, Money Laundering, and Other Financial Crimes." GAO-04-464R, February 20, 2004.

———. "Terrorist Financing: U.S. Agencies Should Systematically Assess Terrorists' Use of Alternative Financing Mechanisms." GAO-04-163, November 14, 2003.

Hearings. "Multinational Petroleum Companies and Foreign Policy." U.S. Senate Subcommittee on Multinational Corporations, Part 7, 1974.

Hearings. "Federal Response to OPEC Country Investments in the United States." U.S. Senate Subcommittee on Commerce, Consumer, and Monetary Affairs, Part 1, 1979.

Hearings. "Political Contributions to Foreign Governments." U.S. Senate Subcommittee on Multinational Corporations, Part 12, 1975.

Hearings. "Terrorism Two Years After 9/11." U.S. Senate Subcommittee on Terrorism, Technology and Homeland Security, Judiciary Committee, August and September 2003.

International Petroleum Cartel. Eighty-Second Congress, Second Session, Committee Prince no. 6, 1952. U.S. Government Printing Office.

"Multinational Oil Corporations and U.S. Foreign Policy." Report of the U.S. Senate Subcommittee on Multinational Corporations, January 2, 1975.

National Commission on Terrorist Attacks upon the United States. Staff report to the Commission (John Roth, Douglas Greenburg, Serene Wille), August 2004.

"9/11 and Terrorist Travel." Staff Report of the National Commission on Terrorist Attacks Upon the United States (Thomas R. Eldbridge, Susan Ginsburg, Walter T. Hempel II, Janice L. Kephart, Kelly Moore), August 2004.

Report by the Senate Subcommittee on Multinationals, January 2, 1975 (Part 3) and hearings, Parts 6 and 7.

"Saudi Arabia: Terrorist Financing Issues." Congressional Research Service, Alfred B. Prados and Christopher M. Blanchard, Update December 8, 2004, Library of Congress.

Statement of Mr. Jean-Charles Brisard, CEO, JCB Consulting, on terrorism financing, before the Committee on Senate Banking, Housing and Urban Affairs, October 22, 2003.

TRIAL TRANSCRIPTS AND FILINGS

Abdelghani Mzoudi Proceedings, Testimony of the witness Zakeri, on Friday, the 30th of January, 2004, 9:00 A.M., in Hamburg, Criminal Justice Building, Stenographic record: Rudolf Burdinski.

Thomas E. Burnett et al. vs. Al Baraka Investment and Development Corp, U.S. District Court for the District of Columbia, Case No. 1:02CV01616(JR), 2002, amended 2002 and 2003.

Oran Almog (the "Franco plaintiffs") et al. vs. Arab Bank, PLC, U.S. District Court Eastern District of New York, Case No. CV 045564, December 21, 2004.

SPECIAL COLLECTIONS

ARAMCO HISTORY PROJECT, GEORGETOWN UNIVERSITY

The Joseph A. Mahon Papers consist of forty-seven folders of material, primarily reports and typed commentaries/reviews authored or collected by Aramco executive Joseph A. Mahon concerning Aramco administration and management, employee recruitment and training, and community development, as well as oil production and the waterfront development of Ras Tanura.

This collection, and particularly the interview transcript with Mr. Mahon (Folder 47), is part of the Aramco History Project, with Paul J. Nance as coordinator, together with Peter C. Speers, Mary Norton, and Robert L. Norberg.

Mr. Mahon began his career with Aramco in 1951, in the engineering department in New York City. The following year he was transferred to Saudi Arabia, where he was first assigned to the refinery operations in the refining and shipping center at Ras Tanura. Later he was assigned to the oil production operations in the town of Abqaiq.

In 1961, Mahon was appointed program coordinator, reporting directly to

Aramco's president, and charged with overseeing the company's budget and planning
activities. In subsequent years, Mahon was director of planning and served as
secretary of the company's management committee. In 1976, he was elected vice
president of engineering and construction, and two years later was promoted to
senior vice president of corporate services. He retired in 1982.

The William E. Mulligan Papers primarily consist of personal and official
correspondence, reports, manuscripts, and printed materials relating to Mulligan's
career in the Government Affairs Department of Aramco (the Arabian American Oil
Company) from 1946 to 1978. The material is arranged in just over five hundred
folders in eighteen boxes.
   William E. Mulligan was born in 1918 and joined Aramco's Government Relations
Department in 1946. He was involved with boundary work for the Saudi government
in the 1940s and early 1950s and was assigned to Tapline for short periods during the
early construction phase of the pipeline.
   Mulligan held the positions of coordinator of the Arabian Affairs Division,
manager of the Government Affairs Services Department, secretary of the Donations
Committee, and assistant to the vice president, Government Affairs. In his early
years he worked extensively with George S. Rentz, the renowned Arabist. As a
journalist, Mulligan edited the "Sun and Flare" in 1946. During his tenure with
Aramco, he contributed dozens of articles to *The Arabian Sun, Aramco World*
magazine and a number of U.S. publications. Mulligan retired from Aramco in 1978.
   The William E. Mulligan Papers contain an extraordinary amount of highly
unique primary and secondary source materials on the early years of Aramco and
many of the most prominent Western figures in Arabia at the time. Included are
manuscripts and correspondence of George S. Rentz, H. St. John B. Philby,
Thomas C. Barger, Dame Violet Dickson, David S. Dodge, and Parker T. Hart. Also
included is an immense amount of biographical materials on Saudi government
officials and businesspeople, including members of the royal family, Sheikh Ahmed
Zaki Yamani, Suliman S. Olayan, Adnan M. Knashoggi, and many others.

Aramco and Its World: Arabia and the Middle East, edited by Ismail I. Nawwab, Peter
C. Speers, Paul F. Hoye; main research and writing, Paul Lunde and John A. Sabini;
caption research and writing, Lyn Maby. Dhahran, Saudi Arabia: Aramco, 1980, part
of the special collection at Georgetown University.

Aramco Handbook, by Roy Lebkicher, George Rentz and Max Steineke with
contributions by other Aramco employees. New York—part of the special collection
at Georgetown University.

Aramco reports on Al Hasa and Oman, 1950–1955. Farnham Common: Archive
Editions, 1990—part of the special collection at Georgetown University.

Saudi Aramco and Its World: Arabia and the Middle East, edited by Ismail I. Nawwab,
Peter C. Speers, Paul F. Hoye; with principal research and writing by Paul Lunde,
Lyn Maby, and John A. Sabini. Imprint Dhahran, Saudi Arabia: Saudi Arabian Oil
Company (Saudi Aramco), 1995, part of the special collection at Georgetown
University.

CONFERENCES AND SYMPOSIA

Report. "Terrorist Financing: Report of an Independent Task Force." Sponsored by the Council on Foreign Relations, October 2002, Maurice R. Greenberg, chair; William F. Wechsler and Lee S. Wolosky, project co-directors.

"Saudi Arabia, Enemy or Friend?" Middle East Policy; 3/22/2004; Hussein Shobokshi. An edited transcript of the thirty-fifth in a series of Capitol Hill conferences convened by the Middle East Policy Council. The meeting was held on January 23, 2004, in the Dirksen Senate Office Building with Chas. W. Freeman, Jr., moderating.

"The United States and Saudi Arabia: American Interests and Challenges to the Kingdom in 2002." (Symposium: the United States and Saudi Arabia). (Transcript)(Statistical Data Included)(Panel Discussion) Middle East Policy; 3/1/2002; Fareed Mohamedi.

MEDIA TRANSCRIPTS

Conan Neal. "Analysis: US–Saudi Arabia Relations in the Context of the War on Terrorism." *NPR Talk of the Nation,* October 16, 2001.

INDEX

Yale Glee Club, 62
Yamani, Sheikh Ahmed Zaki, 75
  and Aramco, 43, 46
  dismissal of, 121–22
Yamani, Sheikh Ahmed Zaki (cont'd):
  as hostage, 76
  land awarded to, 56
  and oil embargo, 43, 46, 50
  as oil minister, 43
  and Saudi oil reserves, 86, 88
Yamani, Mai, 22–23
Yemen:
  USS Cole attacked in, 168
  U.S. weapons to, 115–16
Yom Kippur War, 47, 48–50

Zaire, 115
Zamel, Abdelraham al-, 60
Zawahiri, Ayman al-, 37
Zenith Corporation, 61
Ziegler, Ron, 84
Zionism, 38, 44–45, 54, 58, 175n
Zola, Émile, 62
Zorinsky, Edward, 110
Zubaydah, Abu:
  capture and interrogation of, 3–5, 10,
    14
  confession recanted by, 5
  contacts named by, 4–6, 7, 8, 9, 10, 14,
    182
Zubayq, Muhammad Sharif al-, 35

GERALD POSNER is the award-winning author of nine books, including *Why America Slept: The Failure to Prevent 9/11* and *Case Closed: Lee Harvey Oswald and the Assassination of JFK*. A frequent commentator on television talk and news shows, Posner has also written for many publications, including *The New York Times, The New Yorker, Time, Newsweek, The Wall Street Journal*, and *U.S. News & World Report*. He lives in Miami Beach with his wife, the author Trisha Posner. Visit his website at www.posner.com.